THROUGH THE THREAD OF TIME

THROUGH THE THREAD OF TIME
Southeast Asian Textiles

The James H W Thompson Foundation Symposium Papers

Edited by Jane Puranananda

RIVER BOOKS

Published by the James H.W. Thompson Foundation
6 Soi Kasemsan 2, Rama I Road,
Bangkok 10330
Tel. (66) 2 216-7368
Fax. (66) 2 612-3744
www.jimthompsonhouse.com

First published and distributed in Thailand in 2004 by
River Books Co., Ltd
396 Maharaj Road, Tatien,
Bangkok 10200
Tel: (66) 2 225-4963, 2 225-0139, 2 622-1900
Fax: (66) 2 225-3861
Email: riverps@ksc.th.com
www.riverbooksbk.com

A River Books Production.
Copyright collective work © River Books 2004
Copyright text and photographs © The James H W Thompson Foundation 2004,
except where indicated otherwise.

Publisher Narisa Chakrabongse
Design Suparat Sudcharoen
Production Paisarn Piemmettawat

ISBN 974 8225 76 3

Jacket: *Photograph of Southeast Asian textiles from the collection of
Khun Chutinart Songwattana and designed by Paisarn Piemmettawat.*

Printed and bound in Thailand by Sirivatana Interprint Public Co., Ltd.

CONTENTS

Foreword   6

Introduction   7

Map of Southeast Asia   9

CAMBODIA
1 Textiles at the Khmer Court, Angkor   *Gillian Green*   10
  Origins, Innovations and Continuities

2 Weaving in Cambodia   *Bernard Dupaigne*   26

INDONESIA
3 Motif and Meaning in Indonesian Textiles   *Helen Jessup*   31

4 The Use of the *Pahudu* String Model   *Marie-Helen Guelton* 47
  Lau Pahudu Weaving from East Sumba, Indonesia

LAOS
5 Textiles for the Living and the Dead – *A Lao Case* *Mattiebelle Gittinger* 66

6 Baby or Elephant Cloth?   *Karen A. Bunyaratavej* 83
  Wrappers in Laos and Thailand

MYANMAR
7 The Saopha at Home and Abroad   *Susan Conway*   91
  Shan Court Dress in the 19th Century

THAILAND
8 Fit for a King   *John Guy*   97
  Indian Textiles and Thai Court Protocol

9 Lan Na Male Dress in Peace and War   *Susan Conway*   112

10 *Chuan-tani* or *Lima Cloth*   *Somboon Thanasook* 124
   Cloth in the Lower Region of Southern Thailand

VIETNAM
11 The Representation of Textiles in Cham Sculptures *Emmanuel Guillon*   134

12 Cham Weaving in Vietnam   *Gerald Moussay*   152

13 Traditional Costumes of the Hmong in Vietnam   *Christine Hemmet*   162

EXHIBITION
14 Tilleke & Gibbins Textile Collection   172

FOREWORD

When in 1957 the American James H. W. Thompson began constructing a Thai teak house in Bangkok on a canal across from a Cham weaving village, he set in motion the events that would lead to the publication of this work. While alive, he welcomed hundreds of visitors to his unique home filled with art treasures. Then on Mach 27, 1967 he mysteriously disappeared in the highlands of Malaysia. In an act of great generosity his only heir, nephew Henry Thompson, donated the house and its contents to establish the James H. W. Thompson Foundation, ensuring that a continuing stream of visitors would enjoy the famous cultural landmark. Under the Foundation's charter, proceeds derived from operating the House and Museum must be used to support the conservation, preservation and dissemination of Thailand's rich artistic heritage through research projects, publications and seminars.

For many years the Trustees of the Foundation have wanted to undertake a major cultural event focusing on textiles. On August 2nd and 3rd, 1999 this goal came to fruition with the textile symposium "Southeast Asian Textiles through the Thread of Time". Renowned guest lecturers from around the world were invited to participate in this academic dialogue which drew a large audience of textile enthusiasts. Unfortunately, plans to publish the papers from this conference had to be postponed due to unforeseen difficulties.

However, in 2002 when the Foundation broke ground to build a new Textile Museum on land adjacent to the Jim Thompson House, the decision was made to proceed with publication of the papers. Due to the time lapse, all the scholars who participated in the symposium were contacted and asked to update and revise their work, if needed. Thus, the present publication is the result of their kind efforts in assisting the completion of this project.

There are many people to thank for the success of the textile symposium and the publication of this work. Sadly, for health reasons former President, H.S.H. Prince Subhadradis Diskul, who had been a valuable supporter of the Foundation was unable to participate. However his long-term guidance and support remain at the heart of this project. Professor Smitthi Siribhadra, Foundation Board Member and Thai scholar, assisted this project in many ways including leading the symposium speakers on a stimulating post-conference visit to the northeast. Foundation President Professor William Klausner and Board Member William Booth had the vision to ensure that this project was carried out in a manner that would meet the highest standards of the Jim Thompson legacy and of academic excellence. Jean-Michel Beurdeley, a well-known and highly respected member of the Asian art community, was a driving force in bringing speakers together to participate in the symposium. Overseeing the entire project and handling the many important administrative details was Foundation Board Member Eric Booth, assisted by Beverly Jangkamonkulchai of the Jim Thompson Silk Company.

In terms of preparing this publication, the Foundation is deeply appreciative of the advice and support of M. R. Narisa Chakrabongse and Paisarn Piammattawat of River Books. In addition, grateful appreciation must be expressed to David Lyman for sharing his beautiful Tilleke & Gibbins Textile Collection for use in this book and at a special exhibit held during the symposium.

Finally, warm thanks and deep appreciation go to the twelve speakers who each, in their own way, made such a valuable contribution to *Through the Thread of Time – Southeast Asian Textiles*. Through their scholarship our understanding and appreciation of Southeast Asian textiles has been greatly expanded.

It has been my great pleasure to meet and work with such a wonderfully talented group of people.

Jane Puranananda
The James H. W. Thompson Foundation

INTRODUCTION

A common thread amongst the many civilizations of Southeast Asia has been the great importance placed on textiles. However, today the rich heritage of textiles is slowly fading from the memory of many Southeast Asian cultures. For a variety of reasons, the art of weaving and the meaning and importance placed on textiles has diminished. In even the most remote areas, long-held beliefs and traditions relating to the role and function of textiles are losing their vitality and validity.

Through the Thread of Time – Southeast Asian Textiles presents the efforts of twelve highly respected scholars and art historians to share their knowledge, expertise and research in a field which, ironically, is growing in academic interest even as weavers and old textiles disappear. The guest lecturers, who participated in the James H. W. Thompson Foundation symposium, were given carte blanche to speak on any Southeast Asian textile topic of their choice. As a result, the symposium provided a rich spectrum of ideas, themes and images and served as the basis for the publication of this work.

The papers found in this volume, although based on the symposium lectures, have in many cases been expanded or updated with new information. For reference purposes, the articles included here have been arranged under the modern nations to which they are predominantly related. However, certain articles actually span more than one country, and of course, the historical papers predate modern geographical boundaries.

At the conference, a few of the papers were presented in French or Thai, with the speaker assisted by a translator. However, for this publication, the Thai and French texts have been translated into English. In terms of editing, every attempt has been made to retain the original voice and ideas of the writer.

As to the texts included in this volume, the only deviation from the original list of topics is the addition of a second paper by textile expert Susan Conway on 19th century Shan court dress. Since the time she presented her paper, Conway has expanded her research. She thus offered to provide an additional article with valuable new information.

The reader will note that this volume ends with a selection of textiles which were exhibited during the symposium. These are from the Tilleke & Gibbins Collection in Bangkok. This collection is a valuable resource on Thai, Lao and regional weaving. The James H. W. Thompson Foundation is most grateful to David Lyman for allowing photographs of this collection to be included here.

Arranged in alphabetical order by country, this volume begins with topics under the heading of Cambodia. The first article by Gillian Green provides a fascinating study of ancient Khmer textiles. Through art historical detective work, Green has constructed a convincing account of what types of textiles were used in the ancient Khmer court.

In contrast, Bernard Dupaigne presents a paper that touches on the other end of the spectrum of Khmer textiles by documenting weavings and village culture he studied while living in Cambodia in the late 1960's and 1970's. His report begins with a poignant reminder of the difficulties in pursuing research in the region. Sadly, the Khmer Rouge killed many of the students who assisted him with his research.

The subject of Indonesia textiles is so rich that an entire symposium could easily be devoted to this topic alone. Both the articles included under this heading contribute in very different ways to our understanding of the complexity of this subject. In her article "Motifs and Meanings in Indonesian Textiles" Helen Jessup provides a fascinating overview that focuses on cultural heritage. As an art historian, Jessup explores the various influences on Indonesian civilization and how this bears on the symbolism found in the weaving.

In contrast, Marie-Helen Guelton provides a technical and extremely precise documentation of weavings from East Sumba. The work is based on a detailed study of textiles found in private collections in Paris. Guelton was assisted in this research by enthnologist Danielle Geirnaert, who supplied new unpublished data.

The James H. W. Thompson Foundation was extremely honored to have the renowned textile expert Matiebelle Gittinger participate in the symposium. Her paper reports on field work involving the customs and weaving of three different Tai groups (speakers of the Tai Lao language) in remote areas of northern Laos. While weaving still continues in this part of Laos, as she documents, the meaning and use of whole categories of textiles are being altered beyond recognition.

The other paper listed under the Laos heading, which also includes research in Thailand, was given by Karen A. Bunyaratavej. Her ability to understand the Tai dialects spoken by the groups she interviewed greatly enhanced Bunyaratavej's first-hand account of her research. Through interviews conducted in both Laos and Thailand she investigates and solves a puzzling question about the use and meaning of one particular type of cloth.

The James H. W. Thompson Foundation is very grateful for Susan Conway's contribution to the symposium. Little has been written about the Shan States of Myanmar; thus, her paper provides an insightful introduction into this unique topic. Additionally, her research on Shan dress compliments and links with her original presentation on Lan Na court attire, making this an important addition to this volume.

The James H. W. Thompson Foundation was also extremely fortunate to be able to include John Guy, Senior Curator of Indian and Southeast Asia Art of the Victoria and Albert Museum, in the list of symposium speakers. His paper, under the heading of Thailand, gives a fascinating and well-illustrated historical account of Siamese court dress. He includes information about textiles produced in India for the Thai market.

Also under the Thailand heading is Susan Conway's other article, which presents historical insights on the Lan Na court. For a long time the unique and diverse culture that flourished in the northern Thai Lan Na kingdoms had been greatly overlooked. By specifically focusing on the rich cultural traditions of this area, Conway adds a new dimension to Siamese cultural history.

The third paper listed in the Thailand section was written by Somboon Thanasook, who is a researcher of Thai textiles living in southern Thailand. In this case, the reader benefits from a study presented by a native scholar who intimately understands the culture and traditions of his region. Southern Thailand has long been linked in trade with the Malay Peninsula, thus the beautiful weaving described in this paper reflect this connection.

Under the heading of Vietnam, French scholar, Emmanuel Guillon gives an intriguing introduction to ancient Cham textiles based on a study deduced from sculptural representations. As the origins of the Cham civilization date to the 6th century A. D., this is a challenging task due to the limited amount of available archeological material. However, through his descriptions, fabrics and costumes represented in stone come alive.

Gerald Moussay, lived and worked in Vietnam for many years, until he was unable to undertake further research there for political reasons. He studied the customs and textiles of the Cham people, an ethnic minority presently living in southern Vietnam. Moussay collected information and data about the traditions and ceremonial weavings of the Cham, and provides a very concise account of the Hindu and Muslim influences that underline their textiles.

Finally, also listed under Vietnam, Christine Hemmet gives an engrossing account of the textile traditions of the Hmong minority groups living in Vietnam. Her paper is richly illustrated with excellent photographs she took while doing research amongst these people living in remote mountainous regions. She documents a society and way of life that is currently under much pressure to change.

Through the publication of this volume, The James H. W. Thompson Foundation has hoped to act as a catalyst to further research, analysis, and the sharing of information in the field of textiles. We believe this volume represents an important step in placing on record valuable knowledge and ideas.

The subject matter contained here is extremely diverse, representing an interesting melange of topics and fields of interest. Even as the memory of textiles and weaving traditions disappear, this volume demonstrates that there is much to record, remember and preserve. Hopefully this work will encourage others to pursue new avenues of research into the fascinating field of the roles, function and design of textiles.

Jane Puranananda
The James H. W. Thompson Foundation

CHINA

BANGLADESH

DHAKA

Bay of Bengal

MYANMAR

VIETNAM

HANOI

LAOS

Gulf of Tonkin

HAINAN
DAO

VIENTIANE

RANGOON

THAILAND

BANGKOK

CAMBODIA

ANDAMAN ISLANDS (INDIA)

MERGUI ARCHIPELAGO

PHNOM PENH

Gulf of Thailand

SOUTH CHINA SEA

ANDAMAN SEA

BRUNEI

BANDAR SERI BEGAWAN

MALAYSIA

KUALA LUMPUR

Strait of Malacca

MALAYSIA

SINGAPORE

SUMATRA

BORNEO

INDIAN OCEAN

INDONESIA

JAVA SEA

JAKARTA

BALI SEA

JAVA

9

TEXTILES AT THE KHMER COURT, ANGKOR
Origins, Innovations and Continuities

Gillian Green

Elegant and enigmatic, the costumes depicted on stone and bronze images of deities and kings of the pre- and Angkorian periods subtly signal those universal indicators, status and beauty. Interestingly many of these costume forms are still in evidence, hardly altered, in modern Cambodia.

Although no textiles appear to have survived from Angkorian times, an analysis of their forms and patterns depicted on sculpted images invites more detailed examination of a number of issues often taken for granted. Indeed finding answers to questions about the sources of the fabric, clothing conventions and styles (long the subject of serious research) actually opens up a mine of information supplementing that gained by historical and archaeological researches. Overall it is clear that a sequence of changes occur over the centuries. With a starting point at the mid-first millennium AD, the dates of the earliest available images, a sequence of innovations become apparent and indeed, these changes have been used as an aid to date the images themselves. They are manifested in novel patterns, fabric types and also the styles in which fabrics are draped. These innovations serve in addition, to distinguish royalty and the elite from those lower down the social scale whose simple, unpatterned cotton cloth costumes remain unchanged from that day to this. This paper aims to demonstrate that developments such as these are an inherent feature of the so-called Indic impetus which had such a profound influence on indigenous Khmer religion, aesthetics, architecture and society.

Primary sources of information include epigraphic inscriptions from which a contemporaneous textile vocabulary can be elicited. Visual evidence comes from depictions of costume and also non-costume textile uses sculpted in stone, cast in bronze and carved in relief. Finally, there exists a single surviving literary source in the form of observations recorded by a Yuan dynasty, Chinese emissary, Zhou Daguan who spent a year at the Khmer court at Angkor at the very end of the thirteenth century AD.

Inscriptions both in the vernacular, Old Khmer, and in Sanskrit, the language used in sacred context of the temples, have been intensively studied. This distinction, between sacred and secular, itself may suggest the origin, indigenous or introduced of any particular item referenced in an inscription (fig.1). Saveros Pou's dictionary (1992) has been seminal to interpreting inscriptional information. She has compiled Old Khmer and Sanskrit words deciphered from stone tablets in Romanised form and the dictionary's entries are glossed with their meanings at the time of inscription. Further she has included

Fig. 1 Sanskrit text inscribed on a door frame in the Roluos group of temples, 9th century AD

their modern Khmer counterparts, also transliterated, together with their meanings and pronunciations. Lastly, many of the inscriptions, concerned as they were with listing possessions, be they slaves, riches or land, extend our knowledge of Khmer life beyond the temples and palaces.

Combing through Pou's dictionary, words relating to textiles may be selected. Even though their specific features are generally unknown, these words can be categorised into: styles of costume, types of cloth, techniques and technology and dyes. Some twenty words are glossed as costume forms; thirteen relate to types of cloth suitable for clothing and five to non-costume use; eight words to techniques and tools applicable to textile production, three to dyes and therefore colours; and three to materials from which fabric could be prepared. A selection is listed in Table 1. Some inscriptional words, only slightly modified, are still used in modern Khmer suggesting a remarkable continuity between then and now, in types and techniques as well as in the traditions they represent.

Moving from carved inscriptions to what can be learned from carved images, there are numerous surviving examples of figures in the round as well as bas relief images. Images in the round generally depict human and animal deities and semi-deities of the Hindu pantheon. Buddhism contributes images of bodhisattvas and, in the latter period images of the Buddha and royalty, who commissioned their own sculpted portraits in Buddhist mode. Reliefs, however, portrayed a broader canvas illustrating vibrant depictions of the great Indian epics, the *Ramayana* and *Mahabharata*, or recorded historical exploits of Khmer warrior kings. The images portrayed not only the elite but also Khmer people of the lower echelons of society – soldiers, peasants, slaves and those involved in crafts and economic activities. The most notable examples of the epics are at Angkor Wat and of everyday life at the Bayon (figs. 2, 3). Common to all these forms of imagery is the fact that textiles are omnipresent in all these contexts. They are not merely supplementary to the artistic vision but are an integral part of Khmer life.

Fig. 2 Ceramic pot throwing and sticky rice making, bas relief, Bayon, 12th century AD

Fig. 4 Victory banners, bas relief, Bayon, 12th century AD

Fig. 5 Fans and parasols, bas relief, Angkor Wat, 12th century AD

Looking at the detail in these images, textiles are used in two broad contexts: decorative and utilitarian, mainly in the form of royal regalia and furnishings in palaces and temples, and costumes. We will examine the former first. Regalia includes fans, long vertical "victory banners", parasols, all prominent processional items accompanying, for example, warrior kings into battle (figs. 4, 5). Roofed litters made by attaching a piece of fabric to carrying poles balanced on porters' shoulders become transport for royal princesses while elsewhere, a brahmin can be seen borne along by his helpers (fig. 6, 7). Animal trappings are part of royal regalia. Round, patterned cloths are seen on the backs of horses, water buffalo and elephants, these revered animals often sporting an additional head cloth.

Fig. 6 A Khmer princess being transported in a litter, bas relief, Angkor Wat, 12th century AD

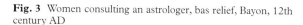

Fig. 3 Women consulting an astrologer, bas relief, Bayon, 12th century AD

Turning to textiles used as furnishings, we see a panoply of parasols made with patterned material on a relief depicting a relaxed Suryavarman II (fig. 8). The king is seated on a patterned and fringed sitting cloth laid on an upholstered couch firmly stuffed with what was undoubtedly locally-grown kapok. Both fabrics are patterned with the same four-petalled flower fabric. Fans constructed of two oblong panels with patterned fabric stretched across them are apparent as well as other forms made of palm leaves or peacock feathers. Inside the royal palace patterned fabrics are employed as roll-up blinds (fig. 9) and blinds to shade window spaces (fig. 10), and curtains made of plain fabric loosely tied back ornament palaces and temples (figs. 11, 12).

Fig. 7 Hindu ascetic being transported in a litter, bas relief, Angkor Wat, 12th century AD

Fig. 8 Suryavarman II relaxing on a couch, bas relief, Angkor Wat, 12th century AD

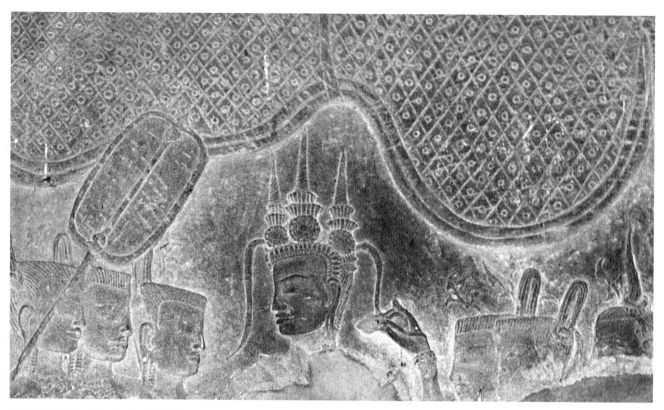

Fig. 9 A fabric blind edged and rolled up with a cord, bas relief, Angkor Wat, 12th century AD

Fig. 10 A patterned fabric blind partially covering a balustered window space, architectural form, Bayon, 12th century AD

Fig. 11 Curtains made of unpatterned fabric seen in a palace, bas relief, Bayon, 12th century AD

14

Fig. 12 Curtains draped round a sacred space enclosing a *lingam*, bas relief, Bayon, 12th century AD

Admittedly the evidence for the use of textiles for the various regalia and furnishing items mentioned above is only circumstantial – their forms and patterns may represent flights of fancy on the part of individual carvers. Yet there exists the eyewitness account of Zhou Daguan who records the use of litters, parasols and banners made of fabric at the Khmer court. Furthermore, the patterns on these observed forms do resemble the patterns on the costumes of the people portrayed in the contemporaneous bas reliefs and sculptures.

There is another group of furnishing textiles whose presence is more subtle because what at first glance may appear to be merely decorative bas relief patterns on temple walls, may well represent textile hangings. In particular representations of two patterns illustrate this point. One, made of intersecting roundels enclosing a floral motif, is carved on stone bas reliefs both at Angkor Wat and the Bayon (fig. 13). At Angkor Wat the pattern appears on the inside surfaces of doorframes and at the Bayon on blinds partially covering a number of balustered windows (fig. 10). The pattern itself is ancient, as evidenced on a four thousand year-old ceramic pot excavated from Mohendjo Daro in the Indus Valley. A number of examples of this pattern created in different media are contemporaneous with the Angkor period.

One is seen on the hipwrapper of a thirteenth-century Javanese stone image of Ganesha (fig. 14). An extant fragment of Indian export cotton cloth recovered from excavations at Fustat, old Cairo is patterned with these same intersecting roundels (fig. 15). The second example, seen on stone bas reliefs on some inner window

Fig. 13 Closeup of intersecting roundel pattern on a door frame, bas relief, Angkor Wat, 12th century AD

15

Fig. 15 Detail of intersecting roundel pattern on a fragment of Indian export, mordant-printed cotton cloth excavated at Fostat, dated to mid-13th century AD. (Sketch based on fragment, Ashmolean Museum, Oxford)

Fig. 14 Intersecting roundel pattern on hipwrapper of a stone Ganesha image from Java, 13th century AD. (Photograph by kind permission of John Guy, Victoria & Albert Museum, London)

Fig. 16 Roundel motif containing two confronting phoenixes, bas relief, Angkor Wat, 12th century AD

frames at Angkor Wat (fig. 16), is of a roundel motif enclosing two confronting phoenixes. The motif is remarkably similar to that on a thirteenth century Chinese silk canopy cloth embroidered with an almost identical image.

These bas relief patterns compared with actual textiles or those represented in other media, are evidence of the existence and therefore likely availability of the actual textiles. Such textiles would undoubtedly have been luxury items affordable only by the wealthy. Archaeological researches have shown that kings' palaces, though ornate, were wooden structures where textile furnishings, including curtains and blinds, would have made a dazzling display. But both these media, textiles and wood, share a common destiny in tropical climates – a short life span. Stone represented permanence, and so was the medium of choice for construction of temples, the homes of the gods. Embellishing a temple wall with durable bas relief patterns representing perishable luxury textiles would therefore be an entirely appropriate solution.

India and China, the likely provenance assigned to the excavated textiles, suggest the source of the fabrics represented at Angkor. Both areas were renowned textile manufacturers, India known for its great quantities of cotton, and China for silk textiles. The Silk Road and its byways extending into South and Southeast Asia may well have been the route by which such textiles found their way to Khmer courts. In addition maritime trade between Southeast Asia and India and, China, had been well established long before the Angkor period.

Turning now to the costume uses of textiles in daily life, upper body coverings, except perhaps for jewellery, are not worn by the Khmer except in the case of warrior kings and soldiers who wear upper body garments of two quite specific forms. One is a short bodice with the lower edge ending above the waist (fig. 17), and the second a longer jacket reaching to the hips (figs. 18, 19). Both forms are short-sleeved. Pattern motifs are varied: four-petal flowers, "solar discs", spots looking remarkably as though resist-dyed, and floral motifs contained in bands or squares. Most also have a characteristic feature of a

Fig. 17 Khmer soldiers wearing short bodices patterned with a "solar disc" motif, bas relief, Angkor Wat, 12th century AD

row of small discs, perhaps shiny pieces of mica, along the edges.

The prevalent form, however, is a lower body garment, termed here a hipwrapper. While all participants in Khmer life – human and mythological – wear hipwrappers of one form or another, the extent of coverage of the lower body ranges from minimal to mid-thigh to ankle length. Hipwrappers are constructed from unstitched rectangular lengths of cloth worn with the selvedges forming the waist and hem borders. Images reveal that over the centuries some fifteen distinct styles of hipwrapper had been in favour and that progressively more exotic fabrics had become available with which to ring the changes. Early in the Angkorian period plain or simple warp-striped lengths were in vogue but by the ninth century, pleated cloth had become very popular (fig. 20). Come the twelfth and thirteenth centuries,

Fig. 18 Khmer soldiers wearing belted, long jackets with an all-over floral pattern, bas relief, Angkor Wat, 12th century AD

Fig. 19 Khmer soldiers wearing what appears to be two long, patterend jackets, bas relief, Bayon, 12th century AD

Fig. 20 Flouncy, pleated skirt cloth worn by a semi-deity, bas relief, Roluos group, 9th century AD

cloth patterned with random or ordered designs of floral motifs in the central field became popular. Often the end panels of these cloths are patterned with geometric designs in weft-oriented bands (fig. 21).

Hipwrappers may be worn in two basic forms, the difference relating to the way the cloth is actually draped on the body. One is a *sampot chawng kbun* a length of cloth wrapped around the waist and knotted at the waist. The simplest form constructed with a narrow length of plain cotton, is knotted at the back, then one of the ends passed between the legs to the front and that end slipped under the waistband cloth and allowed to hang down the front. This minimal form of *chawng kbun* is seen on bas reliefs of rank-and-file soldiers, probably slaves of hill-

Fig. 21 Skirt cloth with floral patterns in centre field and weft-oriented patterned bands in the endpanels, bas relief, Bayon, 12th century AD

19

Fig. 22 "Minimal *chawng kbun*" worn by prisoners, bas relief, Bayon, 12th century AD

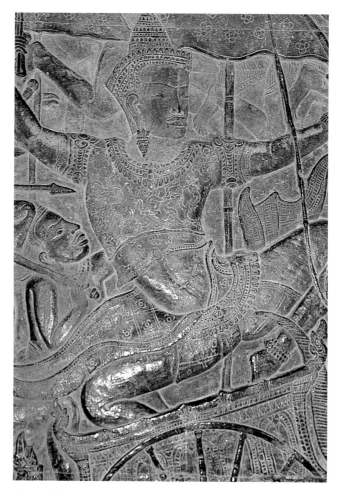

Fig. 23 "Flared *chawng kbun*" with a floral pattern teamed with a patterned bodice worn by a warrior, bas relief, Angkor Wat, 12th century

tribe origin; on captured Cham soldiers; and on ascetics and manual labourers (fig. 22). If, however, the cloth is knotted at the front, the two ends of cloth passed between the legs and slipped under the waistband or belt at the back, a more elaborate form is created and this is the most familiar form *sampot chawng kbun*. One version is termed a "flared" *chawng kbun* while the other is termed a "pocket fold" *chawng kbun* (figs. 23, 24). More flamboyant fabrics are employed on persons of higher rank, kings or high-ranking soldiers.

The other form is termed a skirt cloth *sampot* which differs from *sampot chawng kbun* in that the cloth hangs unhindered from waist to ankle. Consisting of a short length of fabric simply wrapped round the body, skirt cloths are cinched either with a belt or by being knotted at the waist (fig. 25). If a longer length is used, the vertical end panel may be pleated into a bundle, folded over at the waist, and the fold, tucked in at the waist, allowed

to drape forward (fig. 26). Novel cloth patterns with decorative bands in the end panels appear in the later Angkorian period. So as not to conceal these patterns new forms are devised so that these patterned sections are prominently displayed (see fig. 21).

Both forms of hipwrappers are quite easily reconstructed today from the depictions on the sculpted images. But there are two particular forms which initially present problems for reconstruction. One is the elegant style worn by apsaras depicted on bas reliefs at Angkor Wat (fig. 27). The other is the dashing *chawng kbun* worn by a number of male deities (fig. 28). In both instances the problem is that in whatever way a single length of rectangular cloth is manipulated and manoeuvred, the forms cannot be recreated.

In the case of the apsaras' costume, a possible explanation can be deduced from the meticulous depiction of their garments on the bas relief images. The arching

Fig. 24 "Pocket fold *chawng kbun*" with a pendant sash tucked into the belt over the right hip, worn by a guardian, relief at Banteay Srei, 10th century AD

Fig. 25 Skirt cloth knotted at waist, worn with an elaborated belt by an apsara, relief, Banteay Srei, 10th century AD

Fig. 26 Skirt cloth worn by Uma with the endpanel pleated and tucked in at the waist like a modern-day Indian sari, Bakong, 9th century AD. (Coffin Collection, Plate no. VI-20-A-18a. Courtesy National Library of Australia)

21

Fig. 27 Elegant costume worn by an apsara. It most likely consists of two lengths of cloth, one secured over the other, bas relief, Angkor Wat, 12th century AD

Fig. 28 Pleated "pocket fold *chawng kbun*" worn by a deity, Angkor Wat. A second length of fabric forms a pendant sash draping centrally while a third length drapes from one hip to the other. The panel of fanned out pleats above the waist are formed by the end section of the "pocket fold" end panel which, turned back on itself, is secured under the belt. The other end panel of the hipwrapper has been passed between the legs to be secured at the back. (Coffin Collection, Plate no. XXVII-19-D-7. Courtesy National Library of Australia)

panels at the waist are invariably shown emerging from underneath the waist edge of the skirt cloth. One may speculate that the subjects were wearing not one but two garments, one on top of the other. Suppose the underneath garment was tied in *chawng kbun* fashion and its two long ends, after knotting, were swept up while the skirt cloth was secured over it, then these ends would emerge over the skirt cloth, exactly as depicted. This interpretation is supported by the fact that the arching cloth panels and the overlying skirt cloth are always differently patterned. In addition another feature relating to widths of cloth becomes apparent. The underlying cloth does not need to be a wide piece of fabric as is apparent, whereas the overlying skirt cloth clearly is constructed

from a length wide enough to extend from waist to ankle.

The construction of a knee-length *chawng kbun* seen on many images of male deities can be recreated by recognising that the decorative "fishtail" or "anchor" shape is not just a draped section of the *chawng kbun* but is a separate item formed by a second, narrow length of cloth. The term "pendant sash" *ban muk* has been introduced to describe this item. It is slipped up, under and round the belt and allowed to drape down with one end longer than the other. Some images sport one or even two additional pendant sashes either side of the central one.

These two forms are, therefore, examples of sophisticated composite styles requiring not only a minimum of two lengths of cloth but also cloth of differing widths.

Fig. 29. Skirt cloth worn by a female figure. This cloth appears to be made of several lengths of the same width stitched together to form a wider, weft width reaching from waist to ankles, bas relief, Preah Khan, 12th century AD

This issue of widths is very important. It is clear that some costumes worn by Khmer people are made from a narrow length of cloth such as that woven on a simple backstrap loom. The minimal *chawng kbun* being an example of this. But this narrow length is just not wide enough to reach from waist to knee or to ankle as seen in more elaborate images. Neither are the furnishing fabrics, curtains and wall hangings depicted on bas reliefs, typical products of a simple backstrap loom either in form or decoration.

These very practical considerations make one wonder about the sources of textiles used by the Khmer at Angkor, by the elite in particular. Backstrap loom weaving is an archaic technique used by many peoples around the world including the indigenous Khmer. Zhou Daguan remarked on seeing backstrap loom weaving in the thirteenth century and in fact this simple technique is still practised by Cambodian hilltribes to this day.

With regard to elite Khmer costumes there is, of course, the possibility that if several lengths of backstrap loom woven cloth are stitched together along the selvedges, then a wider piece would result. But then horizontal seams would be apparent in all hipwrappers constructed in this fashion. Although details such as folds, pleats, knots and patterns are meticulously depicted by the sculptors, horizontally-oriented seams are so far evident in only one case. This is on an image of a female deity at Preah Khan who wears a skirt cloth with a number of distinct, evenly spaced horizontal seams (fig. 29).

Is there any evidence that the indigenous Khmer of the Angkor period wove cloth other than simple backstrap loom widths? One could look to the bas reliefs at the Bayon where other craft activities are clearly depicted, but no looms of any kind are seen. Inscriptions reveal a vocabulary referring to weaving and to spinning but not specifically to a loom capable of weaving a wider length of cloth.

So the question must be asked from where did the Khmer elite obtain the decorative, wider-weft, patterned cloth from which to style their ankle-length costumes and palatial furnishing materials so clearly shown in the images?

One source was close to home. Zhou Daguan mentions that Siamese weavers supplied 'dark silk damask' cloth for Khmer use. He also recorded that cloth sourced from further afield – Champa and India – was much sought after. But what about sources from further afield? Archaeological evidence of land-based trade routes and historical evidence of contacts between the Khmer and other domains point to likely sources. Suryavarman I and II, for example, actively fostered contact with the Indian Chola dynasty during their twelfth century reigns. China is also recorded to have exported coloured silk cloth to southern entrepots. So it appears that cloth, lending itself to forms other than those dictated by backstrap loom lengths, could have been sourced from India and China. These wider widths would facilitate creation of styles new to the indigenous Khmer tradition.

New styles, it seems, were motivated by influences from abroad. Evidence indicating that Indian costume forms themselves were a major impetus for these new styles can be deduced from comparison with Indian forms. Moti Chandra (1973) analysed depictions of costumes and textiles on Indian sculpted and painted images and from linguistic sources going back to antiquity. Comparing traditional Indian forms with Khmer forms analysed in the same way, remarkable resemblances can be seen. It can be argued the Khmer *sampot chawng kbun* form equates to the Indian *"dhoti"* and that the Khmer pendant sash mimics the Indian *"patka"*. Khmer skirt cloths, with a bundle of pleats tucked in at the waist, resemble the Indian *"sari"* and the skirt cloth simply knotted at the waist, the Indian *"lunghi"*. The cropped bodice and jacket styles worn by Khmer warrior kings and soldiers conform to the style and usage depicted on Kushan and Gupta images of Indian kings, deities and warriors published by Chandra.

In short, it seems quite plausible that the Khmer elite derived both the models for novel costumes from India as well the bulk of the textiles with which to create them. Although Chinese-sourced silk cloth was most likely available to the Khmer, Chinese costume styles, as visualised on contemporaneous silk paintings and tomb relics, were not adopted by the Khmer. But motifs appearing on Chinese embroideries and other textiles do suggest that Chinese-sourced luxury cloth could have been used as wall hangings in an elite Khmer context.

Costumes and textiles represented in stone and bronze, this discussion argues, provide substantial evidence to add to historical and archaeological research of the lives of Khmer people of the Angkorian period. They represent significant innovations in form and luxury additions to the textiles embellishing the lives of upper echelons of society. In contemporary Cambodia weaving of textiles and wearing of traditional costume remains a powerful expression of the enduring importance of cloth in Cambodian culture.

References

Chandra, M. 1973, *Costumes, Textiles, Cosmetics and Coiffure in Ancient and Mediaeval India,* Oriental Publishers, Delhi.

Pou, S. 1992, *An Old Khmer-French-English Dictionary,* Centre de Documentation et de Recherche sur la Civilisation Khmere, Paris.

Footnotes

[1] The Angkorian period is defined as the seventh to mid-fifteenth centuries AD.

[2] Watt, J. & Wardwell, A. 1997, *When Silk was Gold. Central Asian and Chinese Textiles,* The Metropolitan Museum of Art, New York, p. 197.

[3] All words appearing in italics are transliterated modern Khmer words.

[4] The phrase *sampot chawng kbun* derives from *sampot* meaning a length of cloth for covering, *chawng* meaning to bind and *kbun* meaning a cover for the private parts.

[5] *Pamn muk* literally means "to cover (v)/cover for (n) - the front" and is also used for non-costume items with the same function, such as a dais cover on which an image is placed.

[6] The striations indicated on the skirt cloth may be interpreted as a representation of beaten barkcloth rather than woven lengths.

TABLE 1

WORDS RELATING TO COSTUMES AND TEXTILES DERIVED FROM ANGKORIAN PERIOD STONE INSCRIPTIONS

Reference: Saveros Pu, 1992, *Old Khmer-French-English Dictionary*

COSTUME	TYPES OF CLOTH
amval, amron - wrapround	*kansen
kupen - a cover for private parts	*kamvar*
canleyk - lower garment	*kapata*
camnvat - a headdress	*kjo*
chnvat - turban	*kdan
pangat - that which secures, belt made of fabric	*pan-en*
thyam - kind of garment	*thyam*
daup - rag, loin cloth	*thyay*
yo, yau - upper garment, kind of shirt, cloth for making it	
snap - cover, coat, lining	
spai - shawl wrapped round the breasts and over the left shoulder and left hanging down the back	
srapac - cloth, garment ?	
srom sarom - envelop, seath, scabbard	
sati - woven cloth worn to cover below the waist	

Key: * indicates that the item has an equivalent in modern Khmer.

TABLE 2

MODERN KHMER FORM OF SOME TRANSLITERATED INSCRIPTIONAL WORDS

MODERN KHMER	**MEANING**
chawng	to bind
kbun	a cover for the private parts
aaw	upper body garment; length of cloth for making it
kaniuh	to twist different yarns for weaving
pidaan	extension, curtain or canopy
ban	to cover or hide (v)
kiet	to tie firmly
sutr	silk
krapas	unspun cotton
dop	loincloth as worn by mountain people
kansen	a lightweight, all-purpose cloth
kantol	bark cloth
tung	banner

WEAVING IN CAMBODIA

Bernard Dupaigne

I propose to present information about some relatively unknown Cambodian textiles, which, for the most part, I studied at weaving villages during the period 1968-1970 when I was teaching at the Faculty of Archaeology in Phnom Penh.

During those two years I had a chance to study Cambodian crafts in the villages which were often distant and difficult to reach. I was often accompanied by some of my students, whom I wish to thank. Unfortunately most of them were killed during the Khmer Rouge regime.

After the destruction, which occurred during the war and under the Khmer Rouge government, silk weaving has today become very important once again in Cambodia. However, a large variety of textiles have now disappeared. The villages were ransacked, often abandoned and destroyed. The weaving tradition was lost, and the most difficult weaving techniques are not practiced any more. Even though the women have preserved the tradition of wearing silk skirts to festivals, ceremonies and temples, the economic situation has become more complex for them. Frequently they have neither time nor possibility to practise long and delicate weaving techniques, which would have created the most beautiful textiles (fig. 1).

Fig. 1 Ceremonial skirt worn in the palace. Museum of Phnom Penh

The raising of silk worms

The raising of silk was still important in Cambodia in 1970. A large number of farmers produced on their own the silk yarn necessary for weaving, despite a Buddhist interdiction not to kill any living beings (given that the chrysalis in the cocoons were boiled alive before becoming butterflies).

The raising of silk worms was done mostly to the north and the south of Phnom Penh, around the rivers Tonle Sap, Bassac and Mekong, in the provinces of Takeo, Kandal and Prey Veng. The other important centres were in the Cham villages surrounding Kompong Cham on the Mekong river, around Kampot close to the sea, but also in a few villages in the north of the country, mainly at Phnom Srok in the province of Battambang. The raising of silk worms requires a large number of mulberry trees. It was therefore limited to only those provinces which are well-irrigated, and along the streams and rivers.

A capable weaver could raise four batches of worms in one year, during the rainy season from May to January. Three hundred female butterflies could lay enough eggs for a final production of 20 to 30 kilos of silk cocoons. An average batch could therefore provide two to three kilos of silk yarn four times a year, resulting in the production of 10 kilos of silk yarn per family.

To the south-east of Cambodia, along the two banks of the Mekong river close to the Vietnamese border, the breeding of silk worms was largely practised by Vietnamese immigrants. These people did not have land for cultivation and being unable to grow rice; their main economic activity was thus the raising of worms and the separation of cocoons to make silk yarn.

The dyeing of the yarn was generally done by the weavers themselves. There are no dyeing specialists. Vegetable dyes were still well known – the yellow colour was made from the bark of *prahout* (*Garcinia villersiana*), which was used as the base for other colours. The red colour was made from cochineal (*Laccifer lacca*), which is a parasite bush insect, or stick-lac. *Leak,* the blue colour, was obtained from the fermentation of indigo leaves called *trom* (*Indigoferia tintoria*), which is a plant grown in great numbers on the island of Mekong near Kompong Cham. In the province of Kandal, 37 kilometres south of Phnom Penh, there existed the enduring tradition of weaving yarn dyed in black colour by soaking it several times in a solution of fruit called *makloeu* (*Diospyros mollis*). These black dyes were used especially to make trousers for the Chinese and the Vietnamese.

Silk weaving

Silk weaving using hand-weaving equipment produced by village carpenters and specialised craftsmen was still very important in the provinces of Takeo, Kandal, Kompong Speu and Prey Veng. This provided additional income necessary for the Khmer farmers.

The technique used was the weaving of two or three smooth rows to make cotton scarf *krama*, or silk skirts; the weaving with additional smooth rows for the design (such as *lobak*, which is silk cloth with geometrical designs produced in the isolated villages in Kompong Speu province, srok of Phnom Sruoch), *sin* cloth with designs at the lower end – with flower designs in silk, silver or gold, *tcharebap*, woven with golden or silver threads, with eight additional smooth rows to make the design.

The Cham people, expelled after the fall of the Champa empire in the 15th century and attacked by the Annam empire, came to take refuge in Cambodia in the 17th century. As they did not own land, men worked as sailors or fishermen, women as weavers, continuing the rich textile tradition of the Hindu Cham of Vietnam. Three Cham regions produced very high-quality silk: in the provinces of Kampot and Kompong Cham, and to the north of Phnom Penh, all the way to Kompong Luong, along the Tonle river. (fig. 2)

The Malay immigrants, or "Javanese", Chvear, settled down to the north of Phnom Penh as well. They lived in different villages from the Chams, but also being Muslim, they created as in Kleang Sbek, elaborate weavings such as weft-patterned multi-coloured silks for wedding ornaments, or weft-patterned silk weavings (following the Malay and Sumatra tradition) to make turbans and men's wedding trousers. (figs. 3, 4, 5)

Fig. 3 Cham man wearing a traditional turban at a wedding ceremony, Kleang Sbek, Kandal province

Fig. 4 Ancient stitched silk band. Displayed during a Cham wedding ceremony. Chraing Chamres, Kandal province

Fig. 2 Large ikat silk material, displayed at wedding ceremonies. Mosque, tree of life and vessels, dragons, elephants, torpido fish (skate), other types of fish and birds

Fig. 5 Decoration of houses during wedding ceremonies. Silk stitched from silk thread "Chvear", Prek Reing, Kandal province

Cham people also produced *plangi* (tie-dye), women's dresses, manuscript covers, dyed after weaving with series of catches at different places, according to a specific motifs, and with coloured dyes.

The *sarong* of Muslim men, Cham and Mala, were made using warp ikat. In this case, it was the warp thread itself which was dyed, using a series of bindings made with banana fibers: the weaving was then simple, the design appeared already on the warp thread.

The *hôl* weaving

In former times the Khmers knew about weaving with paperboards to produce silk bands (fig. 6) for tying the manuscripts on *olles*, palm paper carved with a sharp knife. As in Burma, these silk bands could be decorated with sacred writings in *pali* language.

However, the most popular weaving technique is the technique of *hôl*, used to make women's skirts. Here the *ikat* is made from yarn: the warp is plain, but the yarn is prepared beforehand by a series of bindings and successive dyeing, thus making a design on the yarn thread. The most important centres for the Khmers are the province of Takeo (srok of Bati), and for the Chams the river villages along the Mekong, in the province of Kompong Cham.

The entire surface of the silk skirt worn by women at festivals is designed with geometrical or floral patterns. The most beautiful ones, which are long and difficult to make, are produced by the Khmer and the Cham people. The motifs include animals, crabs, birds, dragons, birds surrounding the tree of life, as well as angels and *kinari* (birds with a female human face), solar signs, which are the same as those known in the ancient art of Iran.

In former times elaborate designs were made by the Malays of Prek Reing, north of Phnom Penh, for the tapestries decorating the bride's house. Found on these rare weavings, in addition to birds, are dragons, snakes, crabs, trees of life, representations of great ships which reflect the memory of the naval tradition of the Malay people, temples, white elephants and torpedo fish (skate).

Weavings showing the life of Lord Buddha

The Khmer farmers had the same custom as the Thais, to donate their most beautiful weavings to Buddhist temples, especially for the *pidan*, canopy for the statues of Buddha in the temples. Some textiles could date to the 19th century. They disappeared during the pillage of temples by the Khmer Rouge. Only two ancient textiles remain in the museum in Phnom Pehn (fig. 7).

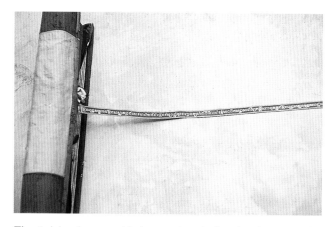

Fig. 6 A band woven with the paperboards, for tying the manuscript on *olles*. Temple of Prek Cheng Kran, Prey Veng province

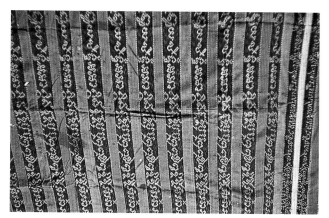

Fig. 7 Silk ikat with Buddhist inscription

Fig. 8 Life of the Buddha. The future Buddha in his palace, and his departure on horseback, protected by a parasol

Fig. 10 The future Buddha in his palace, surrounded by his wife and his son, his followers and the angels. Buddha meditating in the forest. Buddha resisting the attack of the tigers

The *pidan* donated to the temples, made using the *hôl* technique, detail the various episodes in the life of Lord Buddha (fig. 8).

Siddharta Gautama, the future Buddha, was in his palace, (fig. 9) surrounded by his wife the Princess Yasodhara, and his son Rahula. Framing the palace are birds, the tree of life (linking earth with the sky, the axis of the world), two white elephants with their mahouts, and dragons (fig. 10). Sometimes there is Brahma, the four-headed god who "watches over the four corners of the world" on top of the palace's roof.

The "Great Departure" is commonly represented. The prince leaves the palace at night. The angels, *devata*, or celestial divinity, hold up his white horse so that the noise of its shoes will not wake up the princess and her

followers. The Buddha is also protected by a parasol they hold (fig.11).

At the foot of the tree of life, the future Buddha meditates in the forest, fasting as ascetic, and suffering mortification (fig. 12). Underneath the *pippal* tree, he was attacked by the demons in the form of tigers, who try to make him give in. Reaching "Enlightenment", the

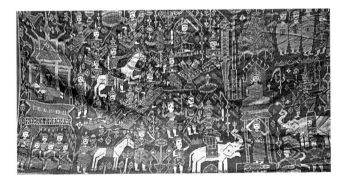

Fig. 11 The prince leaves his father's palace with the white horse, protected by the angels holding a parasol, while his wife is still asleep. A group of followers and concubines. Buddha in meditation. Buddha in asceticism in the forest. The Goddess Thorani cutting her hair to give water to the kingdom surrounded by the royal white elephants, ridden by their mahouts. Source: Srok de Bati

Fig. 9 Buddha in his palace The royal white elephant

29

Fig. 12 Buddha in meditation

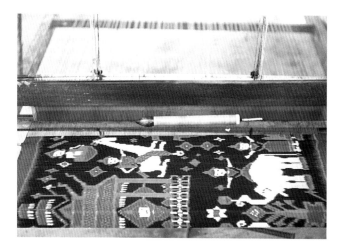

Fig. 13 Life of Buddha, woven in 1968. The prince in his palace, then the prince leaving the palace, the white elephants, ridden by their mahouts, in front of the tree of life

prince cuts his long hair with his sword, signifying by this simple gesture his renouncement of the secular world of desires and sufferings.

On several woven textiles the goddess Preah Torani wrings out her long black hair, thus providing water to the Khmer kingdom.

These superb elaborated textiles, so rich in history, can be found only in some rare collections. High quality copies are now produced in the north-east of Thailand. Nowadays we can still find Cambodia textiles with these designs, but made of a coarser quality and changed from the original use (fig. 13). We can even find some heresy in their use in the form of skirts for tourists.

Silk weaving, which disappeared during the war, reappeared in Cambodia about ten years ago. The quality remains good, but due to the migration of the population and the disruption in the chain of transmission of knowledge, the designs have become more uniform and simplified, whereas in the past, each production centre had its own recognisable style. Fortunately, at present the efforts to rehabilitate the farmer-craftsmen are bearing fruit, and Cambodian weaving will be able to rediscover a part of its past glory.

MOTIF AND MEANING IN INDONESIAN TEXTILES

Helen Ibbitson Jessup

The diversity and richness of the textile traditions of Indonesia make any attempt to create a comprehensive epistemology virtually impossible. There are many ways to approach the subject: analyses can be made on the basis of geography, of technique, of material, of function, among others. Many valuable and stimulating studies that focus on these aspects have been made, especially during the past twenty years. The approach in this paper focuses on motifs drawn from a wide variety of Indonesian cultures, textile types and techniques with the aim of explaining their symbolism, as distinct from their identity. As an art historian, rather than a textile specialist, I have based my analysis on the belief that textiles can be usefully examined in the total context of the culture from which they spring, and therefore I will draw on sculptural and architectural images as well as on those found in cloth.

It is generally agreed that although there are five chief elements in the web of Indonesian civilisation, the most important primary cultural sources are two: an underlying Austronesian social organisation, regarded as original, and an Indic entity that was grafted on. This is of course an over-simplification: the Austronesian characteristics were not autochthonous, but imported into the archipelago over a long period beginning at an indeterminable date around 2000 BCE, or earlier. Their place of origin in Southwest China, in the area now known as Yunan, and the techniques and motifs they brought with them, were consistent with those evident in Neolithic culture.

The second wave of influences, the Indic, is also problematic. First, their Indian sources cannot be identified with any certainty. Are they the areas of Buddhistic evolution in the north, or perhaps Sri Lanka? Or do the influences come from the trade-connected south? Or from Gujerat, the centre of important textile trade? Second, the dating of the arrival of these influences is equally uncertain. We know that trade between Europe and the Middle East, on one end of the axis, and China on the other, was established before the beginning of the first millennium of our era. Its overland route, via what is usually called the Silk Route, would not have affected the Indonesian archipelago or even mainland Southeast Asia, but its maritime route would certainly have linked Indonesia with India and China. In fact, the first written evidence for the existence of any of the Indonesian polities comes from fifth-century copies of third-century Chinese dynastic records, which mention visits from emissaries from the archipelago.

Later, a third cultural influence, the arrival of Islam in the late thirteenth century, and its gradual domination of the religious beliefs of the archipelago by the seventeenth century, deeply affected Indonesian culture. In terms of political organisation, so did the presence, from the sixteenth century, of European colonial powers, the last of the external influences. The fifth influence on Indonesian culture, that of China, was very early, and of great importance, although it has always been underestimated. Like the Austronesian and the Indic, it is undateable.

An examination of artifacts from the Shang period that are contemporary with the Austronesian migrations reveals that their motifs have many similarities with the motifs of what is generally considered the prototype of Austronesian culture, namely, the Dong-son civilisation of the Bronze-Iron age. Dong-son dating is itself problematic: some Vietnamese archaeologists have recently pushed its suggested dates back as far as 2000 BCE. So long as this applies to its origins (rather than the specific culture that flourished in Vietnam from about 700 BCE until the third century CE and was noted from the production of the eponymous Dong-son drums), there is some basis for the concept. Such a date would coincide with Shang bronze-making, which was well established at that period and which marks the gradual transition from the culture of Neolithic, often nomadic peoples of prehistoric China, to the imperial civilisation. As I shall attempt to show, many of the motifs of Dongsonian artifacts are very close to those found on Shang and Zhou bronze objects.

The parallels between the proto-Chinese and the Austronesian motifs can be seen clearly in the use of

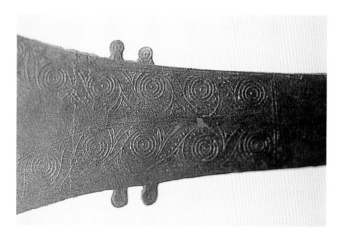

Fig. 1 Ceremonial standard. Roti, Bronze-Iron Age, bronze. Museum Mpu Tentular, Surabaya. Photo D. Bakker for National Gallery of Art, Washington, DC

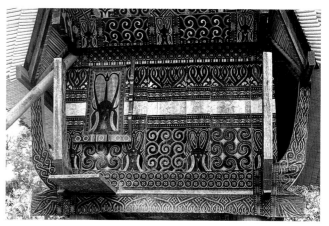

Fig. 3 Carving motif. Toraja, South Sulawesi, 20th century, wood. Photo Helen I. Jessup

Fig. 2 Vessel. Madura, Bronze-Iron Age, bronze. Museum Nasional, Jakarta. Photo Helen I. Jessup

running and interlocked spirals, as on a *hu,* a Shang bronze ceremonial vessel from the twelfth century BCE and a bronze ceremonial tablet of the Bronze-Iron age from Roti (fig. 1). Sometimes the spirals are looser and more open, as can be seen on a *yu,* a bronze ceremonial vessel, also Shang, from the twelfth or eleventh century BCE and a Bronze-Iron age vessel from Madura (fig. 2). The same kind of motif has persisted and can be seen in contemporary Indonesian architectural motifs carved on a house from Toraja in South Sulawesi as well as in the border of a woven textile from Aceh (figs. 3, 4).

The similarity of motif is also apparent in the depiction of stylised heads on a Shang *fang jia,* or bronze ritual wine vessel (12th-11th century BCE) and a ceremonial axe from the Bronze-Iron age from Roti (figs. 5, 6). Can we infer a direct inheritance in the occurrence in historical time of such monster heads as a *kala* head from thirteenth-century Candi Kidal as well as an example from Bali (figs. 7, 8)?

Fig. 4 Border motif. Aceh. Photo Helen I. Jessup

Fig. 5 *Fang jia* (ritual wine vessel). Shang, 12th–11th century, bronze. Freer Gallery of Art, F 35.12

Fig. 6 Ceremonial axe. Roti, Bronze-Iron Age, bronze. Museum Nasional Jakarta. Photo D. Bakker for National Gallery of Art, Wahsington, DC

Fig. 7 *Kala* head. Candi Kidal, East Java cave, Bali, 13th century, stone. Photo Helen I Jessup

Fig. 8 *Kala* head. Goa Gajah cave, Bali, 11th century, stone. Photo Helen I. Jessup

The use of objects adapted from everyday life (such as axes and vessels for food and drink) as ceremonial artifacts suggests that the people who made and used them were still close to an animist set of beliefs inherited from ancestors rather than a structured exotic religion. The focus is apparent in the illustrations on Dong-son drums. These comprise stars, geometric elements like triangles and circles, and meander patterns like spirals (fig. 9). They also present images of ships, birds, warriors with plumed head-dresses and elaborate boats with high curving prows (fig. 10). It is notable that representations of boats are not found on contemporary

33

Fig. 10 Drum, detail showing boat. Dong–son culture, c. 300 BCE-300 CE, bronze. Museum Nasional, Jakarta. Photo Helen I. Jessup

Fig. 9 Drum, Dong-son culture, c. 300 BCE–300 CE, bronze. Museum Nasional, Jakarta. Photo Helen I. Jessup

Chinese bronzes, suggesting that it was the migrating Austronesians for whom the boat was significant. The link between the myths of origin of many Indonesian peoples, in which the ancestors are said to have arrived by water, and the depiction of boats, is clear. Boats are important symbols in an archipelago, and especially in the parts of Indonesia where the Austronesian elements have remained strongest, namely, the areas where Hindu-Buddhist culture did not penetrate so deeply. It is in one of the areas that had less contact with Brahmanism that the ship has the greatest mythological importance: Lampung in southern Sumatra.

The famous ship cloths of Lampung, hung in the houses of the more prominent families at times of ceremonial transition, need little introduction, whether they are the magnificent long *palepai* that are thought to represent ships of the soul or the dead (figs. 11, 12), or

the smaller *tampan,* which were in less exclusive use (figs. 13, 14). Boats are significant treasures, or *pusaka,* in eastern Indonesia, where they can be found in *songket* textiles (fig. 15). An extraordinary example of sacred communal treasure can be seen in an eastern bronze boat that may date from early in our era and which resembles figures depicted on Dongsonian drums (fig. 16). Another instance of the association of the ship with the rite of passage connected with death occurs in the coffins, or spirit boats, of the Torajan people (fig. 17). Within the historical period, we find among the reliefs of Borobudur the depiction of a boat that is similar in many ways to the wooden sailing vessels that ply Indonesia's waterways to this day (fig. 18).

If the boat symbolism of contemporary Indonesia's myths of origin is closely related to Austronesian forms, the sets of patterns that involve swastika, or *banji,* motifs are clearly more closely connected with ancient China. The design on a *lei,* an earthenware Shang ritual wine

Fig. 11 *Palepai.* Semangka Bay, Lampung, Sumatra, 19th century, cotton with supplementary weft. Collection Holmgren-Spertus # I-276

Fig. 12 *Palepai.* Kalianda, Lampung, Sumatra, 19th century, cotton with supplementary weft. Collection Holmgren–Spertus # I-387

Fig. 13 *Tampan*. Lampung, Sumatra, 19th century, cotton with supplementary weft. Collection Holmgren-Spertus # I –114

Fig. 15 *Songket* weaving. Sumbawa Besar, early 20th century, silk with supplementary weft. Raja of Semawa. Photo John Gollings

Fig. 14 *Tampan*. Lampung, Sumatra, 19th century, cotton with supplementary weft. Collection Holmgren-Spertus # I-132

Fig. 16 Ceremonial boat. Flores, Dong-son culture c. 300 CE, bronze. Photo Hugh O' Neill

Fig. 17 Spirit boats. Toraja, South Sulawesi, early 20th century, stone. Photo Helen I. Jessup

Fig. 18 Relief of boat. Candi Borobudur, Central Java, c. 800 CE, Photo Helen I. Jessup

Fig. 19 *Lei* (ritual wine container). Shang, 12th –13th century BCE, bronze. Freer Gallery of Art #39.42

container (fig. 19), is perhaps a precedent for a frequently used motif in both graphic technique, as in the *prada,* or gold leaf, decorations on a courtly Cirebon *dodot* cloth (fig. 20) and in weaving, shown in a warp ikat cloth from Central Sulawesi (fig. 21). It is to be noted that one of these textiles comes from Sulawesi, an area less affected by Indic culture than the central islands of Java, Bali and Sumatra, and the other from the north coast of Java where Chinese trading influences were strongest.

Not only myths of origin and rites of passage employ imagery derived from both Austronesian and

Fig. 20 *Dodot* cloth. Cirebon, West Java, early 20th century, cotton with gold leaf *(prada)* work. Private collection. Photo Helen I. Jessup

Fig. 21 *Galumpang* (shoulder cloth). C. Sulawesi, 20th century, cotton, warp ikat. Private collection. Photo Helen I. Jessup

Chinese sources. The Tree of Life is also a universal symbol, invoking fertility and the links between the Upper and the Lower worlds. It is found in a Western Zhou *hu* of the ninth century BCE and also in a Lampung *palepai* (figs. 22, 23). Like the boat and *banji* motif, the Tree of Life is frequently invoked in the regions of Indonesia where Austronesian influences are less diluted, as seen in a woven mat and a wall hanging, both from Kalimantan (figs. 24, 25), and in a ceremonial seat of honour, or *pepadon*, from Lampung (fig. 26). It is also often seen in places on the north coast of Java where Chinese influences were pervasive. The *kekayon*, or tree motif centrepiece of a set of shadow puppets from Cirebon, reveals strong Chinese influence (fig. 27). In such regions there is a clear predominance, in patterns connected with identity, of geometric motifs derived from the Austronesian sources that resemble proto-Chinese designs. In Baun and Savu in the east, woven cloths contain coded information about social group, position, age and sex (figs. 28, 29).

Fig. 22 *Hu* (ceremonial vessel). Western Zhou, 9th century BCE, bronze. Freer Gallery of Art #13.21

Fig. 23 *Palepai*, detail. Lampung, Sumatra, 20th century, cotton with supplementary weft. Private collection. Photo Helen I. Jessup

Fig. 24 Sleeping mat. Kalimantan, 20th century, split bamboo. Private collection. Photo Helen I. Jessup

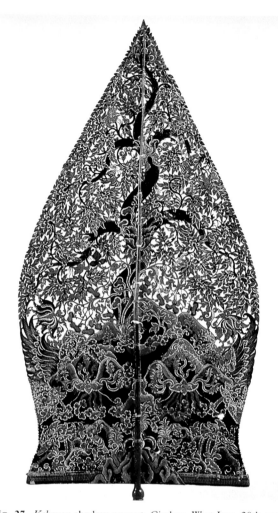

Fig. 25 Wall hanging. Kalimantan, 20th century, split bamboo. Private collection. Photo Helen I. Jessup

Fig. 27 *Kekayon* shadow puppet. Cirebon, West Java, 20th century, water buffalo hide, horn, pigment. Kraton Kasepuhan. Photo John Gollings

Fig. 26 *Pepadon* (ceremonial seat). Lampung, Sumatra, 19th century, wood. Museum Nasional, Jakarta. Photo John Gollings

Fig. 28 Shoulder cloth, Kai Ne'e *natam kosat* motif indicating female member of Raja's family. Baun, West Timor, 20th century, cotton ikat with supplementary weft. Raja of Baun. Photo Helen I. Jessup

Fig. 29 Hip wrapper, motif indicating social group *kobe rena hebe* and *ae hubi*. Savu, West Nusatenggara 20th century, cotton ikat with supplementary weft. Raja Haba family, Kupang. Photo Helen I. Jessup

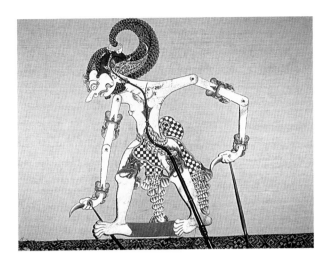

Fig. 30 *Wayang kulit* figure of Bima. Cirebon, West Java, 19th century, water buffalo hide, horn, pigment. Private collection. Photo Helen I. Jessup

An important Austronesian concept expressed in textile form is that of duality. Indeed, many eastern Indonesian peoples have myths of origin involving the link between male and female twins that begin as a single egg and demonstrate that any whole comprises two complementary portions. Plaid and checked weavings found everywhere in Indonesia are symbolic of this dualism, where the complementary elements of the warp and weft create the whole, and reconcile the apparently contradictory forces of the vertical and the horizontal, the light and the dark, and in the deepest implication, life and death. Perhaps the most famous expression of dualism in cloth is to be found in the black and white checks of *kain poleng,* which today can be seen pervasively in Bali draped around statues, trees and temple structures. It has a protective power and is worn in processions to deter and exorcise evil spirits as well as by warriors like the Pandava hero Bima (fig. 30).

The examples cited suggest that the symbolism connected with existential concerns – myths of origin, rites of passage, identity, protection – draws in many cases on the visual material of the earliest ancestors of the Indonesian people. In contrast, almost all symbolism connected with rank, power and kingship derives from the Hindu-Buddhistic civilisation that was grafted on the autochthonous Indonesian culture early in the first millennium of our era. Perhaps the most powerful and important of these is the image of the mountain. Java and Bali have a volcanic and mountainous terrain where imported Hinduistic conceptions of the mountains as home of the gods would have had a strong resonance with the religious and royal rituals that Brahman priests introduced to the courts from as early as the fifth century.

The most famous of the mountain images in Indonesia is certainly the cosmic mountain of Borobudur (fig. 31). Indian cosmogony so pervaded the

Fig. 31 Candi Borobudur. Central Java, c. 800 CE. Photo Helen I. Jessup

Fig. 32 Crown. Banten, West Java, 18th century, gold, rubies, diamonds, emeralds, pearls. Museum Nasional, Jakarta. Photo John Gollings

Fig. 33 *Sumping* (ear decoration). East Java, 14th –15th century, gold. Tropenmuseum, Amsterdam. Photo John Gollings

Fig. 34 Palace gate. Klungkung, Bali, 18th century, brick. Photo Helen I. Jessup

courts of Indonesia that the mountain form came to be equated with royal power, as can be seen in the mountain form of the eighteenth-century royal crown of Banten (fig. 32) and a fourteenth-century royal *sumping,* or ear decoration (fig. 33). The mountain motif was translated into architectural form in the gates of royal palaces in Bali, like that in Klungkung (fig. 34), and into textile form in the batik pattern *sumeru* (meaning the sacred Hindu Mount Meru) that is restricted to the Susuhunan of Surakarta (fig. 35). It should be noted, however, that despite the central importance in Indian belief of Mount Meru and the encircling peaks of other sacred mountains, the mountain (like the Tree of Life) is a universal symbol that may also be seen in Chinese objects like an Eastern Zhous or Western Han *po-shan-hsiang,* or incense burner, of the fourth or third century BCE (fig. 36). Similarly, the pervasive *tumpal* motif, one

Fig. 36 *Po-shan-hsiang* (incense burner). Eastern Zhou/Western Han, 4th –3rd century BCE, bronze, Freer Gallery of Art # F47.15

Fig. 35 Batik, *sumeru* motif. Surakarta, 20th century, cotton. Private collection. Photo Helen I. Jessup

Fig. 37 *Tumpal* motif with spirals. Dayak, Kalimantan, 20th century, wood carving on house. Photo Helen I. Jessup

Fig. 38 Ritual food vessel. Western Zhou, 11th –10th century BCE, bronze. Arthur M. Sackler Gallery #S87.0352

Fig. 39 Plan, Candi Borobudur

of whose meanings may be as a mountian symbol of Indic origin, is found in both batiked and woven cloth (fig. 37), but can also be seen in Chinese art such as a Western Zhou eleventh to tenth century ritual food vessel (fig. 38).

Central to Indian cosmogony is the diagram of the cosmos, which can be in mandala form (like the plan of Borobudur, fig. 39), with a circle set in indented squares, or in circular form implying infinity, with strong directional identity focussed on the cardinal directions and (slightly less) on the sub-cardinal directions. This motif is one of the most important in Central Javanese batik art and is the basis for the *kawung* pattern for which the immediate inspiration was the *patola* cloths that came from Gujerat. It can be seen in the pattern of a Surakarta batik (fig. 40) as well as in a *geringsing* double ikat cloth from Bali (fig. 41). It is interesting that the pattern has an everyday name in Minangkabau (fig. 42), where it is

Fig. 40 *Kawung* motif. Yogyakarta, Central Java, 20th century, cotton batik. Private collection. Photo Helen I. Jessup

Fig. 41 *Geringsing* cloth. Tenganan, Bali, 20th century, double ikat cotton. National Gallery of Australia # 1982.2308. Photo John Gollings

Fig. 42 *Kawung* motif as "split peanut". Minangkabau, Sumatra, 20th century, silk. Private collection. Photo Helen I. Jessup

Fig. 43 *Ceplok nitik ksatriyan jelamprang* motif. Surakarta, Central Java, 20th century, cotton batik. Private collection. Photo Helen I. Jessup

called "split peanut", with an underlying meaning of two halves making a whole rather than of a Hinduistic diagram of the cosmos. This cosmic conception underlies a related motif, the *jelamprang*, which consists of an eight-pointed figure that looks like a flower and a star, as in the motif *ceplok nitik ksatrian* (fig. 43). Like the *sumeru* and the *kawung*, the *jelamprang* is a so-called proscribed pattern, that is, one that (at least in earlier social codes) may only be worn by certain members of the ruling families of Central Java. It is extremely ancient, being represented with great precision in openwork copper alloy seals from western Central Asia that date as far back as the late third millennium BCE.

What is the basis of the forbidden nature of these restricted patterns? They are not overtly symbols of power in the sense that the mountain is. It is possible to speculate that they refer to ancient links between the rulers of Java and the Hindu gods, particularly Visnu and Siva, that led to posthumous association between god and ruler leading to a *devaraja* identity for the dead king, when his spirit was fused with the divinity whose protection he sought.

These relationships were of course restricted to royalty, but in the intervening centuries as the courts became Islamic, the royal Brahmanic implications have been forgotten. Such an explanation would account for the proscribed nature of the *sawat* motif, for example, as illustrated in the *sawat semen gunung* pattern of the Paku Alam of Yogyakarta (fig. 44) and in the *ceplok putri ringgit* motif of Surakarta (fig. 45). It might also account for the meaning of the *parang rusak* motif that is restricted to the Sultan of Yogyakarta, his consort and his children (fig. 46) and to a similar hierarchy in the Surakarta court. When viewed in the context of the cosmogony of

Fig. 44 *Sawat semem gunung* motif. Yogyakarta, Central Java, 20th century, cotton batik. Private collection. Photo Helen I. Jessup

Fig. 46 *Sawung* motif. Yogyakarta, Central Java, 20th century, cotton batik. Private collection. Photo Helen I. Jessup

Fig. 45 (left) *Ceplok putri ringgit* motif. Surakarta, Central Java, 20th century, cotton batik. Private collection. Photo Helen I. Jessup

Fig. 47 (Opposite) Crown. Gowa, South Sulawesi, 15th century (?), gold, diamonds *Istana Gowa-Makassar.* Photo John Gollings

the circle, where the north (with the colour blue-black) is occupied by Vishnu, and the east by Siva, with the colour white, a median orientation between these two directions results in a northeast diagonal. This produces a balance between dark and light and between the two chief gods of the courtly culture, Visnu and Siva, whose resolution of power struggles was necessary for cosmic harmony. This directional mandate still applies today in Balinese architectural projects.

The final motif to be discussed is that of the *naga*, or serpent. Again, we are concerned with a universal symbol involving the power of the underworld, water, fertility and royal power. *Nagas* play important roles in Hindu mythology, in Austronesian-derived myths of origin and in Chinese legends (in the form of the dragon) alike, not to speak of the resonance of the serpent in Mexican, Nordic and Judaic myths, among others. Though the connotations are male in China and India,

Fig. 48 *Harda walika* (ceremonial vessel). Banjarmasin, Kalimantan, 19th century, silver, rock crystal, gold. Museum Nasional, Jakarta. Photo John Gollings

45

they can be female in Southeast Asian legends. One of the founding myths of the Khmer, for example, concerns a *naga* princess. Like the mountain, the *naga* pervades imagery of the royal courts of Indonesia and appears in many media, including the royal crown of Gowa (fig. 47), the ritual object Harda Walilka from the court of Banjarmasin (fig. 48), Naga Sapto, a royal *kris* from Surakarta (fig. 49), a *saput* cloth from Bali (fig. 50), and the Mangkunagaran batik *geringsing naga segara* (fig. 51). A ritual food container from China, a late eleventh or early twelfth century Western Zhou *fang-ting* (fig. 52) offers another source illustrating the myriad strands that enriched Indonesian motifs and complicated their meanings. The scope of this paper precludes tracing these connections more closely, but their pervasiveness hints at the deeply syncretic nature of Indonesian culture, of which its textile arts are a rich and integral expression.

Fig. 49 *Kris,* Naga Sapto. Surakarta, Central Java, 17th century, iron, nickel, gold, diamonds, wood. Private collection. Photo John Gollings

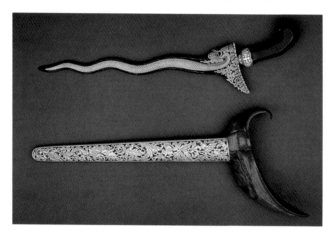

Fig. 51 *Geringsing naga segara* motif. Surakarta, Central Java, 20th century, cotton batik. Private collection. Photo Helen I. Jessup

Fig. 50. *Saput* Cloth, *songket* weave. Klungkung, Bali, 19th century, silk, cotton, gold thread, chemical dyes. Museum Bali, *Denpasar.* Photo John Gollings

Fig. 52 *Fang-ting* (ritual food container). Western Zhou, 11th-12th century BCE, bronze. Feer Gallery of Art #F50.7

USE OF THE *PAHUDU* STRING MODEL
Lau Pahudu Weaving from East Sumatra, Indonesia[1]

Marie-Hélène Guelton[2]

The Equator passes through the Indonesian archipelago encircled by the Indian Ocean, the South China Sea and the Pacific Ocean. This archipelago is composed of about 13,500 islands scattered around about 5,000 kilometres from east to west and 2,000 kilometres from north to south and comprising more than three hundred fifty ethnic groups.

The island of Sumba is part of Nusa Tengarra Timur in the central south of the archipelago (map fig. 1 from a guide book). It is divided in two districts: western and eastern corresponding to linguistic and cultural differences. In contrast to western islands (like Sumatra) located on the trade roads, the culture of Sumba is less influenced by foreign exchanges and the population is thus relatively homogeneous. The models and textiles studied here all come from the same area in East Sumba: Pao, Rindi and Waingapu.

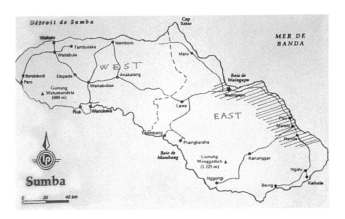

Fig. 1 Map of Sumba divided in two districts: West and East. (Drawn from a guide book)

The *lau pahudu*, (fig. 2) is a woman's tubular skirt worn by the noblewomen in special ceremonies as weddings, ritual dances and burials. It is the equivalent of the man's mantle or hip cloth known as *hinggi*. In Sumba both *lau pahudu* and *hinggi* like other textiles and pigs are part of the gifts which the family of the bride offers to the family of the groom in exchange for buffalo, spears,

Fig. 2 *Lau pahudu*, noblewoman's skirt, full view. The lau pahudu worn as a tubular skirt by the noblewoman for special ceremonies is the equivalent of the man's mantle or hip cloth known as *hinggi*. These textiles, being woven and worn in the same context, have similarities in their iconography. We can see zoomorphic patterns such as horse, fish, bird, and deer. The deer, for instance, symbolises royalty. East Sumba, first half of 20th century. 147 cm (weft, in 2 widths) x 122 cm (warp, circular). AEDTA Collection inv. no. 3009.
Photo Bruno Le Hir de Fallois

and costly gold ornaments. Thus the textiles have a sacred role and even their actual making is sacred.

The *hinggi* is usually woven and worn in pairs, one on the shoulder, the other one wrapped around the waist. It is not mentioned in the records if such is the case for the *lau pahudu* as well, but according to Danielle Geirnaert it is not unusual to observe a woman wearing a pair of *lau pahudu*, one as a sarong and the other one as a *slendang* on the shoulders. These textiles are woven in cotton. This fibre is widely grown in Sumba as in most parts of Indonesia. Each step of preparation is accompanied by special rituals.

As *hinggi* and *lau pahudu* are woven and worn in the same context, they have similarities in their iconography. We can see zoomorphic patterns such as horse, fish, bird, and deer. The deer, for instance, symbolises royalty. The same iconography is also observed on accessories like sculptured tortoise shell combs and the fabulous gold omega-shaped ear ornaments called *mamuli* worn by the women. *Mamuli* like textiles play an essential role in the elaborate gift exchanges that bound Sumba society together, in marriage negotiation for instance.

Supplementary warp weaving technique is used (associated or not with a warp-*ikat* pattern and stripes). This technique, rarely seen in Indonesia, requires a special skill and is executed on a body-tension loom with two types of warps, one for the ground, one for the pattern. To program this supplementary warp, a special string model, called *pahudu* is needed (fig. 3). It is prepared as a guide before weaving with strings in the warp direction and with small bamboo or palm sticks in the weft direction.

We will be studying here eleven examples of *pahudu*. We have given special attention to technical details such as material, colour, type of weave, set up and iconography. Recognized experts have been rather more interested in the design and symbols. Other well-known researchers such as Rita Bolland, or Sylvia Fraser-Lu have worked more particularly on the loom or on the weaving of the *lau pahudu* rather than on the *pahudu* itself although it actually precedes the whole concept.

The string models *(pahudu)* from the AEDTA collection were acquired in 1992 from a traveller who himself had collected them from an East Sumba family near Pao. According to him, the women in that family were not weaving any longer and instead of burning the *pahudu* upon the death of the last woman-weaver as is the custom, they had finally agreed to part with them. It is difficult to date them: the most accurate (fig. 3), fine and skilfully crafted, might be the most ancient and

Fig. 3 *Pahudu,* string model, full view, front. It is prepared as a guide before weaving with strings in the warp direction and with small bamboo or midrib palm sticks in the weft direction. The design is readable in one direction but it is used in another direction. East Sumba, late 19th, early 20th century. 49 cm (strings) x 42 cm (sticks). AEDTA Collection, inv. no. 2969. Photo Bruno Le Hir de Fallois

could date to the late 19th or early 20th century.

In this *pahudu*, as in the others studied, the motif can be read in one direction but it has actually been worked and used in another direction perpendicular to the design. The pattern is traditionally created by a noblewoman but it can also be created at her request by her servant.[4]

The design consists here of a horse mounted by a human figure. The horse is widely represented in the Sumbanese iconography: "The Dutch prized Sumba's ponies as cavalry stock and established their first permanent station on the island in 1866 to ensure a steady supply of mounts".[5] As a consequence, Sumba's 19th century trade in horses generated large new revenues for the princes, stimulating the production of textiles and imported new materials (as chemical dye, threads...). The horse imagery implied power and riches. Around the horse there are other geometric or animal-shaped

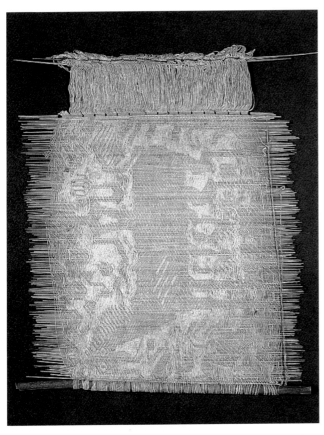

Fig. 4 *Pahudu*, string model, full view, back. When the cotton strings are not intertwined on the obverse, they float freely on the back. East Sumba, late 19th, early 20th century. 49 cm (strings) x 42 cm (sticks). AEDTA Collection, inv. no. 2969. Photo Bruno Le Hir de Fallois

selves which are transmitted from generation to generation. By nature, *pahudu*-based iconography changes only gradually, if at all, in spite of foreign influences.

Without looking too closely one could think that the set up consisted of many small strings whereas actually it is a continuous one going back and forth between two rods just in the same way as the circular warp will be set up on the loom (fig. 5).

In order to avoid an entanglement of the threads during the set up, they are made to pass above and under two small sticks used as cross-rods. As it is illustrated (fig. 6, page 50) we can see three threads above and one under. To facilitate their counting out they are tied (sometimes with a colour thread as here) by bundles of 16 to 20 threads. This method has been observed on each of the twelve models studied, whatever their origin (For recapitulative chart of *pahudu* technical structure see fig. 28, page 63). In this case there are 274 warps for a pattern 36 cm wide which means a density of 7-1/2 threads per cm.

The sticks, extremely fine here, (about 1 to 2 mm in diameter) total 195 for the pattern on a height of 33 cm which amount to a density of 6 wefts per cm. It is usually considered that the sticks are made of bamboo, but Warming and Gaworsky mention "*lidi* sticks" and according to an Indonesian woman participating in the symposium this is the midrib of a palm widely grown in the area. *Lidi* is also a kind of reed which is commonly used for brooms in this region. When looking closely at the sticks, most of them seem to have more suppleness than bamboo and to be closer to palms. The cotton used

motifs but much smaller and not easily decipherable. On the left hand-side, there appears to be half of a Tree of Life possibly reminiscent of Hindu iconography or more probably recalling the head-trees symbolising head-hunting.

Technically, the model consists of cotton strings in the warp direction, corresponding to the supplementary warps on the loom and in the *lau pahudu* weaving. These strings are interlaced with thin sticks tantamount to the wefts. The interlacing is of a weave type: here a 3/1 twill, S or Z direction (fig. 5). We will explain later why the weave is not quite a twill.

When the cotton strings are not intertwined on the obverse, they float freely on the reverse (fig. 4). For the next step, the weaving itself, this model is used as a guide to placing pattern rods to set the design in the supplementary warp. It is a means to preserve the actual weaving technique but also the tradition of the patterns them-

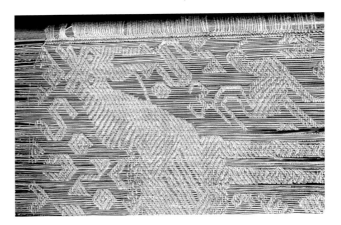

Fig. 5 *Pahudu*, string model, detail. The cotton string is continuous going back and forth between two rods (one at each end as seen here) just in the same way as the continuous warp will be set up on the loom. East Sumba, late 19th, early 20th century. AEDTA Collection, inv. no. 2969. Photo M.-H. Guelton

49

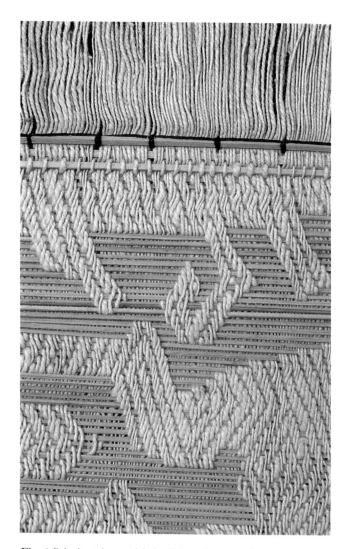

Fig. 7 *Pahudu*, string model, full view. One can easily see here a crocodile with a dragon above, surrounded by smaller various geometrical and animal-shaped motifs such as a bird, a fish, a *mamuli* - an omega-shaped ear ornament. Several East Sumbanese clans believe that crocodilian creatures are among their original ancestors, through marriage. Accordingly, crocodiles are revered. East Sumba, late 19th, early 20th century. 64 cm (strings) x 61 cm (sticks). AEDTA Collection, inv. no. 3256. Photo Bruno Le Hir de Fallois

Fig. 6 *Pahudu*, string model, detail. In order to avoid an entanglement of the threads during the set up they are made to pass above and under two small sticks used as cross-rods. As it is illustrated we can see three threads above and one under. To facilitate their counting out they are tied (sometimes with another thread, black here) by bundles of 16 to 20 threads. East Sumba, late 19th, early 20th century. AEDTA Collection, inv. no. 2969. Photo Bruno Le Hir de Fallois

here is an undyed S 2-ply, Z-spun yarn. It seems to have been hand-spun and is irregular. The threads are woven in a 3/1 twill, S or Z direction.

Another model (fig. 7) is remarkable both by its iconography and its technique. One can easily see a crocodile with a dragon above, surrounded by various smaller geometric and animal-shaped motifs such as a bird, a fish, a *mamuli* (an omega-shaped ear ornament).

As for the crocodile, several East Sumbanese clans believe that crocodilian creatures are among their original ancestors, through marriage. Accordingly, crocodiles are revered. They may not be killed or eaten and they are associated with the afterlife: a crocodile-infested river

has to be crossed to the underworld. Also, young aristocrats are called "children of the crocodile and whale". The dragon for its part is of a foreign source, taken for instance from Chinese ceramic ware, introduced in Indonesia as it is mentioned by Mattiebelle Gittinger.[9] As for the bird and the fish, they are common place in Sumba.

From the technical viewpoint it is interesting to note that if the design is created thanks to the diagonal twill, the crocodile teeth are drawn with the floating warps. We can notice also that at one end just after the cross-rod there are threads bundled together between 1 or 2 sticks in order to flatten them out (fig. 8). Unlike the precedent example, the 2/1 twill, Z direction is less accurate and has some irregularities at the ends. The interlacing is slacker and the threads and sticks densities (146 and 203) are lower by comparison to the size of the design. The cotton also is of a different quality: it is a Z-twist cabled-yarn, S 2-ply, Z-spun. It seems to be factory-produced.

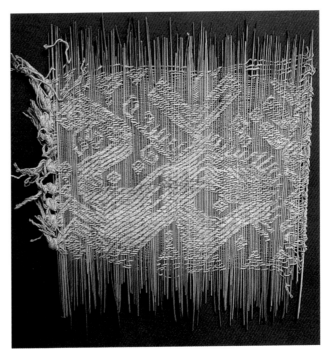

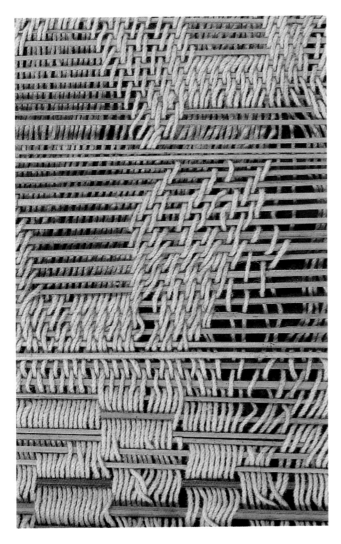

Fig. 8 *Pahudu,* string model, macrophotograph. At one end just after the cross-rod there are threads bundled together between 1 or 2 sticks in order to flatten them. Unlike the precedent example, the 2/1 twill, Z direction, is less accurate and has some irregularities at the ends. The cotton thread is a Z-twist cabled yarn, S 2-ply, Z-spun. East Sumba, late 19th, early 20th century. AEDTA Collection, inv. no. 3256. Photo Bruno Le Hir de Fallois

Among the *pahudu* still extant, some have a design more difficult to decipher and less precise. The craftsmanship can be also of a lesser quality (fig. 9). It can be interpreted as a mythical animal half-rooster, half-dragon. The interlacing is in 3/1, twill, S direction but the ends are not of the same fineness as the other examples. There are neither cross-rods nor end rods which results in the slackening of the threads. This model, probably badly kept, has a particularity: a warp originally continuous but which is now coarsely knotted at one end. The sticks are also slightly thicker and more irregular (2 to 3 mm in diameter). The thread used is a S 2-ply yarn, Z-spun probably hand-spun, rather irregular.

Fig. 9 *Pahudu,* string model, full view. The design is difficult to decipher and less precise. It can be interpreted as a mythical half rooster half dragon. The ends are not of the same fineness as for the other examples. There are neither cross-rods nor end rods which results in the slackening of the threads. East Sumba, probably early 20th century. 37 cm (strings) x 34 cm (sticks). AEDTA Collection, inv. no. 3011. Photo Bruno Le Hir de Fallois

Most *pahudu* have only one pattern repeat but we did encounter several with two or three repeats. We have in fig. 10 (page 52) a two-repeat *pahudu:* on the right hand-side, an animal looking back like a deer in ancient Chinese iconography, but with some elements similar to a dragon, and to the extreme right a design that could be a stylised serpent. On the left-hand side, we can see a partially ruined design. The two designs are separated by a cross-rod and sticks. Though a certain number of sticks are missing, in the remaining part, we can see the mirrored design, maybe a lion's hinder parts, by reference to the same type of motif in a *hinggi* for example (AEDTA collection, inv. no. 3253, unpublished). These lion patterns are said to be inspired by Dutch coats of arms.

This specimen is of particular interest with its two different weaves. On the one hand, there is a very precise interlacing in a 3/1 twill, Z direction with particular well-defined cross-rod and thread bundles for the main design. And on the other hand, there is an interesting

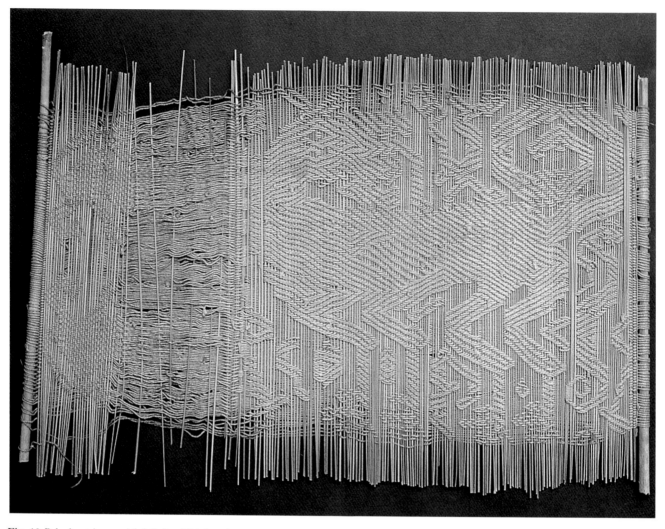

Fig. 10 *Pahudu*, string model, full view. This item has two pattern repeats separated by a cross rod and sticks: on the right hand-side, an animal looking back like a deer in ancient Chinese iconography, but with some elements similar to a dragon, and to the extreme right a design that could be a stylised serpent. On the left-hand side, we can see a partially ruined design, in mirrored image, maybe a lion's hinder parts. East Sumba, probably early 20th century. 65 cm (strings) x 43 cm (sticks). AEDTA Collection, inv. no. 3015. Photo Bruno Le Hir de Fallois

modification in the thread weave. It is a derived tabby with double warps and not a twill. This type of weave is never mentioned in relevant publications and so far we have never encountered such a structure in the weaving of *lau pahudu*.

We can also observe this type of structure in fig. 11 (AEDTA no. 3016, full view). This *pahudu* (badly preserved) represents a dragon with scales. The design has been made denser by the tight weave structure of a derived tabby with double warps and the scales are patterned thanks to extended tabby floats of 2 threads to 2 sticks[12] (fig. AEDTA no. 3016, detail).

So far all the specimens described have a zoomorphic iconography but geometric designs can also be found. Usually they are based on hook-shaped geometric patterns as shown in fig. 13 (AEDTA no. 3014, full view). These particular shapes date from very ancient times in the Indonesian textile iconography, from the Dongson civilisation from Vietnam (400 BC-300 AD) whose style influenced all Southeast Asia as early as the Bronze Age. The well-known bronze hook-shaped pattern drums were found on the archaeological site of Dongson and other places in Indonesia. The small lozenges are also reminiscent of the *patola ikat* patterns.[13]

Fig. 11 *Pahudu,* string model, full view. This specimen is representing a dragon with scales. East Sumba, probably early 20th century. 50 cm (strings) x 51 cm (sticks). AEDTA Collection, inv. no. 3016. Photo Bruno Le Hir de Fallois

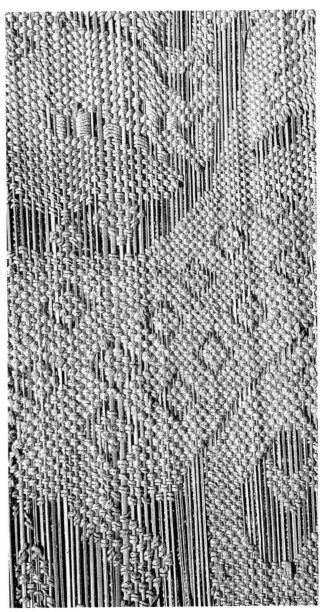

Fig. 13 *Pahudu,* string model, full view. This model composed of 3 pattern repeats based on hook-shaped geometric motifs is unusual in that a dyed cotton is used. East Sumba, probably first half 20th century. 55 cm (strings) x 44 cm (sticks). AEDTA Collection, inv. no. 3014. Photo Bruno Le Hir de Fallois

Fig. 12 *Pahudu,* string model, detail. The design has been made denser by the tight weave structure of a derived tabby with double warps and the scales are patterned thanks to extended tabby floats of 2 threads to 2 sticks. East Sumba, probably early 20th century. AEDTA Collection, inv. no. 3016 Photo M.-H. Guelton

This model which is composed of three geometric pattern repeats is also unusual by the fact that a dyed cotton is used. In all the examples quoted in the relevant literature the cotton is undyed because the design in the weaving must appear quite clearly against the dark background. Yet here it is of a dark red colour that could be a natural dye. It is difficult to establish whether the design was woven on a darker background or whether such a colour was merely used on the model. It is known that there was a trend in the thirties in *lau pahudu* weaving of using yellow threads against a red background or the reverse. This model could date from that period.

Fig. 14 The design of this *pahudu* which is partially ruined in the middle could represent two confronting animals. It is programmed with three thread qualities. East Sumba, probably first half of 20th century. 58 cm (strings) x 58 cm (sticks). AEDTA Collection, inv. no. 3017. Photo Bruno Le Hir de Fallois

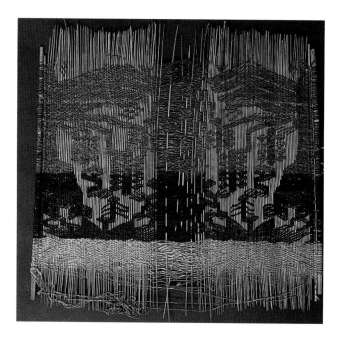

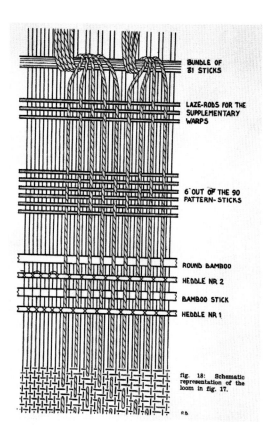

BUNDLE OF 31 STICKS

LAZE-RODS FOR THE SUPPLEMENTARY WARPS

6 OUT OF THE 90 PATTERN-STICKS

ROUND BAMBOO
HEDDLE NR 2
BAMBOO STICK
HEDDLE NR 1

fig. 18: Schematic representation of the loom in fig. 17.

Fig. 14 also has three colours. The design of this *pahudu*, which is partially ruined in the middle, could represent two confronting animals. It is produced with three thread qualities:

• an undyed cabled-yarn, Z 3-ply, S-2 ply, Z-spun cotton;

• a marled brown-black cotton, S 2-ply Z and 4-ply Z apparently hand-spun;

• an indigo blue cotton, S 5-ply Z-spun.

Each colour is used as a continuous warp. The cross-rod is well defined and the weaving is a 2/1 twill, S or Z direction.

It is impossible to visualise the actual weaving from this model. In the fifties, "positive" and "negative" *ikats* were fashionable: white with a blue design whereas before it was the contrary. This information was given to Danielle Geirnaert by the family of the Raja of Kodi, West Sumba. It could have been that there were *lau pahudu* with those type of colours in East Sumba, or more simply that these threads were used as a means of economising.

Now, we will be describing the type of loom used for weaving the *lau pahudu* and the sashes. In Sumba, like in most parts of the Indonesian islands, they traditionally use a body-tension loom also called back-strap loom. It is an horizontal or slightly inclined loom. As mentioned before the weaving is the woman's work. As seen in fig. 15, she often works seated on a mat or on a very low stool. The back-strap goes around her waist, the woman being seated very close to the front beam. The back-strap and the front beam are tied together by strings. The warp beam is tied to a fixed pole, a post or even a tree. A simple movement of the body either front or back results in an increase or a slackening in the tension of the warp necessary for the weaving.

On the simplest looms, the warp is continuous.[16] It is wrapped without interruption from the front beam to the back beam. The continuous warp also symbolises the cycle of life. As the weaving is progressing, the weaver wraps her work around the front beam. When it is finished, the two ends almost meet and the unwoven warp must be cut. This type of loom has one or two heddles but no comb. It is mostly found in areas where textiles are warp-patterned and with a high density of warps. The weft is then hardly visible.

Here the loom is set up with two warps: one for the ground (foundation warp) and one for the pattern (supplementary warp). The supplementary warp is

Fig. 15 A servant weaving *a lau pahudu* for a noblewoman in Rindi, East Sumba, 1982. She is interlacing a *lidi* stick through the supplementary warp to program the design on a body-tension loom. Photo Danielle Geirnaert

Diagram 1 This technical diagram was established by Rita Bolland and pulished (in 1956) in Bolland Rita, "Weaving a Sumba Woman's Skirt", Lamak and Malat in Bali and a Sumba loom, Royal Tropical Institute, Amsterdam, Nr. CXIX Dept. of Cultural and Physical Anthropology Nr. 53, 1956, p. 49-57, diagram p. 50. It was drawn from the observation of a body tension loom acquired by Laurens Langewis 1934 from East Sumba for the Museum of Rotterdam. (We have coloured the supplementary warps in yellow and the rods and pattern sticks in brown for a better reading)

mounted after the foundation warp in the relevant proportion. Whatever their origin or dating in all the studied items, the warp proportion is always 2 foundations for 1 supplementary. The number 2 is also symbolic: it is 1 + 1 companion.[17] At the end of the weaving, the cloth is stretched between the two beams before cutting the continuous warp.

To better understand the set up of the loom and the resulting weaving we have examined a technical diagram drawn by Rita Bolland and published in 1956 (diagram 1).[18] (We have coloured the supplementary warps in yellow and the rods and pattern sticks in brown for a better reading). This drawing was made from the observation of a body-tension loom acquired by Laurens Langewis in 1934 from East Sumba for the Museum of Rotterdam. Both loom and drawing are complementary to the textile structure analysis.

On the lower part of the drawing we can see the cloth being woven and above the loom set up with its different parts. The foundation warp is in black, the supplementary warp in yellow. Here also, the warp proportion is 2 foundation warps for 1 supplementary warp. The loom is equipped with 2 heddles for weaving the tabby foundation weave. As described by Rita Bolland[19] "between these two heddles in the warp is a flat, bamboo stick, 3 cm in width". Over this stick are passing all the warps going through the loops of heddles no. 2, plus all the supplementary warps. This stick has no function in pattern weaving.

Behind heddle no. 2 we find a bamboo in the warp, over which are passing the supplementary warps only.

Because of this the weaver has these thick pattern-threads lying level in front of her, ready to have the pattern laced in with the aid of many thin bamboo sticks, as we can see on the left hand side. They have been inserted thanks to the *pahudu* placed near the loom before weaving. Only six have been represented here. They are laced with the supplementary warps in a kind of 2/1 twill, in S direction.

We can see in the fabric that the pattern is bound in 4/1 twill. So, "each stick is used twice in the formation of sheds, once together with heddle no. 1, and afterwards once with heddle no. 2, then the stick is pulled out of the warp and the next stick's turn is up. When all the sticks have been employed, they are placed in again"[20] if the design is repeated in the fabric. It is obvious here that the weave is not quite a twill. A twill weave would be created by using heddles (minimum 3 for a 2/1 twill for instance) and not by selecting the warp with pattern-sticks. This selection of the warps allows more freedom in the pattern.

Above, we can see laze-rods used to keep the supplementary warps parallel and at the same level during the weaving. They help also to replace the bamboo sticks. At the top of the diagram are the foundation warps in groups of 4 or 5 wrapped around a bundle of sticks. This is used to regulate the tension of the supplementary warps without modifying the tension of the foundation warps. The pattern demands more length of yarn than the foundation fabric because of the floating on the front and back. Then with the aid of a sword stick, the weaver raises the warp threads set by each pattern stick to create a shed for the passage of the weft thread.

The set up of the loom as well as the weaving demands a great skill specially to balance the tension of the two warps. The more precious the ritual fabric, the more skill will be needed by the weaver.

Fig. 16 is a *lau pahudu* from the AEDTA collection. As for all these skirts, it is composed of two widths of cloth woven separately and then sewn together. Traditionally, these two widths are woven on the same loom: the lower part with the main pattern and the upper part with the plain weave and small motifs. The width is about 60 cm. In this case, it uses only a part of the supplementary warp with different pattern, or the supplementary warp is inserted in the foundation warp at the same level. The lower width here comprises two types of pattern techniques:

- the warp *ikat*

- and the supplementary warp weaving

According to Sylvia Fraser-Lu, such a *lau* which includes bands of warp ikat as well as supplementary warp is called *lau pahudu padua*.[21] And to Danielle Geirnaert the significance of *padua* is linked to the ritual of *padu* which enables the exorcism of all the transgressions of the world. The animal-shaped motifs represent dogs and lobsters. Lobsters are widely represented in the Sumbanese iconography and are part of mythical animals associated with the afterlife passage. The supplementary warp pattern contrasting on the dark ground, represents a pig which is part of the marriage exchange from the bride's family. There are also birds and trees.

Fig. 17 *Lau pahudu,* woman's skirt, front detail. The supplementary warp pattern contrasting on the dark ground, is representing a pig which is part of the marriage exchanges for the bride givers. The supplementary warps are of undyed cotton but a few details have been daubed in yellow to touch them up. AEDTA Collection, inv. no. 3443. Photo Bruno Le Hir de Fallois

56

In this textile, the supplementary warps are of undyed cotton but a few details have been daubed in yellow to touch them up (fig. 17). This technique is often observed and probably recalls certain old Sumbanese golden textiles dating from the nineteenth century. This is a mark of good quality. The yellow dyeing could be *Curcuma longa*.[22] Like numerous yellow dyes, the colour is directly applied on the fabric and not obtained by immersion or mordants. So the colour is less enduring. We can also see traces of yellow at the back of the motif (fig. 18).

On the reverse of the fabric the supplementary warps are floating freely when they are not used at the front as for the *pahudu*. Nevertheless they can be bound by a supplementary weft in some places as we can see on the detail. According to some specialists like Rita Bolland, the more precious sarongs dating from the nineteenth century, like those kept in the famous collections in Holland, were usually woven with a supplementary binding weft on the reverse. In the *lau pahudu* dating from the mid-twentieth century and later this technique has often disappeared.

Like for the *pahudu*, the supplementary warp is an undyed cabled S-twist cotton thread, S-2 ply, Z-spun. This yarn is regularly twisted and is probably hand-spun. The foundation warp is a black Z-spun cotton yarn. The black colour seems to be a natural dye. In Sumba, a ferruginous mud, or indigo dye mixed with tannin is traditionally used to obtain this dark shade.

Fig. 18 *Lau pahudu*, woman's skirt, back detail. On the reverse of the fabric the supplementary warps are floating freely when they are not used at the front as for the *pahudu*. Nevertheless they can also be bound by a supplementary weft in some places. AEDTA Collection, inv. no. 3443. Photo Bruno Le Hir de Fallois

Fig. 19 *Lau pahudu*, woman's skirt, back detail. The supplementary warps are bound by a black cotton supplementary weft. AEDTA Collection, inv. no. 3443. Photo Bruno Le Hir de Fallois

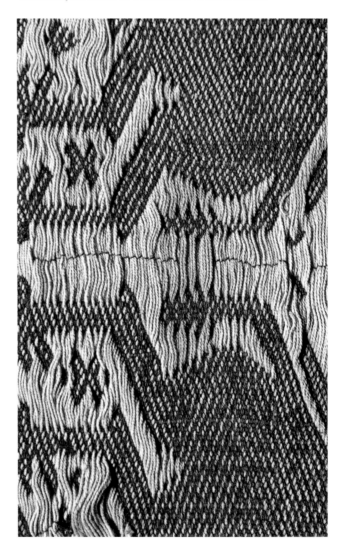

The weave structure of the pattern is a 3/1 twill, S or Z direction. The foundation warp density is 30 threads per cm and the supplementary warp density is 15 threads (warp proportion: 2 to 1). The foundation weft is of the same quality as the foundation warp but the thread is double or triple. The weft density per cm is 7 threads. After the weaving, the quality of the sewing of the widths is extremely important in the case of the *hinggi*.

There are no notable *lau pahudu* in the AEDTA Collection but in other well-known collections a few specimens dating from the 19th century have extremely elaborate decor with beads, shells, fringes or tufted embroideries.

Fig. 20 is another type of *lau pahudu* from the AEDTA collection. The two widths of this skirt have a supplementary warp pattern but no warp *ikat*. The upper part design is fairly straightforward with its small geometric motifs and stripes whereas the lower part decor is more elaborate with deer, snake, birds, and tree.

We can notice that deer are represented with the tail up symbolising the prestige of virility (fig. 20). In this case, the weaving, the dyeing and the sewing are not of a very good quality even though the textile is traditional and probably made for a ritual like the previous one. According to Danielle Geirnaert's investigations, Sumbanese people say that the textiles with "flaws" have to be given back to foreigners. The foundation warp is in local cotton, hand-spun, and indigo dyed. The indigo is very weak. It was probably achieved with only a few baths. The weaving is rather loose and the warp and weft densities are smaller than in the first example. The supplementary warps are floating freely on the reverse without supplementary binding weft.

We know that by the early 20th century most Sumba women were weaving for trade but also to preserve their tradition. For the last twenty years, the weaving of the *lau pahudu* has been decreasing to the benefit of a new type of textile also woven with supplementary warp

Fig. 20 *Lau pahudu*, woman's skirt, detail. In the lower part of this *lau pahudu*, the deer is represented with the tail up symbolising the prestige of virility. In this case the weaving, dyeing and sewing are not of a very good quality even though the textile is traditional and probably made for a ritual like the previous one. East Sumba, first half of 20th century. AEDTA Collection, inv. no. 3009. Photo Bruno Le Hir de Fallois

pattern. It is a kind of long sash, or even banner or just a long patterned strip of cloth for commercial use.

This is confirmed by travellers and dealers who recently travelled to Sumba like John Gillow. He reported in 1992 that "long sashes are also woven in the same technique with repetitive motifs of human figures and animals. The tourist demand for these pieces is now so high that, breaking with tradition, young men as well as women are now weaving them on traditional looms with very long warps". We currently find many specimens in shops and galleries in Paris, and it is interesting to analyse the evolution of their technique and motifs even though their significance has changed.

In the example illustrated (fig. 21) the pattern is no longer white on a dark ground but red on a yellow ground. The composition is unusual: some figures are readable in the weft direction and others in the warp direction. Given the length of the textile, almost three meters, it must have been woven on a loom set up with a discontinuous warp rather than a continuous warp.

The human figure designs recall the ancient *lau pahudu* but their style is more codified and lacking life. According to textile dealers, they are considered to represent the ancestors or are in memory of the clan victims of head hunters. There are also birds, hook-shaped motifs... This kind of textile is often sold to foreigners as "ceremonial sashes". According to Geirnaert, they are not traditionally used but they could replace the traditional Indonesian *slendang* during official ceremonies.

The weaving is very fine, the warps and wefts are cabled or plied factory-produced cotton yarns. The warp and weft densities are as high as those of the first *lau pahudu* analysed. The warp proportion is again 2 foundation warps for 1 supplementary warp. We have observed that the weave structure is a kind of 2/1 twill, S or Z direction. On the reverse the supplementary warps

Fig. 21 *Hikung* (?), sash or banner, folded. The pattern is no longer white on a dark ground but red on a yellow ground. The composition is unusual: some figures are readable in the weft direction and others are in the warp direction. East Sumba, probably for the trade market, late 20th century. 270 cm (warp) x 45 cm (weft). AEDTA Collection, inv. no. 3254. Photo Bruno Le Hir de Fallois

59

Fig. 22 *Hikung,* sash or banner, back macrophotograph. On the reverse of the fabric, the supplementary warps are regularly bound with a supplementary weft every 2 cm. We can clearly see here that the binding of the weft is taken from the yellow foundation warp and occurs every 2 supplementary warps (corresponding to 2 proportions). AEDTA Collection, inv. no. 3254. Photo Bruno Le Hir de Fallois

Fig. 23 *Hikung,* sash or banner, back macrophotograph. When the supplementary binding weft is not necessary, it is left floating along 2 cm of the selvage. This technique of binding is the same as the technique in the ancient *lau pahudu* dating from the nineteenth and the early twentieth century. AEDTA Collection, inv. no. 3254. Photo Bruno Le Hir de Fallois

Fig. 24 *Hikung,* sash or banner, detail. The animal shaped-pattern is a simplified version of the fantastic animal observed on the ancient *pahudu* (fig. 10, AEDTA no. 3015). A few details of the pattern are also daubed in pale blue and yellow, for decoration only. Weavers know that yellow daubing is traditionally a mark of good quality, so they tend to overdo it. East Sumba, for the trade market, late 20th century. 207 cm (warp) x 57 cm (weft). Stromboni Collection, Paris. Photo M.-H. Guelton

are regularly bound with a supplementary weft every 2 cm (fig. 22). We can clearly see here that the binding of the weft is taken from the yellow foundation warp and occurs every 2 supplementary warps (corresponding to 2 proportions). When the supplementary binding weft is not necessary it is left floating along the selvage (fig. 23) for 2 cm. This technique of binding is the same as the technique in the ancient *lau pahudu* dating from the 19th and early 20th centuries.

The specimen illustrated in fig. 24 dates from the last ten years. The pattern is yellow on a red ground. These colours recall the fashion of the thirties. The animal shaped-pattern is a simplified version of the fantastic animal observed on the ancient *pahudu* (fig. 10). A few details of the pattern are also daubed in pale blue and yellow, only for decoration. Weavers know that yellow daubing is traditionally a mark of good quality, so they tend to overdo it…We do not know whether the weavers continue to prepare models for their new production of weaving. It would be interesting to know if they create new designs or if they are only inspired by ancient ones.

The last example studied here has been woven two or three years ago. It is kept in a gallery in Paris and is labelled as *hikung*. The textile dealer mentioned that they are used as banners in East Sumba (fig. 25). According to records and Danielle Geirnaert's information, ceremonial banners are never traditionally used in this area, but it could be a new fashion to decorate the modern houses in Sumba for weddings or festivals. Whatever the

Fig. 25 *Hikung*, sash or banner, folded. The pattern of this *hikung* could represent ancestors as for the ancient *lau pahudu*. Whatever the use, the pattern is readable in the warp direction and in consequence the textile has to be presented vertically. East Sumba, for the trade market, late 20th century (1996-1998). 127 cm (warp) x 37 cm (weft) Stromboni Collection, Paris. Photo M.-H. Guelton

Fig. 26 *Hikung* sash or banner, detail, front. The pattern is woven with supplementary warps as previously but the foundation weft is a thread composed of 3 or 4 assembled yarns with different shades of blue, creating a marled effect. Stromboni Collection, Paris. Photo M.-H. Guelton

61

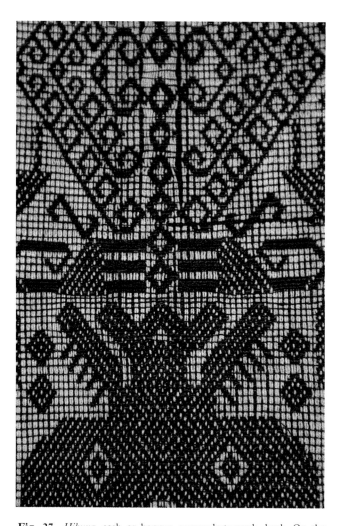

Fig. 27 *Hikung*, sash or banner, macrophotograph, back. On the reverse, the supplementary warps are bound by a supplementary weft every 2 or 3 foundation wefts. It is the finest binding we have analysed and it would be interesting to compare it with the earliest *lau pahudu* kept in the museum collections. After years of ignorance we assist to a "come back" of the finest technique of weaving. Stromboni Collection, Paris. Photo M.-H. Guelton

use, the pattern is readable in the warp direction and in consequence the textile has to be presented vertically. The pattern could represent ancestors and recalls the human figures observed on the ancient *lau pahudu*. It is remarkable by the large size of the human figures. The significance of the design looses strength as it gains in size.

This example is also particularly interesting for the technique of weaving. The pattern is woven with supplementary warps as previously but the foundation weft is a thread composed of 3 or 4 assembled yarns with different shades of blue, creating a marled effect (fig. 26). On the reverse, the supplementary warps are bound by a supplementary weft every 2 or 3 foundation wefts (fig. 27). It is the finest binding we have analysed and it would be interesting to compare it with the earliest *lau pahudu* still kept in the museum collections. After years of lack of knowledge we see here a "return" to the finest techniques of weaving.

According to Danielle Geirnaert the technique of binding had disappeared in the late seventies and early eighties. In 1982, she met two representatives of the department of education and culture in East Sumba. They were invited by Mrs Mboy, the governor's wife of Nusa Tenggara Timur to revive and promote traditional art, and the women's role in this area. This new quality of textile could be the fruit of this cooperation.

This work would be more complete with additional comparative specimens from other collections. It would also have been interesting to study the use and significance of these textiles for the Sumbanese people, and how they differed from times past. It would seem nowadays that there are two productions, a domestic and a commercial one: are they strictly compartmentalized or is there an interchangeability between them?

Fig. 28 Recapitulative chart of the *pahudu* string model structure.

Inv. n°	Motif	Pattern repeat (warp x weft)	Cotton Warp number / material		Lidi sticks number/ diameter		Ends (set up of the warp)	Structure
AEDTA n° 2969	A human figure mounted on a horse, geometric motifs, volatile.	36 cm x 33 cm.	274 threads	Undyed S 2-ply, Z-spun yarn.	195 sticks (pattern); 7 (cross rods).	1 to 2 mm.	Circular warp grouped by 16 threads). 2 wooden end rods. 2 sets of cross rods.	3/1 twill, S or Z direction.
AEDTA n°3010	Geometric hook-shaped diamond motifs.	About 24 cm x 24 cm.	212 threads + 2 (twining).	Undyed, S-5 ply, Z-spun yarn.	130 sticks (pattern); 4 (cross rods).	1 to 3 mm. 5 mm.	Cut and knotted warp at 1 end (grouped by 20 warps). 2 wooden end rods.	3/1 twill, S direction. Extended tabby (with 2 or 4 warps and 2 sticks).
AEDTA n° 3011	Mythical animal half rooster half dragon.	About 30 cm x 25 cm	136 threads (rather low density).	Undyed cotton, S-2 ply, Z-spun yarn.	139 sticks (pattern); 2 at one end.	2 to 3 mm (irregular).	Cut and coarsely knotted warp at one end. No end cross rods.	3/1 twill, S direction.
AEDTA n° 3012	Horse. Bird.	About 27 cm x 27 cm.	174 threads.	Undyed cotton, cabled Z 3-ply, S-2 ply, Z-spun yarn.	90 sticks (pattern) + 5 cross rods.	2 to 3 mm.	Circular warp (grouped by 20 warps). 2 wooden end rods. 2 set of cross rods.	Double warp tabby (fine structure). 2/1 twill, Z direction.
AEDTA n° 3013	Hook- shaped motif; half diamond geometric pattern.	About 37 cm x 11 cm; 37 cm x 13 cm (2 pattern repeats).	220 threads.	Undyed, S 2-ply, Z-spun yarn.	71 + 76 sticks (2 patterns) + 10 (cross rods).	1 mm.	Circular warps (grouped by about 16 warps) 2 wooden end rods. 2 sets of cross rods.	3/1 twill, S and Z directions. Extended tabby (by 3 threads to 2 sticks or 5, 7 threads to 2 sticks).
AEDTA n° 3014	3 hook-shaped geometric designs.	About 40 cm x 17 cm; 40 cm x 18 cm; 40 cm x 12 cm (3 pattern repeats).	246-250 threads.	Red brown, S 2-ply, and also S 7-ply, Z-spun yarns.	64 + 62 + 57 sticks (patterns); 4 + 7 + 11 (cross rods).	2 mm.	Cut and knotted warp at one end (grouped by 20 threads). 2 wooden end rods.	3 sets of cross rods. 3/1 twill, S direction. 2/1 twill, S direction.
AEDTA n° 3015	Deer or dragon (?), stylised serpent. Mirrored design : a lion hinder parts (?).	20 cm x 32 cm; 39 cm x 33/36 cm (2 pattern repeats)	230 threads (uncomplete).	Undyed, cabled Z 3-ply, S-2 ply, Z-spun yarn.	37 + 154 sticks (patterns); 2 + 6 + 2 (cross rods).	1 to 2 mm.	Circular warp (grouped by 20 threads at the cross rods). 2 wooden end rods. 3 sets of cross rods.	Tabby double warp. 3/1 twill, Z direction.
AEDTA n° 3016	Dragon.	About 45 cm x 40 cm.	300 threads.	Undyed, S 2-ply, Z-spun yarn.	142 sticks (pattern); 4 (cross rods).	2 to 4 mm (irregular).	Cut and knotted warp at one end (grouped by 20 threads). 2 wooden end rods. 2 sets of cross rods.	Tabby double warp. Extended tabby (scales).
AEDTA n° 3017	2 confronting animals (uncomplete)	25 (?) cm x 42/44 cm; 20 (?) x 42/44 cm (2 uncomplete pattern repeats).	422 threads : (224 indigo + 138 brown-black + 60 undyed).	3 yarns : undyed cabled Z 3-ply, S-2 ply, Z-spun; marled brown-black S 2-ply Z and 4; indigo blue S 5-ply, Z-spun yarn.	70 + 73 sticks (patterns); 1 + 7 +3 (cross rods).	1 to 2 mm.	Circular warp (grouped by 20 threads). 2 wooden end rods. 3 sets of cross rods.	2/1 twill, S or Z direction.
AEDTA n° 3256	Crocodile, dragon, fish, volatile.	57 cm x 47/50 cm.	292 threads.	Undyed, cabled Z 2-ply, S 2-ply, Z-spun yarn.	203 sticks (pattern) + 9 (cross rods)	About 3 mm.	Circular warp (grouped by 20 threads). 2 wooden end rods. 2 sets of cross rods.	2/1 twill, Z direction.
B. Aubert Collection	Deer (?), volatile	48 cm x 41 cm.	268 threads	Undyed, cabled Z 3-ply, S 2-ply, Z-spun yarn.	215 sticks (pattern).	About 2 mm.	Cut and knotted warp at one end (grouped by 20 threads). 2 wooden end rods.	3/1 twill, S and Z direction.

Fig. 30 Recapitulative chart of *Lau Pahudu* weave structure

Inv. n°, specimen, main design	Textile dim. Pattern repeat	Warp material	Warp proportion & thread count per cm	Weft material	Weft proportion & thread count per cm	Weave structure
AEDTA n° 3009 *Lau pahudu.* Confronting deer. (fig. p.)	122 cm (circular) x 147 cm (in 2 widths) Pattern repeat: h. 74 cm, w. 32 cm. Unit: h. 37 cm, w. 32 cm.	Foundation: cotton, Z-spun, indigo, red, yellow. Supplementary: cotton, cabled Z, 3 S 2-ply Z, undyed.	2 warp systems. 2 foundation to 1 supplementary. Count: foundation 24, supplementary 12.	Foundation: cotton, Z-spun, 1 or 2 ends, no noticeable twist, pale grey.	Only 1 weft system. Count: 8 picks.	Warp-faced tabby weave, striped, supplementary pattern warp bound in 3/1, 5/1, 7/1 twill.
AEDTA n° 3443 *Lau pahudu.* Pigs. (fig. p.)	129 cm (circular) x 132 cm (in 2 widths). Pattern repeat: h. 68 cm, w. 12 cm. Unit: h. 34 cm, w. 12 cm.	Foundation: cotton, Z-spun, black, grey, red. Supplementary: cotton, cabled Z, 3 S 2-ply Z, undyed.	2 warp systems. 2 foundation to 1 supplementary. Count: foundation 30/32, supplementary 15.	Foundation: cotton, Z-spun, dark grey, paired. Binding: cotton, Z-spun, dark grey.	2 weft systems. 1 foundation weft to 1 occasional binding weft (very irregular). Count: 7 picks (foundation), irregular (binding).	Warp-faced tabby weave, striped, warp ikat, supplementary pattern warp bound in 3/1, Z twill and occasionally bound on the reverse. Daubed after weaving.
AEDTA n° 3254 *Hikung* (?), sash or banner. Human figures (fig. p.)	270 cm (warp) x 44.5 cm (weft). Pattern repeat: h. 102 cm (divided in 3 parts?), w. 44 cm. Unit: h. 35 (?) cm, w. 34 (?) cm.	Foundation: cotton, S 2-ply, Z, yellow. Supplementary: cotton, cabled S, 3 S 2-ply Z, orange, blue.	2 warp systems. 2 foundation to 1 supplementary. Count: foundation 22, supplementary 10/11.	Foundation: cotton, Z-spun, 3 ends, no noticeable twist, yellow. Binding: cotton, Z-spun, yellow.	2 weft systems. 1 foundation weft to 1 binding weft every 9 picks. Count: 7 picks (foundation), 1 binding weft every 9 picks.	Warp-faced tabby weave, striped, supplementary pattern warp bound in 3/1, Z twill on the front and also bound on the reverse.
AEDTA n° 3879 *Hikung* (?), sash or banner. Deer and human figure. (not illustrated)	197 cm (warp + fringes) x 39 cm (weft). Pattern repeat: h. 53 cm x w. 39 cm. Unit: h. 33 cm x w. 39 cm.	Foundation: cotton, S 2-ply Z, blue, red. Supplementary: cotton, S 3-ply Z, undyed.	2 warp systems. 2 foundation to 1 supplementary. Count: foundation 20, supplementary 10.	Foundation: cotton, Z-spun, 3 ends, no noticeable twist, black. Binding: cotton, Z-spun, black.	2 weft systems. 1 foundation weft to1 binding weft every 1.5cm, 2 cm, 3 cm (irregular). Count: 7 picks (foundation), irregular (binding).	Warp-faced tabby weave, striped, supplementary pattern warp bound in 3/1 (occasionally 2/1), S or Z twill on the front and bound on the reverse. Daubed after weaving.
Stromboni collection *Hikung*, sash or banner. Confronting deer, geometric pattern. (fig. p.)	207 cm (warp) x 57 cm (weft). Pattern repeat: h. 47cm x w. 55 cm. Unit: h. 23 cm x w. 26 cm.	Foundation: cotton, S 2-ply Z, orange. Supplementary: cotton, S 3-ply Z, pale yellow.	2 warp systems. 2 foundation to 1 supplementary. Count: foundation 22, supplementary 11.	Foundation: cotton, Z-spun, 3 ends, no noticeable twist, orange. Binding: cotton, Z-spun, orange.	2 weft systems. 1 foundation weft to 1 binding weft every 4 picks. Count: 8 picks (foundation), 4 (binding).	Warp faced-tabby weave, striped, supplementary pattern warp bound in 3/1 or 2/1 S or Z twill on the front and also bound on the reverse. Daubed after weaving.
D. Stromboni collection. *Hikung*, sash or banner. Human figure. (not illustrated)	193 cm (warp) x 50 cm (weft). Pattern repeat: h. 47cm x w. 55 cm. Unit: h. 23 cm x w. 26 cm.	Foundation: cotton, S 2-ply Z, blue. Supplementary: cotton, S 3-ply Z, undyed.	2 warp systems. 2 foundation to 1 supplementary. Count: foundation 22, supplementary 11.	Foundation: cotton, Z-spun, 3 ends, no noticeable twist, black. Binding: cotton, Z-spun, black.	2 weft systems. 1 foundation weft to1 binding weft every 7/8 picks (irregular). Count: 8 picks (foundation), 1 (binding).	Warp-faced tabby weave, striped, supplementary pattern warp bound in 2/1, S or Z twill on the front and also bound on the reverse. Daubed after weaving.
D. Stromboni collection. *Hikung*, sash or banner. Human figures. (fig. p.)	127 cm (warp) x 37 cm (weft). Pattern repeat: h. 120 cm x w. 55 cm. Unit: cannot be determined.	Foundation: cotton, S 2-ply Z, blue, red. Supplementary: cotton, S 3-ply Z, undyed.	2 warp systems. 2 foundation to 1 supplementary. Count: foundation 18, supplementary 9.	Foundation: cotton, Z-spun, 4 ends, no noticeable twist, 2 shades of blue. Binding: cotton, Z-spun, black.	2 weft systems. 1 foundation weft to 1 binding weft every 2/3 picks. Count: 7 picks (foundation), 3 (binding).	Warp-faced tabby weave, striped, supplementary pattern warp bound in 2/1, or 3/1, S or Z twill on the front and also bound on the reverse. Daubed after weaving.
M. Biras collection. *Hikung*, sash or banner. Two-headed figures. (not illustrated).	280 cm (warp) x 43 cm (weft). Pattern repeat: h. 48 cm x w. 43 cm. Unit: h. 33 cm x 32 cm.	Foundation: cotton, S 4-ply Z, blue, red. Supplementary: cotton, S 4-ply Z, pale yellow or undyed (?).	2 warp systems. 2 foundation to 1 supplementary. Count: foundation 22, supplementary 11.	Foundation: cotton, Z-spun, 4 ends, no noticeable twist, black. Binding: cotton, Z-spun, black.	2 weft systems. 1 foundation weft to 1 binding weft every 2, 2.5, 3 cm. Count: 6 picks (foundation), irregular (binding).	Warp-faced tabby weave, striped, supplementary pattern warp bound in 2/1, S or Z twill on the front and also bound on the reverse. Daubed after weaving.

1   This work is mainly based on the study of the Association pour l'Etude et la Documentation de Textile dû Asie (AEDTA) collection and also on a few examples from private collections in Paris (Bernard Aubert, Marine Biras Gallery and Dominique Stromboni Gallery). So far the author has not actually travelled to East Sumba but was made aware by Danielle Geirnaert of new unpublished data concerning the interrelation of this weaving with local customs. Danielle Geirnaert is an ethnologist and an Assistant Professor at Paris X University. She is also the President of AFTA (French Association for Textile Studies), Paris. She stayed in West Sumba in 1982 and 1984 and went back in 1996 for her research on textiles, symbols and ethnology. At the same time she also did research in East Sumba.

2   The author is the assistant-curator and technical analysis specialist, AEDTA, Paris. This text was translated from French by Dominique Scott, AEDTA, Paris. The author would like to thank the James H. W. Thompson Foundation and the Jim Thompson Thai Silk Company for the symposium and the present publication. A special thanks to Jean-Michel Beurdeley, Eric Booth, William Booth, Jane Puranananda and their staff for their valuable cooperation.

3   We are thinking of Mattiebelle Gittinger, Brigitte Khan-Majlis present at the symposium, but also Monni Adams, Laurens Langewis, Robert J. Holmgren and Anita E. Spertus, Wanda Warming, Michael Gaworski and Danielle Geirnaert. Of course, this list is not exhaustive.

4   Unpublished information from Danielle Geirnaert.

5   Adams Monni, "System and Meaning in East Sumba Textile Design: A Study in Traditional Indonesian Art", Southeast Asian Cultural Report Series no. 16, New Haven, Yale University, 1969, p. 5-6, 8 and quoted by Robert J. Holmgren and Anita E. Spertus in Early Indonesian Textiles from Three Island Cultures – Sumba, Toraraja, Lampung, The Metropolitan Museum of Art, distributed by Harry N. Abrams, Inc. New York, 1989, p. 30 note 2.

6   Warming Wanda and Gaworski Michael, The World of Indonesian Textiles, Serindia Publications, London, 1981, p 136-138.

7   This has not yet been laboratory tested.

8   Holmgren Robert J. and Spertus Anita E., Early Indonesian Textiles from Three Island Cultures – Sumba, Toraraja, Lampung, p. 26. Forth Gregory L., Rindi: An Ethnological Study of a Traditional Domain in Eastern Sumba, Verhandelingen van het Koninklijk Instituut voor Taal-, Land-en Volkenkunde, Leiden no. 93. The Hague: Nijhoff.

9   Gittenger Mattiebelle, Splendid Symbols, Textile and Tradition in Indonesia, The Textile Museum, Washington DC, 1979, p. 159.

10 The same particularity occurs in three specimens: AEDTA no. 3010, no. 3014, no. 3016. See recapitulative chart of pahudu technical structure, fig. 28.

11 See pahudu AEDTA no. 3015 (fig. 10); no. 3016 (fig. 11). See also recapitulative chart of pahudu technical structure, fig. 28.

12 For the complete analysis, see recapitulative chart of pahadu technical structure, fig. 28.

13 Patola are double-ikat pattern silks woven in Gujarat, India for the domestic and Indonesian market. The were probably imported to Indonesia between the 16th and 19th centuries.

14 This has not yet been laboratory tested.

15 Danielle Geirnaert mentioned such a lau pahudu kept in The Rambu Timba collection, of a noblewoman from Waingapu, East Sumba. This example confirms the use of supplementary warps in different colours in the same weaving. According to the design the supplementary warps are yellow, white and blue on a red ground.

16 See, for example, the diagram of the back-strap loom published in Seiler-Baldinger Annemarie, Classification of Textile Techniques, Calico Museum of Textiles, Ahmedabad, 1979, fig, 9 p. 53. See also Gittinger Mattiebelle, Splendid Symbols, Textile and Tradition in Indonesia, p. 229-231.

17 Unpublished information from Danielle Geirnaert.

18 Bolland Rita, "Weaving a Sumba Woman's Skirt" Lamak and Malat in Bali and a Sumba Loom, Royal Tropical Institute, Amsterdam, Mr. CXIX Dept. of Cultural and Physical Anthropology Nr. 53, 1956, p. 49-57 diagram p. 50.

19 Bolland Rita, op. it. p. 52.

20 Bolland Rita, op. it. p. 52.

21 Fraser-Lu Sylvia, Handwoven Textiles of South-East Asia, Oxford University Press, 1988, p. 199.

22 This has not yet been laboratory tested.

23 For instance see Holmgren Robert J. and Spertus Anita E., Early Indonesian Textiles from Three Island Cultures – Sumba, Toraraja, Lampung, p.35 ñ 39. See also Tropen Museum Collection in Amsterdam inv. A5244 published in Gittinger Mattiebelle, Splendid Symbols, Textile and Tradition in Indonesia, p. 162, fig. 122. And, The Museum of Ethnography Collection in Basel, inv. 4-86.

24 For the complete technical analysis see the recapitulative chart of the lau pahudu weave structure, fig. 30.

25 Gillow John, Traditional Indonesian Textiles, Thames and Hudson, London, 1992, p. 117.

TEXTILES FOR THE LIVING AND THE DEAD –
A Lao Case

Mattiebelle Gittinger

Many of the 38 different ethnic groups which comprise the Lao population once supported vital textile traditions. The relative importance of these customs has waned in the face of changing life styles and increased commercial imports, but among a few groups textile traditions have retained a resilience that speaks to their importance even in the face of change.[1]

Customs associated with members of the Tai Lao language family, in particular the Tai Dam (Black Tai), Tai Daeng (Red Tai) and Tai Kaw (White Tai) are the focus of this paper. These particular groups have moved in relatively recent times from northern Vietnam to the narrow upland valley in Laos, clustering in greater numbers in Luang Nam Tha Province in the northwest of the country and Houa Phan Province in the northeast.[2] Tai is the name of a language family that includes many of the people of Laos, Thailand, as well as minority groups in Vietnam, Burma, and parts of southern China. Thai refers to the citizens of the country of Thailand.

The separate ethnic identity of these upland peoples is readily declared by the people themselves. However, experts increasingly challenge this proclaimed diversity. The Tai Daeng share many traits with the Tai Dam and it has been suggested that they are one and the same group misnamed by early westerners in the region. Some scholars also relate the Tai Dam and the Tai Kaw, saying the latter are a recent "splinter group" from the Tai Dam. The convergence and divergences of the textile forms and customs of these various groups do not suggest a resolution to these questions. Nor did work in these areas address these issues. The ethnic terms used within this paper are those admitted by local populations during work in these areas in 1993 and 1995.

Even in the face of an expressed diversity, these groups share many textile skills. Each utilizes cotton and silk, employs a simple frame loom equipped with two to four heddles, practices supplementary weft and supplementary warp patterning and may use warp or weft *ikat* to pattern their textiles.

Basic Tai Dam Textile Forms

Among the several groups, the Tai Dam are of initial interest because they are thought to be the least affected by outside cultural influences.[3] In particular they have never accepted Buddhism nor experienced the changes that that religion has had on the practices of some of their neighbors. Their most unpretentious cloth is the *khan phuan* a modest white cotton plain-weave rectangle with a plain center and, usually, a line of horse and rider motifs near the fringe ends, fig. 1. Most commonly these designs are worked by supplementary wefts, but occasionally these or simple plant forms are embroidered. The cloth always has a cotton foundation, but the patterns may be in cotton or silk.

Fig. 1 Tai Dam *khan phuan* is typically a plain-weave cotton rectangle with end patterns worked in cotton discontinuous supplementary wefts. Each is approximately 80 x 30 cm.

Inquiry concerning this cloth is usually met with mirthful asides and blushed responses. This is because a young girl may present a *khan phuan* to a favored suitor as a sign of her interest. At one time young men tallied their popularity by the number of the small cloths they could boast. When worn the cloth was lightly folded and hung about the neck. More commonly a man saved the cloth throughout his life and at his death the cloth, or cloths, would be placed in his coffin. While this function is that which the Tai Dam first mention, the *khan phuan* is used on many other occasions.

This cloth is the sign by which a new bride signals to the elders in her husband's family her newly acquired status. She must present a *khan phuan* to her husband's parents and each of his elder siblings. The binding qualities of this obligation were exemplified in the history of one Lao example recorded. A niece living in north Vietnam presented one of the cloths to her uncle when he finally had the opportunity to visit her and her family on a trip from his Lao home. Even though the niece's marriage had occurred far earlier, the "bride" fulfilled her obligation when it became possible to do so. The cloth is seen as a sign of respect and travels in a socially upward direction from younger to older. The name itself, *khan phuan* means "half cloth" with the implication of "unequal halves". This may hint at the relationship between a wife and husband or it may be a simple reference to the size of the cloth which tends to be half a *wa*. A *wa*, the standard Lao cloth measure, is the distance from the middle fingers of outstretched arms, approximately 166 cm.

Most often the cloth is joined with other ritually mandated textiles in gift sets that social custom pre-scribes. In the simplest form the set will include the *khan phuan*, a head cloth (*pio*), fig. 2, and a *phaa puu* also known a *phaa tuum*, fig. 3. In certain instances the flat bag (*pi*), fig. 4, displaces the *phaa tuum* in this basic set. The set forms the core of the several gifts a Tai Dam bride gives to her new mother-and father-in-law which also includes a skirt, blouse, trousers and occasionally a sash. At the time of marriage a young woman could appropriately give this set not just to her husband's mother and father, but also to aunts and uncles for which she might receive a sum of money in return.

The *pio* of the set is a Tai Dam woman's head cloth. It is a long narrow blue-black cotton textile with patterning framed in a compact rectangle at both ends. In most examples today this patterning is embroidered, but

Fig. 3 A Tai Dam *phaa puu* or *phaa tuum* shows a locally woven center panel with patterns worked by supplementary wefts. The cloth is lined and framed by contrasting borders. Sizes vary, but most have an overall dimension close to 160 x 60 cm. The weft of the center panel is 35 cm.

Fig. 2 Two Tai Dam women's head wrappers, *phaa pio* show rectangular end patterns worked in supplementary wefts. In some instances the end panels are embroidered. Each is approximately 135 x 36 cm.

Fig. 4 A Tai Dam flat bag *(pi)* was traditionally part of a man's costume and was a required item in certain ritual gift sets

Fig. 5 An elderly Tai Dam woman wears *phaa pio* with both ends hanging down her back. She carries a woman's traditional basket

seemingly older examples often employ supplementary wefts. At the ends, small tassels or yarn-wrapped circular shapes are applied. As worn by older women, the patterned ends fall over the back, fig. 5. As a young woman demonstrated the headcloth, however, one end fell down the back and the other was flipped jauntily forward toward the forehead.

The *pi* or *yam*, the flat bag is today a common attribute of school children, fig. 6, and tourists, but that has not always been the case. The flat bag was traditionally used by men to carry small personal items while women employed a woven basket worn on the back, fig. 5. Thus the bag inherently carries a male connotation in contrast to the female head cloth, the *phaa pio*.

The *phaa puu*, a cover, is another important cloth among the Tai Dam and has only a few direct counterparts among the textiles of other Tai ethnic groups. (See Bunyaratavej in this volume.) It is a flat patterned rectangle that is entirely framed by two or more contrasting borders. The outermost border is the edge of the cloth lining, usually a white cotton, that is turned to the front and sewn to the face of the cloth. In the better examples the corners of the framing borders are neatly

mitered. The whole rectangle measures approximately 160 cm in length by 60 cm wide. The central panel has a plain weave cotton foundation with cotton and silk supplementary wefts worked in narrow bands of geometric patterns. It is woven in strips approximately 8 meters long by 35 cm wide. These strips generally form part of a household inventory; they are saved to be cut apart as needed such as for the *phaa puu*.[4]

The form of the *phaa puu* is notable within the context of Southeast Asian textiles in that it is bordered and lined. These details are unusual in a region where the more common format is that of a simple unframed rectangle.

The meaning of *phaa puu* is a cloth "to put down, such as a sheet on a mattress," or in some instances this cloth is termed *phaa tuum*, signifying a cloth "for wrapping such as a mother wraps a child." It literally accompanies a person from birth through death and beyond. The cloth covers a child in the cradle, fig. 7, and serves as a carrying cloth, fig. 8. Several *phaa puu* may line the walls of a house at times of appeasing the household spirits, fig. 9. The cloth is placed under and over a corpse and on top of the coffin, figs. 10 and 11. The very num-

Fig. 6 Today most school children in upland Laos carry school supplies in the traditional flat bag

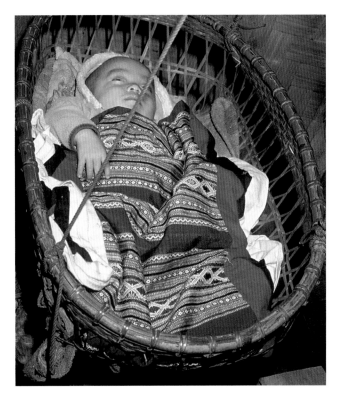

Fig. 7 A *phaa puu* serves as a cover for a Tai Dam baby

ber of these cloths to appear at periods of mourning signals a person's industriousness and degree of respect within the larger community. To paraphrase one Tai Dam informant:

> ...if there is no *phaa puu* on the coffin, it shows the person was not well known during life. He or she has not touched others and, therefore, did not gain respect from others. Many people bring these cloths – the number shows the goodness of the dead person. The house of the dead is also decorated with textiles, if not that person had been lazy.

Textiles in great numbers are central to a Tai Dam funeral which itself is a theater of transcendent beliefs often engaging 200 to 300 people. The Tai Dam believe the body contains 32 *khwan* or life essences (variously translated as spirits or souls) that endow the body with qualities of life.[5] These all leave the body upon death and head for different destinations. That of the body goes to heaven aided by religious practitioners, *mo dam*, and the eldest son-in-law. Once conceived as having multiple levels and conveniences that mirrored the hierarchical levels of earthly society, heaven today is still believed

Fig. 8 Most frequently *phaa puu* are seen as cloths for carrying Tai Dam babies

Fig. 11 A Tai Dam funeral in 1993 showing *phaa puu* covering the coffin as it is taken to the cemetery

Fig. 9 (left) *Phaa puu* line the wall of a Tai Dam house during a spirit appeasement ceremony. In the foreground the elderly sister of the male spirit makes ready presents to be taken to the house altar. These include *khan phuan*, skirts, head wrappers, *phaa puu* skeins of silk, bedding, a flat bag, commercial clothes and antique jewelry. After being accepted at the spirit altar the gifts are returned to the sister

Fig. 10 *Phaa puu* and *phaa pio* cover the walls and, together with a flat bag, cover the body of the dead at a Tai Dam funeral. The disarray of the house interior is a sign of death, as is the white cloth worn by close relatives. Sons and sons-in-law, in particular are required to wear white a this time

to reflect the features of this life, but in a more egalitarian form in keeping with socialistic precepts.[6] Textiles remain a passport to this realm.

Following a death, the main room in the house of the deceased becomes a scene of disarray with dozens of textiles hung over lines, casually strewn over objects and others placed under and over the body of the dead, fig. 10. These textiles are primarily *khan phuan* and *phaa puu*, but also head cloths and purses and increasingly, items made from imported foreign cloth are included. Normally stored neatly in baskets in the sleeping area of the house, the disorder of these textiles now spread around represents the chaos associated with death.

The potency of the symbolism of "disordered" cloth was brought home to the author and her colleagues during their work in a Tai Dam village headman's house. In the course of the interview, textiles to be photographed later had been casually set to one side. After some time the host gently remonstrated the questioners, that while it did not matter to him, cloth so disarranged meant there was a death in the house and this casualness – this disorder – would matter to others.[7]

The ultimate source of these textiles spread at random through the room varies according to Tai Dam informants. Many are the property of the deceased person and the immediate family. A household prepares *phaa puu* for the time of death and at least two of these are buried with the dead. Close relatives may give additional *phaa puu* which are draped over the coffin and after being purified are returned to the owners. These cloths are afterwards never used as covers for children. Other cloth gifts come from friends and mourners, but there is no consistent indication that people in a certain relation to the dead must give specific textiles.

The coffin containing the body is carried to the cemetery in a procession led by the eldest son-in-law of the deceased. He holds aloft a banner and shoulders a flat purse belonging to the house of the dead, fig. 12. This may be the purse a bride presented to her in-laws at the time of marriage. It is later returned. The body is now buried in the cemetery, or among some Tai Dam, the body is cremated.[8] The following day, mourners return to the grave site and erect an elaborate assemblage of grave furniture to assist the dead to the beyond.

Although varying in size and style the following are the essential components constructed at the grave site. A miniature house (*hun noi*) supported on pilings is built immediately above the grave, fig. 13. A skein of silk stretches from the grave through the floor of the house, fig. 14. Extending from the *hun noi* is a wooden

Fig. 12 A son-in-law leads the funeral procession to the grave yard. He wears a shouder bag from the house of the dead and holds a banner aloft

"bridge", often a simple pole, that carries a much smaller house (*huo yin*) and which continues on to an imposing structure that reaches skyward. If the dead had been female this structure, known as *ko hee oh*, is a gigantic wooden pole with limbs that recall the ribs of a wind-inverted umbrella. These ribs or limbs are hung with red or white "flags". From the center of the limbs a tall pole stretches upward carrying a figure of a bird and a basket and terminating, finally, in a finial of an umbrella. If the deceased had been a woman, this configuration appears on the east side of the grave site, if the deceased had been a man, on the west. In its place on the eastern side is the *chow fai yai* – a tall ladder-like form – similarly topped by a figure, now that of a horse, basket and umbrella, fig. 15. To erect the *chow fai yai* a buffalo must be sacrificed which, in current belief, guarantees the deceased access to the highest levels of heaven.[9] The rungs of the ladder are hung with red or white cloths. An additional tall pole carrying a plain cloth banner stretches even higher. Across these structures located in the east, a long pole is lashed horizontally in the upper reaches. At the extremities hang a man's shirt and a woman's blouse. The direction the garment faces indicates if the spouse of the dead is living or dead: if already deceased it faces east, toward the original homeland of the Tai Dam in north Vietnam. If still living the garment faces west.

Various details enhance this assemblage. On the grave itself may be an inverted stool, a suitcase with some of the deceased's clothes, a bottle of alcohol – seemingly items intended for use by the dead. Placed in the house directly over the grave are items necessary in this life now dedicated to the dead. These may include a mat, pillow, mosquito net, blanket, a cloth to put food on,

Fig. 13 A Tai Dam woman's grave site in Luang Nam Tha Province. The house directly over the grave contains cloths, utensils for cooking and eating and other items necessary for this life. The small house connected to this holds a *khan phuan*, a head cloth and a flat bag. These same gifts are also found on the figure of the animal at the top of the pole and, again, under the umbrella that crowns the whole

Fig. 14 On the west side of the house over the grave shown in Fig.13 appear woven banners that were carried in procession by the son-in-law of the dead woman. The skein of silk leading from the grave to the house appears on the left

Fig. 15 The ladder-like structure in this cemetery scene is indicative of a Tai Dam man's grave. The cloths on the "ladder" are red and white indicating a "good" death. When these are black and white it signifies the deceased shed blood at death. The same gift sets that are listed in Fig. 13 would be present here

tea pot, plate, utensils for eating, etc. The extent of these gifts seems to be quite variable. Elsewhere in the grave assemblage, however, there does not seem to be such latitude. A gift set of a *khan phuan*, *phaa pio* and *pi* (flat purse) must be placed in three different locations: the *huo yin*, on the horse's neck (or bird's) and under the crowning umbrella, fig. 16. The male/female symbolism is evident, the ultimate symbolism of the *khan phuan* beyond that of an honorific, is not apparent within this set, however. Tai Dam informants say the soul of the deceased passes from the grave along the silk skein and from the *hun noi* with its worldly items to the *huo yin* which is considered a "cooling house". From there it ascends the pole in the center of the *ko hee oh* or the *chow fai yai* and rides the bird or horse to heaven. It is not clear if the dead is intended to take all of the grave gifts to heaven, but certainly the elements of the textile gift sets are thought to accompany the deceased. When

Fig. 16 At a Tai Dam grave site in Luang Nam Tha the umbrella crowning the grave has fallen allowing the *khan phuan*, flat bag and head cloth to be seen

Virtually all of the items that go to the cemetery stay there. The exception may be the textiles used to cover the coffin during the procession to the grave site. These are *phaa puu* or, rarely, one of the older style "long coats." These may be ritually purified in a simple ceremony at the river's edge and returned to the home of the dead person. The *phaa puu* in the coffin remain with the dead as well as the particularly fine personal clothing of the dead, often saved for this very purpose and, frequently *khan phuan* given to the deceased during his life.

If the dead had been a senior member of the household, on the third day the family returns to the grave to invite the spirit to return to the house to act as a guardian. A small altar located on one of the poles within the house accommodates the spirit. Modest offering may be made at the altar, but in other instances elaborate ceremonies and extravagant feasting honor the spirit, fig. 9. This spirit will one day be replaced by the death of the senior person in the next generation who lives in the house.

The grave furniture is the most remarkable material expression of the Tai Dam. The assemblage celebrates what the society deems a successful life – a mature person with many descendants who has touched other people's lives. It is not available to unmarried people, or to the physically or mentally impaired. The structure at once proclaims the position and wealth of the dead and his family and, by facilitating the ascent to heaven, secures the good will of the spirit. In theory all of this is returned in the benevolence the spirit confers upon the next generation. The grave furniture and all the accouterments decay with time, animals desecrate the gifts and in four to five years the site is barely discernible. Not until another family elder ends a "successful life" is a similar structure built and furnished.[10]

Funeral Customs of the Tai Kaw

In the transition to Buddhist custom among other Tai groups, many of the original forms of these textiles have become blurred. Yet there is a resonance in what exist today to suggest that these textiles and their associated customs were once part of the broader Tai heritage.

A Tai Kaw funeral in Xam Neua in Hua Phan Province in northeast Laos contains echoes of this past. Many items of possible correspondence appeared in the Buddhist context, only now the objects were carried to the wat where in the giving they earn merit for the living and the dead.[11] The small house filled with the necessities of this world, fig. 17, formerly built over the grave, now acts as the conveyance to the temple, the silk and cotton

asked why a man would take a woman's head cloth to heaven the reply was to give to his mother who is in heaven. It seems that the textile gift sets, witness to times of transition during life, are invested with similar functions after death. The textiles are icons of both stability and change.

The textiles seen today on the *ko hee oh* are typically red and white commercial cloth, but on some grave sites they had been woven locally and certainly this would have been the case in the past. Those observed had a red foundation and lines of simple supplementary weft patterning. Informants in certain villages said the white cloths which alternate with the red were once *khan phuan*, but this was never empirically substantiated. Black flags and white flags occasionally replaced the red and white. These appear on the graves of people who had spilled blood as they died, which was considered a bad death.

Fig. 17 Tai Kaw near Xam Neua prepare funeral gifts to be taken to the Buddhist wat to earn merit for the dead just cremated. The small house in front contains rice grains. The structures and concepts in this funeral, though Buddhist, are similar to those of the Tai Dam

Fig. 18 The umbrella to be raised over the Tai Kaw gift tower contains a baseball cap, towel and money which are surely substitutes for the more traditional gift set in Fig.16

fibers are important gifts and the tall poles that reach skyward over the Tai Dam grave are replaced by the towering structure considered to be a *stupa*, fig. 19. The whole is once again crowned by an umbrella sheltering familiar forms of a head covering, here a baseball cap, and a rectangular cloth, not the forgotten *khan phuan*, but a commercial towel, Fig. 18. It is incomprehensible that these items are not founded on older common Tai tradition as seen among the Tai Dam.

Funeral Customs of the Tai Daeng

The Tai Daeng customs are a bit more modest in comparison to the Tai Dam and Tai Kaw. To mark the grave of a senior person, this group equips a small house raised over the grave site with a sampling of the necessities of this life: skirt or trousers, a carrying basket or shoulder bag, shoes, sitting pillows for men or a rattan stool for women, tea pot, cups, etc., fig. 20. The area around the grave is fenced and a small garden and other elements of a homestead are constructed within the enclosure, replicating this life in miniature. Such luxurious grave gifts, however, are the exception for the very wealthy; more commonly seen are graves with a modest crude bamboo roof and a few gifts.

In explaining a funeral, Tai Daeng informants said nine layers of cloth would be placed above and below the body in the coffin for a woman, and seven if the deceased were male. Textiles destined for such use today are long narrow warp lengths of cotton or silk patterned with red, yellow and white weft stripes. The coffin was covered with a *phaa pok luang* which was similar to the striped cloth in the coffin, but carried patterns in some of the stripes, fig. 21.

The face of the dead was reportedly covered by a small square of cloth. Those shown were bits of commercial cloth. A number of people interviewed mentioned using a small square cloth in various other rituals.

Traditionally the Tai Daeng flew banners to signal a death. According to some, the banners were placed on the grave and remained there until they disintegrated, thus explaining the lack of older examples. Inhabitants of a Tai Daeng village south of Xam Neua produced two banners created from commercial cloth and fragments of older cloths, fig.22. According to informants there, the banners are considered the property of patrilineal kin groups whose members have the exclusive right to fly the banner at their home when there is a death. It is

Fig. 19 The Tai Kaw gift frame in Fig.17 has been completely wrapped in cloth and the whole topped with a *"stupa"* crowned with the umbrella in Fig.18. The entire structure is carried to the local *wat* on the following day

Fig. 20 A Tai Daeng grave site in Hua Phan Province shows a similar grave house containing the necessities of this world

Fig. 21 The Tai Daeng in Houa Phan Province cover a coffin with a cloth such as this called *phaa pok luang*. This example had a plain-weave silk foundation with silk weft stripes and supplementary weft patterning. This example was 833. x 36 cm.

probable that most of the long, heavily patterned textiles that have come from Laos in the recent past were once banners or textiles to cover a coffin.

The funeral customs of these three groups are fundamentally the same with minor variations. The dead is supplied with the necessities of this life to enjoy in the hereafter and this giving carries a connotation of reciprocal benevolence from the spirit to the family of the living. Designated textiles are placed in and on the coffin exterior when the body is carried from the house. Some form of banners either plain or heavily patterned announces a death to the larger community and, at least among the Tai Dam sets of designated textile gifts mark stages on the soul's ascent to heaven.

Fig. 22 A Tai Daeng banner flown at the house of the dead to announce a death. This example is made from an older, locally woven segment, attached to a commercial coth

Textile Forms for the Living

The women's skirts which enter into the marriage equation, as well as daily life of all three of these groups raise problems. Far from being unique ethnic expressions as most foreign observers have considered, most styles of skirts today, at least, are woven by two or even all three peoples. This does not seem to be a very recent phenomena.

Seemingly the most modest of the skirts made by the Tai Kaw and Tai Daeng contains very subdued details. In a Tai Kaw example, fig. 23, the warp is a series of fine stripes of red silk and black cotton interspersed with yellow and green silk stripes and a single narrow white silk stripe which demarcates the hem section. Small, apparently random areas of the yellow silk warp were first tied off, then the yarns were dyed indigo resulting in a purple *ikatted* yarn. Two of these *ikat*-worked purple yarns ride in the center of each red stripe adding a pleasing reticulation to the cloth surface. Plain red silk yarns plied with the purple *ikat* yarns form the selvedge. The weft is black cotton which does not show on the tightly woven warp-faced plain-weave textile. Other examples of this type of skirt may not have the selvedge detail, but all are characterized by narrow red (silk) and black (cotton) warp stripes and random warp *ikat* patterning usually located in the middle of the red stripe.

Woven in 1993, the skirt in fig. 23 was a gift from a bride to her new mother-in-law. In 1995 it had not been worn and still lacked a *hua* or waistband. No additional hem section (*tin sin*) would be added to this type of skirt. While appearing in household inventories, in the course of the work among the Tai Kaw and Tai Daeng, this skirt was never seen being worn, possibly it had been relegated to gift exchange alone. It does continue to be woven, however, as witnessed by an example on a Tai Daeng loom. A variation of this skirt carries parallel rows of simple geometric designs worked in white supplementary warps (*muk*), fig. 24. This skirt is woven by the Tai Daeng, Tai Kaw and Phuan, a Tai ethnic group in Xieng Khouang Province.

The skirts that are dependent on warp patterning either as *ikat* or supplementary elements may well be the oldest type for these Tai groups. All other skirts depend on weft patterning techniques which may have entered the local repertoire when longer warps were technically possible. Probably the longer warp arose with the adoption of the frame loom at some time in the distant past. By shifting the patterning to weft elements, the weaver could work a variety of patterns on a single warp, not being restricted to patterning originating in the warp set up.

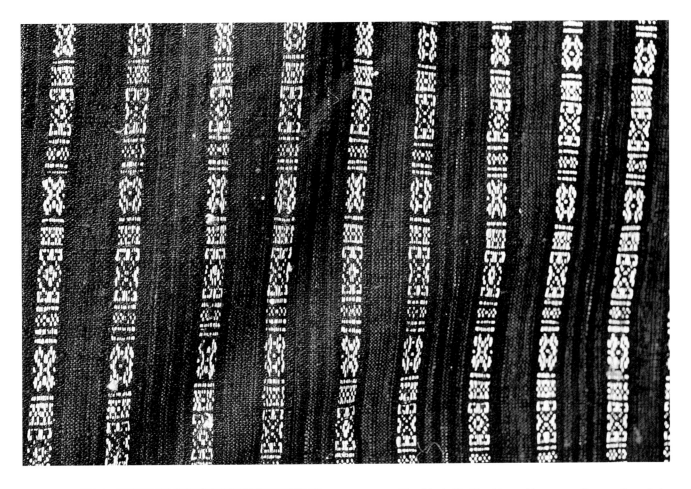

Fig. 24 The skirt in Fig.23, with or without warp *ikat*, may be embellished with narrow supplementary warp *(muk)* stripes. The width of the pattern combination in these stripes lends its name to the skirt, thus one hears of *muk* 2 or, the widest, *muk* 6. Both Tai Daeng and Tai Kaw make this skirt in Houa Phan Province as well as the Tai Phuan people in Xieng Khouang. It has also been reported to be common in Vientiane. (Cheesman 1988: 65)

Fig. 23 A skirt type made by both Tai Daeng and Tai Kaw. This example was a Tai Kaw bride's gift to her mother-in-law. It features narrow black cotton and red silk warp stripes and simple warp *ikat* dashes within the red stripe. Normally the skirt would have a waist band, but not a decorative lower border

Fig. 25 Probably the most commonly seen skirt in Houa Phan Province is this type with supplementary warp stripes and a contiguous border pattern worked in supplementary wefts. These examples are pictured in the Tai Daeng village of Baan Nala; similar pieces are woven by the Tai Kaw

Fig. 26 One of the most complex skirts of the Tai Daeng utilizes the common supplementary warp stripes, now to frame broad rows of alternating blocks of weft *ikat* patterns worked on dark blue and supplementary weft patterns. In the latter, the masterful use of varied colors creates a lively complex visual experience. Variation of this skirt are made with equal dexterity by Tai Daeng and Tai Kaw in Houa Phan Province

In variations of the skirt in fig. 24 the warp *ikat* may, or may not, be present and supplementary weft decoration is added to one edge which when worn becomes the lower margin of the skirt, fig. 25. This skirt is made and worn by Tai Kaw and Tai Daeng and seems to be the most common type in Houa Phan Province today. It was sketched along with other textile designs in a pre-World War II work on the Tai Daeng living in north Vietnam by R. Robert.[12] Although necessarily schematic, the drawings indicate that the Tai Daeng contemporary skirt in fig. 26 was being made at that time. A second skirt drawing indicates that the basic composition of the skirt in fig. 26 was also woven. It is a complex assemblage of weft *ikat* and supplementary warps and wefts. In the drawing from north Vietnam of this type very rudimentary designs are indicated in weft *ikat*. This skirt is currently made in Laos by both Tai Daeng and Tai Kaw women.

Robert's work is interesting for its omissions as well. It includes design forms such as the large animals in the skirt border in fig. 27, but in the context of a shoulder cloth, not a skirt. and no place is there a suggestion of the skirt in figs. 28 and 29. Today both of these skirt types, however, are thought to be signature pieces of the Tai Daeng.

The type is held to be "traditional" not only among the Tai Daeng, but also among the Tai Dam, fig. 30. At least in one instance the type was present in a Tai Kaw collection. The skirt composition, almost always worked on a red silk warp, is of a number of red ground and blue ground *ikat* bands separated by bands of supplementary weft patterning. Stylized dragons and birds are the char-

acteristic figures in the *ikat* although these may be so abstract they are not clearly discernible. The patterning is done in the weft and is oriented vertically when worn.

The lower border, a separately woven element, may be elaborately patterned and ten to twelve inches wide or a narrow, one or two inch modestly patterned addition. The waistband (*hua*) is commonly vertically striped in red; however, in some Tai Daeng examples a dark colored *hua* carries geometric patterns worked in supplementary warps. We were told a daughter would wear this *hua* at the funeral of her mother.

This skirt is rare in the uplands today having been a prime object of collectors over the past eight or nine years. It has generally been given a Tai Daeng origin by dealers and there is a suggestion that the very finest examples were done by this group. The complexity of the earlier *ikat* patterns, requiring at least four dye stages, has been replaced in today's work by simpler all-over *ikat* patterns of a more generic character among the Tai Dam and simple banded patterns among the Tai Daeng. There is also increasingly a trend away from weft *ikat* toward supplementary weft patterning.

That the Tai Dam may have borrowed this style of skirt and, possibly, the skills of weft *ikat* patterning from the Tai Daeng is suggested upon examining the weaving of groups related to the Black Tai. The Lao Song of Thailand are a people thought to be of Tai Dam origin who were forcibly moved to settlements in Thailand in the 18th and 19th centuries.[13] They seem to have practiced no *ikat* work and the woman's skirt is a weft-faced plain weave blue-black cotton with broadly spaced white weft stripes which are oriented vertically as worn. The

Fig. 27 A decorative border of a Tai Kaw woman's skirt. This was considered an older example and was currently used as a model for contemporary skirt borders. Borders of a similar character are common to the Tai Daeng as well

Fig. 28 While commonly recognized as a Tai Daeng style skirt, this type was also made by Tai Dam in Luang Nam Tha and the author saw one example reportedly made by a Tai Kaw. Weft *ikat* bands with red and blue grounds showing dragons or birds alternate with rows of geometric patterns in supplementary wefts. The warp in these skirts is almost always red silk. Collection of Mr. and Mrs. Russell S. Fling, Columbus, Ohio

Fig. 29 A Tai Daeng woman in the Xam Neua area. She wears a skirt with a body similar to that in Fig. 24 and an attached border in a traditional Tai Daeng style. The new skirts in her hands are similar, but simpler versions to that in fig. 26

Fig. 30 A Tai Dam woman in Luang Nam Tha Province wearing her traditional dress, including a skirt similar to that in fig. 28

Fig. 31 A typical Tai Daeng women's head wrapper. This may be folded lengthwise into fourths to create a narrow strip which is then wrapped around the top of the head like a crown. It may also be worn unfolded in which case the large decorative diamond rides on the top of the head with the border cascading down the back of the head and neck. The Textile Museum 1985.31.4 The Ruth Lincoln Fisher Fund

hidden warp is red silk. The skirt, quite voluminous in comparison to the narrow Tai Dam skirt, carries a narrow waist band and lower attached border.[14] Even in photographs made in the 19th and early years of the 20th century, this is the skirt depicted. While skills may be lost over time, this lack of ikat skirts among the Lao Song may suggest a later borrowing by groups left in Laos. If this has been the case, it is perplexing that the borrowing was so limited given the broad interchanges or similarities of forms between Tai Daeng and Tai Kaw.

The extensive sharing of skirt types and designs among these groups casts into relief the lack of sharing of *any* elements in the women's head dresses. The head wrapper of the Tai Dam, fig. 2, the Tai Daeng, fig. 31, and the Tai Kaw (who today say they wear only a plain blue cloth) share no design features nor is one type ever used by an ethnic group other than its own. This remains true also for the head wrappers of other Tai ethnic groups not discussed here. The head dress of these peoples remains inviolate to borrowing more so than any other item of costume.

The lack of weft *ikat* in any of the head dresses also bears notation. As pointed out elsewhere, weft *ikat* pat-terned items among Tai groups in Thailand were traditionally not worn above the waist.[15] Weft *ikat* has been a technique associated with lower body garments – skirts and hip wrappers – which are imbued with concepts of ritual pollution. However these admonitions were communicated, they have been respected by the remotest of these upland groups.

Set within the context of the textile production of the larger Tai linguistic family, the textiles of the Tai Dam and the Tai Daeng present few surprises except in two regards. The absence of the importance of pillows among the Tai Dam, at least among those groups in Luang Nam Tha Province, is noteworthy. From Tai groups in Yunnan, through Thailand and many parts of Laos head pillows (or more rarely sitting pillows) are extremely important elements in gift exchanges. Even beyond the Tai family, pillows were important symbols in life crisis rituals in Southeast Asia.[16] Pillows probably were more important in the past for the Tai Dam. When questioned about this form, a young adult in a Tai Dam village in Luang Nam Tha dismissed the question by saying they were associated "with grandmother's house". However, near the Vietnamese border, Tai Dam reported giving pillows at weddings, and in another instance a Tai Dam living near Vientiane reported guests to a wedding were given small squares of cloth called *phaa maun*, literally "pillow cloth". The presence of pillow usage in a ceremonial context among the Tai Dam, if so, is significant because pillow giving is more closely associated with Buddhist Tai groups. However, even within these Buddhist groups pillow giving is paramount to marriage rituals which are considered secular events so even though pillows are important gifts to monks the original custom may have predated Buddhism in this area.

The carefully framed and lined *phaa puu or phaa tuum* of the Tai Dam while not uncomfortable within the Tai spectrum does claim attention within the Southeast Asian context where framing is not generally found. Only Tai groups seem to use this type of crafted cloth. It is a feature of blankets, baby carriers, some floor mats, and in the Tai Daeng and Tai Kaw houses the door curtains to the sleeping area, fig.32.[17] Possible sources for this framing among the Tai are not apparent.

The symbolic function of the framed *phaa tuum* in the context of the bride's gifts to her in-laws is perplexing. An item used in child rearing and mourning rites seems an inappropriate gesture to an older generation at this particular rite of passage. Consequently, when Tai Dam informants in the opposite side of the country, next to the Vietnamese border said *phaa tuum* there were given only after the birth of a child and at death, a possible source of Tai Dam customs elsewhere suggested itself. Door curtains are never included in the listing of the gifts of a new Tai Dam bride as is always the case among the Tai Daeng and Tai Kaw. However, the Tai Dam houses we visited had wooden doors that secured the sleeping area. If these wooden doors subsumed the role of an older cloth form normally brought by a bride, the curtain would remain to be used in other ways. There are enough similarities between the door curtain form and the *phaa tuum* to suggest the former may have segued into a familiar role once its original function became obsolete.

Summary

Even though we are left with fragments of once strong traditional customs, a picture begins to come into focus from these northern Lao areas of societies in which hand woven textiles were – and often continue to be – a vocabulary used for communication within this world and beyond. At once textiles mediate within a family,

Fig. 32 The interior of a Tai Daeng house in the Xam Tai area of Houa Phan Province showing the curtains leading to the sleeping area

being the signs of the presence and productivity of a bride within her new family. In other instances such as birth and death textiles ameliorate the potential for catastrophe in the scrim they form between the liminal state of birth and existence and the living, the dead and the hereafter. Their disordered presence announces the chaos of death, just as the fomulaic joining and structuring of certain types of cloth and cloth gifts within the ceremonies of death and birth become the emblems of restoring order. The importance of the roles of textiles is still apparent in many of these societies even as there is an apparent simplification in textile forms and the substitution of commercial cloth for the handwoven.

It seems there has been a great amount of sharing in basic skirt types between or among these groups, particularly in those styles predicated on warp patterning. Were some skirts unique to one ethnic group or has the borrowing we witness today a recent phenomena? These questions may never be resolved. The remaining evidence suggests that the Tai Daeng were the most accomplished weavers and may have provided inspiration for their neighbors; too much evidence has been lost to make this an unqualified conclusion. That which is not qualified, however, is the unique character and use of Tai Dam and Tai Daeng headwrappers.

Weaving on traditional looms with cotton, silk and artificial fibers thrives in many of the villages of northern Laos and is actively encouraged by the government. Dealers or members of the Lao Women's Union supply pattern pieces of textiles that meet market demand in Vientiane, Luang Prabang and other markets. This organization also organizes dye courses and handles the marketing of pieces outside the village arena in many instances. All of this emphasis is on commercially viable products that yield a monetary return for the weaver. As this is translated into textiles for local use the results vary. Simplified expressions of traditional forms are common, but more importantly the significance of why these textiles were ritually important is being lost so substitutions or omissions are acceptable. In certain instances whole categories of cloth, such as the long funeral banners, are simply no longer used in any form. Unfortunately, this may be the eventual legacy for the future of weaving through the region.

End Notes

1   A slightly different form of this article first appeared as "Textiles and Textile Customs of the Tài Dam, Tài Daeng, and their Neighbors in Northern Laos," *The Textile Museum Journal* 1995-1996: 93-112. The joint authors were Mattiebelle Gittinger, Karen Anderson Chungyampin and Chanporn Saiyalard. The three shared in field work in 1993 and 1995. In addition to the invaluable contributions of those colleagues, much appreciation goes to the many government officials of the People's Democratic Republic of Laos for the courtesies extended during work in that country and to the many villagers who shared their knowledge and kind hospitality.

2   Stuart-Fox 1993: 112. This movement while originating probably 100 years ago, accelerated after World War II and again during the Vietnam conflict.

3   Sams 1987: 56-57.

4   Many of the long strips of modestly patterned Lao cloth that appeared in dealer's hands 8-10 years ago were probably woven to serve in this capacity or as door curtains.

5   Pitiphat 1980: 32.

6   Evans 1991: 81ff.

7   The association of cloth as death symbols also emerged in a Tài Lue village when we casually mentioned how difficult it was to find long banners. These textiles, hung in the wat to earn merit for the dead, are rarely seen outside the Buddhist temple. An informant said that keeping one in the house would be as if you were waiting for someone to die.

8   Cremation may once have been the right of noble families. See Evans 1991: 92. Today one hears of burial, cremation and grave sites lined with charcoal as practices among the Tài Dam.

9   Evans 1991: 91.

10 The research reflected in this paper entailed visits to graveyards in many Lao areas. Permission to visit graves was consistently sought from village elders in advance and at no time were grave sites entered without an escort from the village.

11 Additional details concerning Tài Kaw funeral customs may be found in Gittinger, Chungyampin and Saiyalard 1995-1996.

12 Robert, 1941 n.p.

13 Sams 1987: 66.

14 See Fraser-Lu 1988:119 Fig. 151.

15 Gittinger and Lefferts 1992: 35ff.

16 Ibid.: 47-53, 114-115.

17 In northern Thailand two types of cloth floor mats and a bed sheet are similarly framed. These too are made by Tài people and are probably related to the framed forms of the Tài Dam and Tài Daeng. See examples in Prangwatthanakun and Naenna 1994:
47, 66, 67.

Works Cited

Evans, Grant
1991   "Reform or Revolution in Heaven? Funerals among the Upland Tài." *Australian Journal of Anthropology.* Vol. 2 no. 1 pp. 81-97.

Gittinger, Mattiebelle and Leedom Lefferts
1992   *Textiles and the Tai Experience in Southeast Asia.* Washington, D. C. The Textile Museum.

Gittinger, Mattiebelle, Karen Anderson Chungyampin and Chanporn Saiyalard
1995-1996 "Textiles and Textile Customs of the Tai Dam, Tai Daeng, and their Neighbors in Northen Laos," *The Textile Museum Journal* Vols. 34 & 35 pp. 92-112.

Pitiphat, Sumitr
1980   "The Religion and Beliefs of the Black Tài, and a Note on the Study of Cultural Origins." *Journal of the Siam Society.* Vol. 68 pt. 1 pp. 29-38.

Prangwatthanakun, Songsak and Patricia Naenna
1994   "Central Thai Textiles" in *Thai Textiles. Threads of a Cultural Heritage.* Bangkok. National Identity Board. pp. 27-47.

Robert, R.
1941   *Notes sur les Tay Deng de Lang Chanh. (Thanh-hoa, Annam)* Hanoi. Imprimerie d'Extreme-Orient.

Sams, Bert F.
1987   *Tradition and Modernity in a Lao Song Village in Central Thailand.* Ph.D Dissertation University of California, Los Angeles.

Stuart-Martin
1993   "On the Writing of Lao History: Continuities and Discontinuities." *Journal of Southeast Asian Studies.* Vol. 24. no. 1 March pp. 106-121.

BABY OR ELEPHANT CLOTH?
Wrappers in Laos and Thailand

Karen A. Bunyaratavej

Introduction

In 1993 and 1995 while carrying out fieldwork in the People's Democratic Republic of Laos*, I came across a textile previously unknown to me. Thus far, scholars and collectors of Lao textiles had mentioned little about this type, even though by this time a few Lao textile publications had already been written. Despite the scarce information regarding this textile, its uniqueness stands out from all the other textiles, such as head cloths, shoulder cloths, blankets and banners, belonging to the Tai people, as perhaps the only textile from the entire repertoire that is surrounded by a border and therefore appears framed-in. Such textiles are known in Laos as *pha tuum* or *pha ob,* meaning "cloth to wrap or surround" and, as the name suggests, is used to wrap a person's shoulders or surround a baby and the person carrying him or her for warmth. Further fieldwork in 1995 carried out in Thailand, though, presented a different perspective. Framed cloths similar to those found in Laos are not associated with people but rather with elephants. The cloth is known as *pha lo hua chang,* literally translated as "elephant head cloth", and is used to cover an elephant's head during Buddhist ordination ceremonies when a young boy enters the monkhood.

How is it that a textile, which stands out from all the other textiles belonging to the Tai people because of its unique form, yet found within the same ethnolinguistic group residing in two geographical locations, can have such different and diverse functions? This leads to a closer inspection of this unique textile and its puzzling functions in order to further investigate and determine the weavers' intention. Was this cloth meant to provide warmth to a baby or intended for an elephant?

Baby Wrappers in Laos

Function

The Lao *pha tuum's* initial role is that of providing warmth to a person, especially during the cold winter days where the sun is hidden behind thick clouds and the air is inundated with mist. The dampness created follows a person throughout their daily chores from dusk until dawn. This cloth's initial superficial function, therefore, is a humble yet important utilitarian one. It is most commonly seen wrapped horizontally around an adult carrying an infant (fig. 1). The cloth sling that anchors the

Fig. 1 Tai Dam mother and baby wrapped in the typical Luang Nam Tha baby wrapper

baby to the person carrying it shifts the baby's weight from arms to shoulder and enables a person free use of their hands. The horizontally and tightly tucked baby wrapper limits the baby's movement but provides the needed warmth. This combination provides the care giver with the mobility to go about the daily chores. During other occasions the *pha tuum* adds warmth to a baby sleeping in its cradle (fig. 2) or to the shoulders of an elderly person (fig. 3). Like most village textiles, the

Fig. 2 Tai Dam baby in Luang Nam Tha sleeping in his cradle

Fig. 3 Tai Dam woman in Luang Nam Tha seeking warmth from her *pha ob*

baby wrapper follows a person throughout his or her life, from birth to death. Hidden behind this basic utilitarian function, though, lies a less obvious one of providing protection against forces and spirits both known and unknown. Its secret meaning, elaborated by a mother of one-month-old triplets, became clear when she would not allow her babies to be photographed until they were properly wrapped and hence protected in baby wrappers. (Gittinger: 1995-6).

This hidden connotation of providing protection becomes even more obvious during life crisis situations, especially situations where a person comes directly into contact with spirits. This occurs for instance during ceremonies such as the house spirit appeasing ceremony or during funerals where a shift and therefore a change of the spirit in residence occurs. During these vulnerable moments not only do the appearance of *pha tuum* intensify in number but their utilitarian function becomes overshadowed by a ceremonious one. (For more detail please refer to the article by Mattiebelle Gittinger in this publication)

This is true with all groups of Tai people in Laos but with stronger conviction in the northern regions where remoteness buffers the people in various degrees from development and dictates from the capital. This together with an unending shortage of cash demands that weaving remains an important and integral part of their daily life. But this rings true even more so with the Tai Dam who at present are not only considered to be the most traditional of all the Tai but still practice much of their animistic beliefs. So this article will focus on the Tai Dam living in Houaphan in the northeast and Luang Nam Tha in the northwest, the Tai Daeng and Tai Kao in the Houaphan area and to a lesser degree the Tai Lue of Oudomxai.

Related Function

In the Houaphan area amongst the Tai Daeng another textile shares the function of a baby wrapper (fig. 4). This textile is a doubled-paneled cloth with a white silk or cotton foundation patterned with continuous supplementary weft usually, but not always, in indigo. One end of this cloth is zoned dyed (Gittinger: 1992) in red. The area adjoining the black and white portion of the textile is patterned with a small band of discontinuous supplementary weft in multiple colors utilizing both silk and cotton yarns. It is not uncommon to walk into a Tai Daeng village in the Houaphan area and see one baby wrapped by a framed-wrapper side by side with a baby

Fig. 4 "Zone-dyed" blanket being used as a baby wrapper in Houaphan

Fig. 5 A village in Sam Tai, Houaphan with three types of cloth being used as wrappers

Fig. 6 A terry cloth, in this case, has replaced that of a hand woven baby wrapper

wrapped in a zone-dyed one (fig. 5). It is unclear why this is, but at the time of this fieldwork the zone-dyed textile is more commonly used as a blanket, where the zone-dyed section is used to indicate the feet end. There are probably practical reasons as to why these zone-dyed blankets have become baby wrappers. Perhaps the extra width and length is more appropriate for the required additional warmth than that provided by the limited size of the framed baby wrapper. Or, perhaps the villagers have sent their framed baby wrappers into the antique trade market, a rather common phenomenon at this time throughout Laos. When worn, the visual effect created by the zone-dyed blanket, with a contrasting indigo and white back and a bright red and multi-color motif front, makes for a very graphic and stunning presentation of the figure wrapped in it.

The Tai Daeng is not the only group that has allowed another textile to take on the function of a baby wrapper. With other groups, blankets and commercially produced textiles have also adopted the role of traditional baby wrappers (fig. 6).

Fig. 7 Baby wrapper from a Tai Dam village in Luang Nam Tha

Fig. 9 Baby wrapper from a Tai Daeng village in Luang Nam Tha

Fig. 8 Detail of Fig. 7

Fig. 10 Baby wrapper from a Tai Daeng village in Houaphan

Form

A typical *pha tuum* has a single center panel woven predominantly with cotton in a plain weave. This panel is patterned with both continuous and discontinuous supplementary weft using silk and cotton threads of multiple colors. The panel is then surrounded with a single or multiple plain, or rather un-patterned, border(s) (fig. 7), the better examples of which having mitered corners (fig. 8). In the Luang Nam Tha and Houaphan areas these baby wrappers are given a lining that is brought forward to the front and stitched down, giving the appearance of having an additional border.

There are variations to this typical form both in terms of the color in the center panel as well as the numbers of layers and colors of the border. This variation is dictated respectively by group and location. For instance, a Tai Dam baby wrapper (fig. 7) has a red center panel with two borders. In contrast, the Houaphan Tai Dam uses a blue lining, while the Luang Nam Tha Tai Dam use a white lining. A Tai Daeng baby wrapper has a blue center panel, but the Luang Nam Tha Tai Daeng finish their baby wrappers with a blue lining (fig. 9), unlike the Houaphan Tai Daeng, who prefer a white lining (fig. 10). The same applies to the Tai Kao in Oudomxai. The Tai Kao baby wrapper has a white center panel and blue borders and lining (fig. 11), while their Houaphan counterpart add a red border and white lining to their white-base center panel (fig. 12). The Tai Lue of Oudomxai add only one border in red (figs. 13, 14) to their white-base center panel and do without a lining altogether. It appears, based on the information collected at the time of this research, that generally the color of the center panel distinguishes one group from another, while within the same group the borders and lining place them geographically.

Color combinations aside, weavers of baby wrappers on a whole share a common trait through the choice of motifs used to decorate the center panel. The same

Fig. 11 Baby wrapper from a Tài Kao village in Oudomxai

Fig. 12 Baby wrapper from a Tài Kao village in Houaphan

Fig. 13 Mother and baby in Oudomxai on the way to market

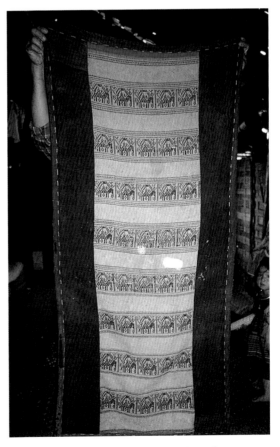

Fig. 14 A Tài Lue baby wrapper in Oudomxai

theme, of small geometric designs such as diamonds and stars, petite floral designs and some animal designs, are evenly scattered throughout the baby wrapper with not one motif dominating another. This theme is preferred and is used over and over again no matter what the group, Tai Dam, Tai Daeng, Tai Kao, Tai Lue or Tai Phuan, where ever the location.

Related Forms

In the course of the numerous interviews that took place inside the houses together with several meals graciously offered by the villagers, I had the opportunity to view home interiors, which also brought me into contact with door curtains (fig. 15). I mention door curtains as they share a similar form to baby wrappers in the sense that door curtains too appear to be framed. Closer inspection though, reveals that the borders that are given to door curtains are cruder and meant to widen its narrow dimension in order to fit the doorframe. The borders lack the refined mitered corners and attention baby wrappers are given, but they draw attention nonetheless.

A comparison can be made with the interior of houses of Lao people living on the other side of the border in Vietnam. Here, the majority do not have wooden wall partitions, but rather the sleeping area is closed off from the living area by woven curtains and married couples use mosquito net-like chambers for additional privacy. One then wonders if door curtains are a later development having to do with change and development effecting the Tai living on the Lao side of the border.

Elephant Head Cloths in Thailand

The use of a framed textile as an elephant head cloth was reported as occurring in northern Thailand in Si Satchanalai, Sukhothai province, the old capital of the Siamese kingdom. In this region the elephant head cloth or *pha lo hua chang* (often abbreviated as *pha lo)* is used as part of the ordination ceremony. The cloth is

Fig. 15 Similar cloth used as a door curtain in Houaphan

Fig. 16 *pha lo* in Uttaradit, Thailand

88

Fig. 17 Ordination ceremony in Si Satchanalai

described as being placed on the elephant's head or rather its neck where the young boy, head shaven and dressed in pure white traditional clothing, sits during a procession to the temple.

In 1993, during a field trip in Sukhothai and Phitsanulok I was unable to witness the ordination ceremony but instead had the opportunity to visit and interview villagers. There were several *pha lo* remaining in the village (fig. 16), but informants knew nothing of their use as an elephant head cloth. *Pha lo* in areas other than Si Satchanalai are used as items to make merit. Villagers reported taking the *pha lo* to temples and donating them to monks. They in turn would use them as floor coverings or distributed the surplus to people of lesser means. *Pha lo* as also used during wedding ceremonies to decorate the house and line the floor for the seating of guest. Another trip to the area in 1999 was done during the time of the ordination ceremony to see how the *pha lo hua chang* was used in Si Satchanalai. I arrived at a household where three boys were about to enter the monkhood. Their heads were being shaved. The newly shaved boys were dressed in white pantaloons and their

torsos were draped with another narrow width white cloth, showing the renouncement of their worldly status. The boys then transformed themselves (fig. 17) to imitate the Lord Buddha while he was still Prince Siddhartha. Elephants were then brought to the front door and handwoven blankets were draped on the elephant's head for the boys to sit on. The novices were paraded through town joining up with other novice-ridden elephants. Together, boys and elephants marched to the temple where the four-legged vehicles circumambulated the abbot three times, symbolic of the boy being sent to a new stage in his life.

A visit to a privately owned local museum gave insight to the history of the *pha lo*. Khun Sathorn, owner of the museum, elaborated that the *pha lo* was traditionally used as a mattress cover during weddings and is often part of the items villagers donated to the temple to make merit. With the introduction of commercial material and its ready availability the *pha lo* has been losing out in popularity. Out of concern for the future of this cloth, he and a small group of friends began finding and promoting new uses for this cloth.

So what appeared to be an elephant's head cloth is actually a ceremonial textile that is used on an elephant's head in a manner that was recently invented in a localized area to give meaning to a textile that is heading towards extinction.

Conclusion

I believe that the *pha lo* found in Thailand were items which the Tai people carried with them when they migrated southwest out of Laos to settle in this country over a century ago. At one point they functioned as baby wrappers and mattress covers and were part of ritual items associated with life crisis situations. With a shift in geography and a change in lifestyle, in particular a change of climate to a warmer one, production of these wrappers as utilitarian items declined. The numbers found in a community began to decrease and those that remained were reserved principally for ritual functions such as weddings and funerals. The same application that villagers associate them with today, such as mattress covers of the bridal couple, wall linings and even coverings for stacks of mattress are, "to make the room beautiful" and are in keeping with the earlier uses of these textiles for times of celebration.

*Based on this research the following article was written: Gittinger, Mattiebelle; Karen Anderson Chungyampin and Chanporn Saiyalard, "Textiles and Textile Customs of the Tai Dam, Tai Daeng, and their Neighbors in Northern Laos" published in *The Textile Museum Journal 1995-1996*, vol. 34 and 35, The Textile Museum, D.C.

Bibliography

Australian National Gallery 1992 "Cultures at Crossroads: Southeast Asian Textiles from the Australian National Gallery", Studies on Asian Art No. 2.

Connors, Mary F. 1996 *Lao Textiles and Traditions*, Oxford University Press, Kuala Lumpur.

Conway, Susan 1992 *Thai Textiles*, Asia Books, Thailand.

Cheesman, Patricia 1988 *Lao Textiles: Ancient Symbols – Living Art*, White Lotus, Thailand.

Fraser-Lu, Sylvia 1988 *Handwoven Textiles of Southeast Asia*, Oxford University Press, Singapore.

Gittinger, Matiebelle and H. Leedom Lefferts, Jr. 1992 *Textiles and the Tai Experience in Southeast Asia*, The Textile Museum, Washington, D.C.

Gittinger, Mattiebelle, Karen Anderson Chungyampin and Chanporn Saiyalard, "Textiles and Textile Customs of the Tai Dam, Tai Daeng, and their Neighbors in Northern Laos" in *The Textile Museum Journal 1996-1996* Vol.34 and 35, The Textile Museum, Washington, D.C.

Howard, Michael C. 1994 *Textiles of Southeast Asia: An Annotated and Illustrated Bibliography*, White Lotus, Thailand.

Maxwell, Robyn 1990 *Textiles of Southeast Asia: Tradition, Trade and Transformation*, Oxford University Press, Australia.

Naenna, Patricia 1990 *Costume and Culture: Vanishing Textiles of Some of the Tai Groups in Laos P.D.R.*, Studio Naenna, Thailand.

Na Ubon, Sunai et al 1993 *Textiles and the Way of Life of the Tai Lao Ethnic Group of the Ubon Line*, Office of the National Cultural Commission, Ministry of Education.

Phanichphant, Vithi, Songsak Prangwattganakun and Patricia Naenna 1994 *Thai Life: Thai Textiles*, The National Identity Board, Office of the Prime Minister, Bangkok, Thailand.

Prangwattganakun, Songsak 1993 *Textiles of Asia: A Common Heritage*, Office of the National Culture Commission, Ministry of Education and Center for the Promotion of Arts and Culture, Chiang Mai University.

Prangwattganakun, Songsak 1993 *Lanna to Langchang* (in Thai), Office of the National Culture Commission, Ministry of Education, Thailand.

Prangwattganakun, Songsak and Patricia Cheesman 1988 *Lan Na Textiles: Yuan Lue Lao*, Center for the Promotion of Arts and Culture, Chiang Mai University.

Visuttiluk, Suddean 1991 "Changes in the Production of Handwoven Textiles in Ban Hadsiew, Amphor Si Satchanalai, Sukhothai Province" (in Thai), Master's Thesis, Faculty of Social Science and Anthropology, Thammasart University.

THE SAOPHA AT HOME AND ABROAD
Shan Court Dress in the 19th Century

Susan Conway

Bordered by China to the north-east, by Laos and Thailand to the east and by India and Bangladesh to the west, the Shan States together comprise160,000 square kilometers, almost a quarter of the country known today as Myanmar or the Union of Burma. The Shan people are defined as descendants of the Tai who inhabited south China from at least the 9th century BC.[1] The Shan live in part of an important and distinctive cultural area that includes Sipsong Pan Na (south-west China), Lan Xang (western Laos) and Lan Na (north Thailand). The people speak a similar language with regional variations and share a sacred script *(tham)*.[2] They practice a form of Theravada Buddhism that remains faithful to what they consider to be the original teaching of the Buddha. There are also similarities in their architecture and arts and crafts.

From the 12th century the Shan States formed a network of principalities and settlements ruled by princes *(saopha)*, chiefs *(myosa)* and village headmen *(ngwegunhmu)*. Some states were powerful like Keng Tung that was comparable in size to Belgium, while small states like Nawngwawn and Mawnang were less than one hundred square kilometres. The Shan Chronicles record that rulers, chiefs and village headmen were linked through a complex web of political treaties and marital alliances and through trade although local feuds and fighting between them was common.[3] Diplomatic visits between states involved envoys travelling in the dry season by elephant, on horseback or riding ponies along a network of paths. Powerful states like Keng Tung and Hsenwi received tribute from minor states and from hill tribe communities. These arrangements were subject to change as the most powerful rulers attempted to dominate as many minor states as they could and the smaller states frequently changed allegiance to suit the prevailing political climate.

The tributary system extended to the major neighbouring powers and Chinese and Burmese envoys travelled to the Shan courts. One of the earliest accounts of interchange comes from the 8th century CE when a Chinese envoy conferred a golden seal on a tributary Shan prince who was escorted by sixty-five horses, their harnesses set with cowrie shells and decorated with gold. The Shan prince was dressed in a coat of chain mail overlaid with a tiger skin. He bowed twice and prostrated himself on the ground facing north in the direction of China.[4] The Chinese envoy presented the prince with gifts that included dress and regalia issued according to Chinese sumptuary law.[5] Tributary relationships did not always run smoothly and the Chinese at times sent armies to suppress the Shan when they considered their loyalty to be in doubt. In one account a Chinese army was defeated "by lightning induced through invocations and abnormal rites."[6] In reality they were probably brought down by disease and inhibited by the difficult mountainous terrain. In the mid 18th century an invading Chinese army was unable to keep its communication lines open and was forced to retreat when supply lines were cut and their horses were stolen and eaten by local forces.[7] A peace treaty brought this particular invasion to an end and diplomatic and trading relations were restored.

The Shan also have a long history of tributary obligations to Burma. In 1556 King Bayinnaung of Pegu subdued the Shan states of Hsipaw and Mong Nai on his way east to conquer the capital of Lan Na at Chiang Mai (north Thailand). The Shan princes were fearful of Bayinnaung's military power and hastily swore allegiance to him. Burmese agents took up residence at the major Shan courts or they operated from a regional centre. The Shan princes were expected to attend Burmese court ceremonies to pay their respects *(kadaw)* to the kings of Burma. At the court of Ava and at Mandalay there were written rules that governed every aspect of these ceremonies, allocating the places where Burmese royalty, court officials and tributary princes were seated in audience according to rank. The kings of Burma also allocated court dress and regalia to the Shan princes as part of this ranking system. Although the Shan princes were tributary subjects, the kings of Burma were always careful not to offend them. This sense of caution penetrated all levels of court life and was expressed in oral history. In Burmese Palace Tales a legendary King of Mandalay muses that the Shan are always ready to rebel and he expresses anxiety in case he should upset them.[8]

The Shan aimed to keep good relations with both their powerful neighbours while attempting to resist as much interference as they could and they appear to have developed an even-handed policy in their tributary gifts. In the 19th century the British envoy Captain McCleod noted that rulers in the northern Shan states sent the same tribute to China as they sent to Burma. This consisted of one gold cup, "tinsel" cloth, silk cloth, a pair of shoes, a cake of salt and a viss each of candles covered with gold leaf, candles covered with silver leaf, candles decorated with gold flowers and candles decorated with silver flowers.[9] At the court of Keng Hung (Cheli), McCleod witnessed the presence of one Chinese and two Burmese officials who took notes on what was said during his audience with the ruling prince.

When the British colonised Burma they sent the reigning King Thibaw into exile in 1885. This action led to the collapse of the Burmese court and the end of traditional tributary systems and sumptuary laws that had allocated dress and regalia to the Shan princes. As colonial rulers, the British introduced their own laws. The Shan princes swore allegiance to Queen Victoria and British officials issued them with patents of appointment recognizing their right to rule. The British promised the Shan princes that they would not interfere with local traditions and customs but would maintain civil order and control foreign affairs. British officers and troops marched through the Shan states to establish British authority, to get to know the Shan royal families and to conduct surveys of the land and the people.

The Shan rulers had for centuries maintained a sophisticated level of communication both between principalities and internationally. Envoys and important guests visiting for short periods were given suitable places to stay and were met with a degree of civility that was appropriate to their rank. Guest quarters in the larger palace compounds accommodated visitors, mostly royal relatives and friends from neighbouring states. Guest rooms could be separated into individual sleeping areas by hanging curtains as room dividers. The servants unfolded kapok-filled mattresses that were stored concertina-fashion during the day and set out on mats at night.

On occasions when large numbers of guests had to be accommodated the ruler ordered the construction of temporary buildings called *tawmaw*. First a circular bamboo frame was built with a steep tiered roof frame that was thatched. The floor was raised above ground level and a staircase was built as an entrance. When constructed as guest quarters the *tawmaw* were given exterior walls of bamboo and woven matting and a small verandah was added. The interior could be divided with bamboo screens or curtains depending on the number of guests it was intended to house. If there was a large gathering several *tawmaw* were put up to provide a meeting hall, kitchens and staff accommodation. If the *tawmaw* was intended for ritual use such as a royal funeral ceremony it might have curtains hung at intervals from the frame instead of bamboo or matting walls. The curtains could be tied back so that large assemblies could watch the rituals. When privacy was needed the curtains were drawn. At the end of ceremonies and gatherings the *tawmaw* were dismantled and the building materials sold to local dealers.

The building of a *tawmaw* was part of traditional Shan hospitality and the British adopted the custom during their period of occupation. They often stayed in *tawmaw* when they visited the Shan princes, chiefs and headmen to settle skirmishes that had arisen following the exile of King Thibaw and the ensuing power vacuum. In a private letter, the British envoy Sir George Scott wrote "The mere fact of getting the chiefs together is most beneficial and after having met once I dare say they will be less likely to fight". He goes on to describe football matches and military band performances that helped create a friendly and informal atmosphere.[10] These assemblies, referred to as "durbars" (a term brought from India), were extensively photographed.

Fig. 1 shows a *tawmaw* erected for British officials in the 1890s when they arrived in Keng Tung to meet the ruling prince and local tributary chiefs. The *tawmaw* is built on stilts with a verandah laid with matting where the ruling prince and British officials are seated on chairs while attendants sit nearby on the floor. Some have taken shelter under the raised floor while others gather outside. A Union flag flies from a corner of the building. Fig. 2 shows a group of officials from the Southern Shan States and their families assembled outside a *tawmaw* in Loi Long.[11] The roof has been covered with woven matting.

Groups of royalty and officials were often photographed against decorative cloth backdrops. In fig. 3 two elaborate embroideries *(shwe chi doe)*, also referred to as *kalaga* have been hung.[12] This type of embroidery was produced in workshops wherever royal courts were functioning and was used by royalty and by senior monks for ceremonial and decorative purposes.[13] The

Fig. 1 Durbar house with Southern Shan State ruler and the British representative

most common subjects portrayed are scenes from the Life of the Buddha, stories from the *Ramayana*, court life with royalty and attendants, hunting scenes, mythical birds and animals and pictures of village life. Lunar calendars and signs of the zodiac were also popular. Some hangings have no story line but portray idyllic landscapes. The technique involves a number of skilled workers. A master artist draws the major designs on a backing of cotton or silk fabric. These designs are copied and cut out in different colours from the main backing cloth and are then transferred to an embroidery frame. Skilled female workers embellish the designs with appliqué, with couched gold and silver thread, with mother-of-pearl and silver and gold sequins, with semi-precious stones and coloured glass. When they are fully decorated each design is sewn in its place on the main backing cloth. Some designs are filled with kapok to give them a two-dimensional look.

Fig. 2 Officials and their families outside a durbar hut, Loi Long Southern Shan State

Fig. 3 *Myosa* of Pinhmi with wives and children

The hanging on the right side of the photograph in Figure 3 is a *shwe chi doe* in traditional form with a border of hexagonal lozenges containing mythical animals and birds and an inner field of court scenes from the life of the Buddha. The hanging on the left of the photograph shows a Chinese style landscape. Although embroidered hangings are seen in many period photographs, printed cotton and plain fabrics were also used (fig. 4).

The photographs also show the type of dress worn by rulers and senior officials. In fig. 3 the *myosa* of Pinhmi poses with his wife and children. He wears a patterned turban cloth, a loose long-sleeved shirt and wide Shan trousers held at the waist with a cloth sash. His sons, seated at his feet are dressed in similar style. In the cold season the rulers wore jackets padded with cotton, as seen in figure 2 or lined with fur, as worn by the *saopha* of Tawngpeng (fig. 4).[15] According to trade records, fur-lined coats were imported from China.[16]

Men are frequently photographed in a similar form of dress. In contrast, women's dress can often be identified with a particular group. In fig. 3 the wives of the *myosa* of Pinhmi are dressed in loose Shan blouses and ankle-length skirts decorated with *luntaya*, a complex tapestry weave pattern.[17] They wear their hair in a topknot decorated with combs and jewellery. In fig. 4 the wives of the *saopha* of Tawngpeng wear Palaung dress with a cotton headdresses in the shape of a hood, long sleeved jackets and tubular skirts.[18] They wear heavy silver bracelets, earplugs and necklaces. The wife seated furthest away from the *saopha* on his left wears Shan dress with a turban, loose fitting blouse and skirt. The state of Tawngpeng had a mixed population of Shan and hill tribe groups and the *saopha* had secured marital alliances with leading families. It was the custom for women to continue to wear the dress of their homeland when they moved to the court of their husband and this accounts for the variation in style of female dress.

94

Fig. 4 *Saopa* of Tawngpeng with his wives

The durbars called by the British and recorded in this group of photographs portray relatively informal gatherings and bear no relationship to the exotic regalia and court dress formerly issued from Burma and worn when the Shan princes went to pay tribute and *kadaw* to the King of Burma. Shan regalia, as prescribed by Burmese sumptuary laws incorporated richly embroidered silk robes with scalloped gold collars and fantastic hats. Chinese tributary dress included silk embroidered robes and turbans. Gilded umbrellas, ceremonial water vessels, betel boxes and jewellery were also recognized as part of the tributary system.

As the British formalized their relations with the Shan courts, they began to distribute titles and new regalia according to sumptuary laws operated by the court of Queen Victoria through her colonial representatives in Imperial India. The *saopha* of Yawngwhe was knighted, given medals and decorations and was entitled to a salute of nine guns. The *saopha* of Keng Tung and

the *saopha* of Mongnai had similar awards. Less powerful princes received titles and medals according to rank.

In December 1902 the British organised a huge durbar in Delhi that was attended by princes and senior officials from all parts of the British Empire. The display of exotic dress, military uniforms and caparisoned animals was the greatest visual spectacle of the age. A group of princes represented the Shan States and were photographed in front of a *shwe chi doe* in exotic court dress that was a legacy of the tributary systems operated from Burma and from China (fig. 5). Displayed on the carpet at their feet are the ceremonial vessels that were their regalia of office. The British had exiled the King of Burma and with his departure the Burmese court had been disbanded. At the Delhi Durbar it was the Shan princes who reflected in their elaborate dress and regalia the history and cultural affiliations that had existed before the British arrived.

Fig. 5 Group of Shan State princes photographed in front of the *shwe chi doe* (1902)

NOTE Dr. Susan Conway is conducting research for a book on the dress and regalia of the Shan States to be published by River Books.

1   Hall, D.G.E., *A History of South-East Asia,* London, Macmillan, 1955 reprint 1968, pp. 10-11.

2   Dodd, William, C., *The Tai Race: Elder Brother of the Chinese,* Cedar Rapids, 1923, reprint White Lotus Press, p. 156.

3   Mangrai, Sao Saimong, (trans.), "The Padaeng Chronicle and the Jengtung State Chronicle" in A. Becker, P. Hook, J. Musgrave and T. Trautman (eds.) in University of Michigan Papers on South and Southeast Asia, No. 19, 1981.

4   Milne, Leslie, *Shans at Home,* London, 1910, reprint Paragon, 1970, p. 13.

5   When the Shan princes were tributary to China they were sent Chinese dress, textiles and regalia, graded according to rank and distributed as part of tributary exchange gifts to be worn on ceremonial occasions.

6   Mangrai, 1981.

7   McCleod, W.C., Captain, "A Journal kept by Captain W.C. McCleod" Parliamentary Papers 1868/1869, Vol 46, The British Library, London.

8   Fielding-Hall, Harold, *Palace Tales,* Harper, 1900, p.72.

9   A viss weighs 3.652 lbs.

10 Scott, J.G., *Burma and Beyond,* London, 1932.

11 The photograph is labelled "Loi Long", the Shan name for the state. The Burmese called the state Taung Baing and the British changed it to Tawngpeng.

12 Tin Myaing Thein states in his book *Old and New Tapestries of Mandalay* (2000) that the term *shwe chi doe* is correct for this type of decorative work and he rejects the term *kalaga*.

13 Tin Myaing Thein, 2000.

14 Chinese designs developed as a result of trade and cultural exchange with China.

15 Sir George Scott (1932) noted that Tawngpeng had been ruled by Palaung and Karen chiefs.

16 Scott, J.G., *Burma: A Handbook of Practical Information* London 1906, reprint Bibliotheca Orientalis, White Lotus, 1999.

17 Worked with up to two hundred shuttles the designs have been well documented and are based on landscapes, particularly mountains, rivers and flowers (U Aye Myint, 1993).

18 The state of Tawngpeng was populated by Palaung, Karen and Shan people.

FIT FOR A KING:
Indian Textiles and Thai Court Protocol

John Guy

In his pioneering study *Siamese State Ceremonies*, H. G. Quaritch Wales provided the following description of the State Audience following the Coronation of King Prajadhipok in 1925. Attached to the Lord Chamberlain's Department, Wales was afforded the unique privilege of observing the proceedings from behind the curtain which separated the king from his subjects:

> The King, wearing full state robes and the Great Crown of Victory entered the curtained off part of the Amarindra Hall... As soon as the King had arranged his robes and signified his readiness, a fanfare resounded and three taps of two ivory blocks were the signal for the curtains to be suddenly drawn to reveal to the waiting officials the King on his throne of audience. The lighting was very cleverly arranged to present the King as the centre of a symmetrical picture of glittering gold. This golden audience throne called *Brah-di-nan Budtan Don* (Golden Hibiscus Throne) is ...highly ornamented and set on a tall tiered pyramid, carved with figures of *devatas* and *garudas*. It was flanked by tables bearing the regalia and by gold and silver trees while above was reared the nine-tiered white umbrella.

Wales then observed, pointedly, that "apart from the attire of the King, this occasion bore little resemblance to the State Audiences of old", lamenting the absence of "(the) antique uniforms such as give the impression of Old Siam". He noted with some satisfaction that "the efflorescence of semi-European styles (of dress) which was evolved in the last reign, but which has happily undergone considerable curtailment during the present one" (Wales: 177-179).

Wales had been in a privileged position within the Siamese court, and his description of state ceremonies provides a unique insight into the transitional nature of royal and court ceremonies in Thailand in early decades of the twentieth century. In fact, what Wales was witnessing was a process of modernisation – westernisation – in court etiquette. This process had been instigated by King Mongkut (Rama IV, r. 1852-68) in the 1860s and was enthusiastically pursued by his son, King Chulalongkorn (Rama V, r.1868-1910). In a portrait photograph taken of King Mongkut in 1857, he presented himself in traditional robes and regalia, as the embodiment of divine rule. The robes and the crown served to evoke the god-king image (fig .1). This portrait, one of

Fig. 1 King Mongkut, photographed in royal robes and regalia. This was one of two Daguerreotype portraits sent by the Siamese monarch to Queen Victoria in 1857. It was in all probability taken by the first Thai trained in photography on equipment sent in 1855 as part of a state gift from Queen Victoria. Photograph courtesy of The Royal Archives © Her Majesty Queen Elizabeth II

Fig. 2 King Sisowath of Cambodia, wearing his royal robes and regalia as a god-king. Phnom Penh, c.1900. Photograph private collection

the first ever taken of a Thai ruler, was prepared expressly to send to Queen Victoria, as part of a state gift from the Siamese king in that year. King Mongkut was alert to the need to present (and represent) Thailand abroad as a modern state not in need of the "civilising forces" of colonialism. As early as 1865 King Mongkut had a photographic portrait taken of himself with the Crown Prince Chulalongkorn, both outfitted in European attire.

Such photographs were not for domestic consumption, but to be sent abroad as part of a diplomatic engagement with the West. For the performance of royal ceremonies at court, dress was strictly traditional: in 1865 King Mongkut had himself photographed enacting the tonsure ceremony for the Crown Prince. Here the king dressed as a heavenly being ('Indra on earth'), attended by members of the nobility *(khunnang)* wearing the long jackets and conical hats of office which have been prescribed since the reign of Phra Narai in the late seventeenth century.

The kingdom of Siam already had a long history of skillfully combining tradition with modernity. It was one

of several mechanisms employed by the Siamese state to strengthen its ability to resist external political pressures and to ensure its survival and welfare. The greatest moderniser was perhaps King Chulalongkorn. He most clearly understood the need to create a monarchy that preserved sufficient trappings of traditional Thai kingship to ensure continuity with the past and to guarantee a place for the institution of monarchy in the future. Like his father, King Mongkut, he understood the importance of using state ritual to preserve the social hierarchy upon which the institution of Thai royalty had been erected. An outward expression of this strategy was the manner in which court dress – ceremonial and civil – was manipulated by royal decree.

It becomes immediately apparent reviewing Thai royalty that it is richly cloaked in the ritual and paraphernalia of brahmanical Hinduism, and that this stands in striking contradiction to Thai society, which is staunchly Theravada Buddhist. The ways in which the apparent contradictions of this situation have been resolved are outside the scope of this paper. Suffice to say that the Thai monarchy has been careful to preserve the mantle of brahmanical authority through which its hereditary rights have been perpetuated, whilst being seen by the broader society as embodying the highest Buddhist virtue of protector of the Buddhist Law (Dharma).

The rituals of kingship in Thai society were made explicit through the use of symbolic dress. The cosmic symbolism was largely drawn from Khmer images of kingship, as can be seen from the early twentieth century Cambodian king dressed in full regalia (fig. 2). He resembles a god, and is specifically linked to the Hindu deity Indra, who presided over and maintained order in the realm of the gods. The Thai kings broadly followed these Khmer conventions, and in the early Chakri era were especially inclined to do so as a means of acquiring legitimacy through association with the ancient Cambodian kingdom. This association of the king with Indra is repeatedly referred to in the imagery of the deity that occurs in many of the textile designs. One of the most dramatic examples shows Indra on his elephant Erawan, surrounded by adoring celestial figures *(thepanom)* (fig. 3). The Khmer derivations of this design, and of the concepts of kingship which underlay it, are underscored by the border design which depicts ferocious monkey-warriors with aquatic tail, a motif directly echoing late-Angkorian relief decorations. The centre-field trellis pattern is read across the textiles, selvedge to selvedge, not along its length, indicating that this cloth

Fig. 3 Ceremonial hanging textile, decorated with the Hindu deity Indra on his seven-headed elephant Erawan, surrounded by adoring *thepanom*, in a trellis design. Coromandel Coast, for the Thai market. Cotton, painted mordant-dyed, resist-dyed and painted. Private Collection

was not intended to be worn (the design could not be 'read' correctly), but rather was intended as a hanging, perhaps as a screening or curtaining device. The iconography of the design certainly suggests that it would be most appropriately hung within the palace.

Designs incorporating celestial deities and demi-gods from Hindu mythology were much favoured for court décor. Such devices served to evoke the other-worldliness of the royal palace, and of its principal occupants. Designs incorporating the attendants of the heavenly realms were especially popular, featuring combinations of *devas* and *thepanom* (celestial devotees), *kinnara* and *kinnari* (male and female half-bird creatures), *gandaravas* (celestial musicians), *apsaras* (celestial maidens), *garuda* and *naga*. A cloth associated with royal use was that with golden *thepanom* on a white ground, bordered by flame-motif and flower cartouche designs (fig. 4). A double-register end border pattern suggests female use, as cloths with triple or greater end border registers were intended for males of ascending rank, as seen on a cloth with gilded flower in trellis design on white (fig. 5). The orientation of both these designs is horizontal, appropriate for wearing as a waist cloth or *pha nung*.

Fig. 4 Skirt-cloth *(pha nung)*, decorated with "golden" celestial worshippers *(thepanom)*. (Coromandel Coast, for the Thai market. Cotton, painted mordant-dyed, drawn resist-dyed and painted. Victoria and Albert Museum, IS 53-1991

Fig. 7 Décor textile *(pha kiao)*, decorated with *kinnari* and *thepanom*, on a blue ground. Coromandel Coast, for the Thai market. Cotton, painted mordant-dyed, drawn resist-dyed and painted. Victoria and Albert Museum, IS. 31–2002. Given by the Friends of the V&A

Fig. 6 Portrait of King Chulalongkorn on the occasion of his Second Coronation, 1873. Photograph formed part of a royal gift to the Siam Exhibit at the 1876 U.S. Centennial Exposition, Philadelphia. Photograph courtesy of the National Museum of Natural History, Smithsonian Institution, Washington

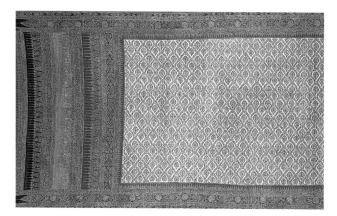

Fig. 5 Skirt-cloth *(pha nung)*, decorated with a glued gold floral motif in a trellis pattern. Coromandel Coast, for the Thai market. Cotton, painted mordant-dyed and resist-dyed, with painted gold. Victoria and Albert Museum, IS 37-1991

The golden celestial demi-deity of fig. 4 is represented in a dance posture, and with hands clasped in veneration. The surrounding flame-leaf design embodies a barely detectable guardian *kirthimukha* in its foliage, a typical Thai decorative device of concealing one motif within another, often suggesting a visual metamorphosis is underway before the viewer's very eyes. The lavish nature of this design, and the close concordance between celestial and royal attire is underscored by a comparison of the golden *thepanom* with the coronation attire and regalia worn by King Chulalongkorn on the occasion of his Second Coronation in 1876 (fig. 6).

The design of *kinnari* and female *thepanom* on a blue ground (figs. 7, 7b, 7c), is another pattern likely to have close associations with the court. Like fig. 3, it probably served as a décor fabric rather than for dress. The motif of the *kinnari* recurs in Thai applied arts of the period, but is relatively rare in textiles, this example being one of the few to have survived. The *kinnari* emit flames from their wings and feet, enlivening the scene with celestial energy. Hung in the appropriately grand palace interiors, such textiles would have enhanced the otherworldly atmosphere which was so consciously striven for.

7b, 7c Details of the decor textile shown opposite

Costume was a key device for demarcating rank and station within the court hierarchy. This was the case in the reign of the famous seventeenth century Siamese ruler Phra Narai (1656-1688), and remained a preoccupation of the monarchy well into the reign of King Chulalongkorn. This paper will examine some of the conventions, decrees and sumptuary laws and the ways in which elements of these were perpetuated into the twentieth century.

The Victoria and Albert Museum has a fine collection of textiles manufactured for Thai court use, most of which are high quality painted cottons produced in India expressly for use in Thailand. These cloths were ordered to Siamese design for use at court, where they were identified as *pha lai yang*. Among this collection are examples which combine exceptionally fine *kalamkari* – wax resist painting – with subjects depicted which have close associations with the court. Some had their designs embellished at the court with glued gold work, when they were known as *pha khian thong* (fig.5).

Many of the shifts in court taste can be chronicled through the V&A's collection. Examples in the collection reflect the courts need to service an increasingly wide network of patronage, especially as part of the elaborate tributary system created in the early Bangkok period (1782-1851). Added to this was the growing democratisation of the Indian textile trade to Thailand, which allowed a greater variety of Indian imported textiles of more common-place quality to be marketed without reference to or interference from the court. Three tiers of Indian trade textiles were circulated in Thailand: those for royal use, those for distribution to the wider court community, and those permitted for commoner use. The bulk of surviving examples relate to the early and middle Bangkok periods, (1782-1910), and it is to these periods that the majority of examples in the V&A collection can be assigned.

A taste for India

Early in the history of Southeast Asian court cultures we witness a predilection for fine textiles, most notably Indian cottons and Chinese silks. As early as 1297 the Chinese diplomat Zhou Daguan provides a description of life at the city and court of Angkor, in which he is explicit about the superiority of Indian cloths, valued for

101

their "skill and delicacy" (Zhou Daguan: 23). It would seem that this attitude to imported Indian textiles was also assumed by the early Thai courts, along with much of the kingship rituals that continued to play such a central role in court life down to the modern period. It is clear that this taste came to include a variety of silks, and gold and silver brocades.

Written records that make reference to Siamese taste in textiles begin to appear as early as the beginning of the sixteenth century. Tome Pires, the Portuguese based at Melaka (Malacca) on the Malay Peninsula from 1512 to 1515, observed that among the merchandise taken from Melaka to Thailand were "Kling cloths in the fashion of Siam". The term "Kling" referred to Tamil-speaking merchants from the Coromandel Coast, most particularly associated with the ports of Masulipatam and Pulicat. Pires' observation is the first direct evidence of Indian cloths being designed expressly for the Thai market. Another contemporary commentator, Duarte Barbosa, states that the ports of Thailand and the kingdom of Pegu in lower Burma received large quantities of Indian textiles from both Pulicat and Cambay (western India), and that these Indian textiles were highly valued. The Coromandel was especially famed for its production of the finest quality painted textiles. At their best, they combined fine cotton fabric with the most refined brushwork and skill of dyeing, achieving a brightness and fastness of colour unrivalled anywhere in the world. It was from these workshops, situated in the hinterland of Golconda and served by the port of Masulipatam, that the agents of the kings of Siam secured the cloths they desired, fashioned, so we are told by the contemporary commentators, in the taste of Siam.

"After the fashion of Siam"

A clue to the nature of the Siamese Indian textile trade in the early seventeenth century is provided by the head of the Dutch VOC factory at Ayutthaya, Jeremias van Vliet, who was director from 1629 to 1634. He makes clear that the Coromandel and Surat painted cottons were imported in great quantities by Thai, Moslem and Hindu traders. What emerges from this and other seventeenth century sources is a picture of a seventeenth century Siam in which the monarch, through his ministers, regularly commissioned high quality painted textiles to Thai design. The court had its own agents who operated from Masulipatam and elsewhere on the northern Coromandel coast, commissioning the designs, and with ships chartered to conduct the trade on their behalf. Van Vliet explicitly states that "His Majesty further enjoys many profits from the trade with Coromandel and China" (van Vliet: 27). Late eighteenth-century sources, such as Francis Light, make clear that this practise was still being actively pursued 150 years later. Siam continuously struggled, not always successfully, to maintain control of its ports on the west coast of the Thai Peninsula to service this India trade. The most vital of these was Tenasserim. Such was the importance of this port to Ayutthaya's prosperity that the governor of that port-city was alone permitted to impose a tax of 6.5% on the Indian painted cotton textiles "which the Moors from Coromandel and other places bring" (van Vliet: 65). Such a concession to a provincial governor confirms the importance of ensuring that the loyalty of this port was not compromised.

We have a remarkably vivid picture of court life at Ayutthaya under King Narai. A series of foreign embassies were received by the king and resulted in the most detailed descriptions of any late seventeenth-century Southeast Asian court. Commentaries by the French envoy resident Simon de Loubère (1678-88) and the priest Nicolas Gervaise (1688) make clear that prosperity of the kingdom was built on international trade of which textile exchange formed a major part. They also stress the role that textiles played in consolidating allegiances through a system of gift exchange and patronage. Gervaise observed that members of the French 1685 embassy from Louis XIV were given presents, including fine cloths, "rich enough to give them an exalted idea of his (King Narai's) greatness and magnificence."(Gervaise; 228-29).

A detailed city map of Ayutthaya was prepared on the basis of these French missions, drawn by Courtaulin and published by Francois Jollian in 1686. It is the first map to indicate the extent of the foreign trading communities resident at the capital. Foreign quarters are identified belonging to Indian, Chinese, Malay, Burmese, Portuguese, French and Dutch trading missions, confirming the city's role as an international entrepot. European merchants resident at Ayutthaya, the most notable of whom was Joost Schouten (sent as chief of the Dutch VOC factory in 1633), make clear that Coromandel and Surat textiles were among the principal trading commodities of Ayutthaya (Schouten:130-148). Whilst some of these were certainly used as goods to be traded on for profit, particularly to Japan, a significant quantity were for the use of the court. As we shall see, these were destined for distribution at court, to the descending ranks of the nobility and others in attendance at court, and to those who came to the court from afar, be they provincial governors, or representatives of vassal states or foreign embassies.

The Siamese court was seen to use Indian painted textiles as one of the preferred items in diplomatic gifts. Father Tachard, who wrote the official account of the French ambassador Chevalier de Chaumont's visit of 1685, made clear that fine textiles featured prominently in the recorded list of gifts received (Tachard: 175). The Persian ambassador Ibrahim Beg recorded similar observations.

Cloths for court

A set of court protocols appear to have emerged in the course of the seventeenth century, if not earlier, which dictated that textiles for attire could be distributed by the ruler as expressions of royal favour. The practice also evolved of using cloths of different qualities as social demarcators. Specifically, they came to denote where the recipient stood in the court hierarchy. Thai sources survive from the early Bangkok period (1782-1851) – to which we will return later – but it is to earlier European commentators that we must turn to for a glimpse into the world of Siamese court etiquette and the hierarchy of cloth. Some form of sumptuary law was already in force in the early seventeenth century that regulated who could wear specific textiles or garments at court. They served to denote rank, alongside other indicators such as gold or silver betel boxes, which were also favoured by the king as gifts to the nobles he wished to promote or reward. The majority of the nobility assumed their rank as a birthright, whilst some were promoted from the ranks of commoners by the monarch. Commoners could be raised to one of the ranks of princes, a necessary elevation before they could hold ministerial office. Through time the greatest power resided with the ministers appointed directly by the king. The granting of royal gifts was an integral part of this patronage system and textiles featured prominently in it, especially in the granting of the right to wear textiles of restricted designs, a clear public display of a recipient's status in the court hierarchy. As van Vliet tells us:

"the mandarins [ministers] are chosen from the noble as well as the not-noble families, but before anyone can become a mandarin he must be raised to nobility by the king, and new names and marks of honour are given to him…Among this nobility everyone receives donations [gifts] in conformity with his quality and rank…The marks of honour given by the king are always carried about with the owner wherever he goes, and by them he is recognised and honoured" (van Vliet: 63-64).

Newly elevated members of the nobility *(somdet)* formed a rank equivalent to but distinct from the hereditary nobility. They were largely drawn from wealthy and influential trading families whose allegiance was often essential for a ruler, especially in times of succession. Chinese, Persian, Indian and Mon families all feature in the histories of the later Ayutthaya period, and they all share a common background – links to their respective foreign merchant communities resident at Ayutthaya. They had came to dominate the offices associated with the Phrakhlang or Ministry of Finance (which included foreign trade), often rising to the highest noble rank of *caophraya*, "minister of state". Their importance becomes clearer in light of the fact that the Siamese monarch was heavily dependent on the revenue of international trade. Over time, these families moved to centre-stage, infiltrating the royal household itself – the Chakri dynasty is descended from Mon families first associated with King Narai's reign. Other families associated themselves with the royal household through intermarriage. These alliances were in place before Rama I founded the Chakri dynasty in 1782. The opportunities for these high-ranking ministers to shape the terms under which international trade was conducted were considerable. Their community links with the foreign trading communities meant they could foster direct trade relations with other Asian countries, ensuring a high level of control.

We are told by van Vliet that the king had, by this time, established an effective monopoly on the trade in a variety of commodities, including the importation of Indian textiles. All were free to import such goods, but their sale was carefully controlled by the crown's agents through the office of the Phrakhlang, which had express responsibility for managing commercial relations with foreigners. Peter Floris, a Dutch agent in the employ of the United English East India Company, complained that in 1612 he was unable to conclude a sale of his consignment of Indian textiles because "other shopkeepers dare not bee so bolde as to buye one piece of cloth till the King bee furnished and his price agreed" (Floris: 73-74).

In the course of the seventeenth century the Siamese monarchy succeeded in consolidating further economic control degree, extending the scope of the royal monopolies. Two harbour-masters, of Indian and

Fig. 8 Floral decoration, from a mural in the ordination hall at Wat Yai Suwannaram, Petchaburi. Late 18th century. Photograph courtesy of Muang Boran, Bangkok

Fig. 9 Detail of fig. 4 showing *thepanom* and *kirthimukha*

Chinese origin respectively, were appointed to supervise trade with Siam's two most important trading partners. The reign of Phra Narai (1656-88) represents a period of unprecedented royal wealth and authority, built largely on international trade. The sources make clear Indian textiles formed a major part of this exchange. Yet we are left with no possibility of identifying extant cloths which may date from this period. Those sent as diplomatic gifts to France in 1686 have not proved traceable.

The issue of dating Thai-market Indian painted cotton textiles presents special problems. Specific designs can be linked to datable objects. Mural paintings from the late Ayutthaya period provide some useful comparisons. The most complete series of murals are those preserved in the ordination hall of Wat Yai Suwannaram, Petchaburi. They probably date to a late eighteenth-century renovation. The stylisation of the flame-leaf motif may be sympathetically compared to the treatment of the same motif in the golden *thepanom* design cloth (figs. 8, 9). Illustrated manuscripts can often be assigned to a particular reign, so providing a date range for the painting style. A manuscript illustrating the legend of Phra Malai, assignable to the early decades of the nineteenth century, demonstrates a distinctive painting style which has close parallels with painted textiles (fig. 10).

Traditional textiles remained an integral part of temple décor and temples in nineteenth-century Bangkok. At Wat Rajabophit, textiles are represented as wall hangings, forming an integral part of the decorative schema of the temple itself (fig. 11). An anonymous photograph taken around 1900 shows the familiar *thepanom* in trellis design common to many Indian painted cottons (fig. 12).

In the first half of the eighteenth century Ayutthaya was plagued by successive Burmese invasions, culminating in the sacking of the Siamese capital in 1767. A devastating consequence of the Burmese wars was the almost complete loss of the written records of the Ayutthaya period, and of any archives inherited from earlier times. The Burmese continued to harass the Thais for some decades thereafter, throughout the reign of King Taksin (1767-1782) and into the reign of Rama I (1782-1809). A direct consequence of these depredations was the relocation of the capital south at Thonburi, marking the beginning of the Rattanakosin or Bangkok

Fig. 10 Thai illustrated manuscript of the Legend of Phra Malai. Gouache and gold on *khoi* paper. Early Bangkok period, c. 1810-1830. Victoria and Albert Museum, IM 41-1931. Given by Mrs E.M. Hinchley

Fig. 11 Mural paintings representing textile designs, Wat Rajabophit, Bangkok. Late 19th century. Photograph c. 1900. Private collection

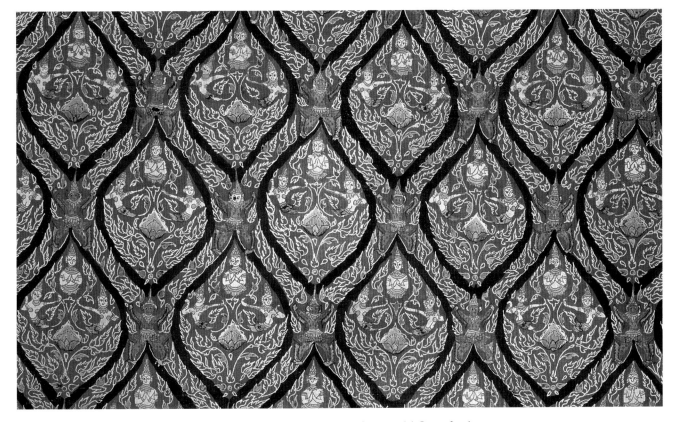

Fig. 12 Skirt-cloth *(pha nung)*, decorated with *thepanom* in a trellis pattern. Coromandel Coast, for the Thai market. Cotton, painted mordant-dyed and resist-dyed. Victoria and Albert Museum, IS 58-1991

era. When a newly founded Chakri household attempted to construct a legitimising history for themselves, they had few written records to draw on and largely had to reinvent a past. In almost all matters of state and court protocol, the new regime had to rely on the memory of recent past practice, leaving the new court to re-build a code of practice through court memorandums and royal decrees.

The early records of the Rattanakosin era, preserved in the *Chotmaihet Ratchakan,* provide detailed accounts of a complex system of patronage built on gift-bestowing by the ruler to his favoured subjects, the receipt of offerings from tributary states, and the formal exchange of gifts with foreign countries. According to Constance Wilson, who has made a study of these records for the early Bangkok period, the archives provide detailed inventories of gifts given and received, but say little about the policies to which these exchanges give expression (Wilson). These must be deduced from the gift record.

An elaborate system of gift exchange with regional vassals was built up in order to establish and consolidate political allegiances. This was an extension of the long established system of holding hostages at the capital, usually princes of vassal or tributary states, and of marrying princesses from such states to further strengthen the allegiance and integration of the periphery to the centre. The receiving of yearly tribute missions underscored these allegiances. The regions were expected to pay taxes in the form of gold and silver flowers, a symbol of allegiance, indeed submission, to the Siamese ruler as the supreme Buddhist sovereign, or *Cakravartin.* Gold and silver flower tribute was extracted, according to the Thai "Palatine Law of 1468" (which regulated royal succession), from twenty towns *(muang).* In addition to their political value, these offerings were expected to have an agreed monetary value, and were periodically melted down for reuse in regalia or religious images. Gold and silver bullion was also received, along with wax, lacquer and other forest products of value to the capital for use in its royal workshops. In exchange for these demonstrations of loyalty, the king was expected to respond in kind, with objects of value and status. The centre normally reciprocated with precious metal utensils, status objects of royal recognition, carefully graded by rank. These were the products of the royal workshops expressly maintained for this purpose. Favoured objects were betel boxes, in gold, silver or niello ware, depending on the rank of the recipient.

Fig. 13 HRH Prince Nilratana, Prince of Alongkot, a son of King Rama II (1811-1867), dressed in brocade robe. Photograph by John Thomson, 1865-66

Textile giving

A key commodity in the cycles of gift exchange was textiles. The expensive items given to senior officials were restricted in their circulation, and yet it was these textiles that provided the most widely distributed item of royal gift exchange. Those appointed to high office would receive the items of court dress appropriate to their office and rank. Those of lesser rank, and members of an official's entourage, would receive textiles of lower quality.

The regions in turn presented examples of their finest local textiles, and imported textiles from outside the realm. Khmer silk *ikat (mudmee)* fabrics were particularly admired at the Bangkok court. The Khmer silks favoured were typically embellished with supplementary gold thread woven into the end-borders. These were judged so that the gold work would be visible when the cloth was worn as *chong kraben* or *na nang* style, and were known as *pha som pak pum.* The number of end-border registers was taken as a sign of rank, and of gender. The Khmer silk *pha nung* with three registers was restricted to the King, that with two to the Queen. This designator extended beyond the royalty category of *pha nung* to all ranks of the nobility and officialdom, so that three registers marked a male cloth, two a female. This is to be seen in numerous Indian sourced painted cotton *pha nung* (compare figs. 4 and 5).

The court also regularly received as tribute fine cotton textiles from Thai Lanna and the precious metal silk fabrics of the southern provinces, especially of Nakhon Sri Thammarat and Songkla. The governors of the Thai provinces and protectorates who paid annual tribute to Bangkok sent both local textiles and imported fabrics, where available (fig. 13). The Malay state Trengganu, still under Thai suzerainty for much of the early nineteenth century, was noted for sending Malay-style gold embroidered cloth (Wilson: 23). The southern provinces also strove to secure supplies of imported Indian painted cotton textiles of a quality and design understood to be acceptable to the court (fig. 14). Early in the reign of Rama I, a nobleman from Thalang (Phuket), on the southern peninsula, placed an order in 1787 with the English country trader Francis Light to procure in India "cloth of a special pattern for the King". The official was the *Yokrabat*, third in rank in provincial government, and appointed by central government to enforce loyalty to the centre. In the same year a Lady Chan, wife of the governor of Phuket, was engaged in procuring Indian textiles from Light, which she proposed to pay for in tin. Officials of this rank would have had a clear understanding of the textiles appropriate for presentation to the Bangkok court on the occasion of the annual royal audience. Among the textiles named by Lady Chan which could clearly have been secured in India were "flowered chintz" *(pha lai dok tang kan)* and "patterned white muslin" *(pha khao kasa na thong na chua)*, both renowned products of the Coromandel Coast and Bengal respectively.

The crown regularly received Indian, Chinese and regional textiles from those officials required to demonstrate their allegiance during the annual sojourn to Bangkok and the royal audience. The court records of the reigns of the early Bangkok period (1782-1868) make clear that the gifting of textiles by the crown was an essential part of court protocol and the political infrastructure that it supported.

As we have seen, the distribution of cloths and garments had been used since the Ayutthaya period as a method of expressing favour, privilege and rank. The Thai sources for the late eighteenth and much of the nineteenth century are less than explicit about the policy

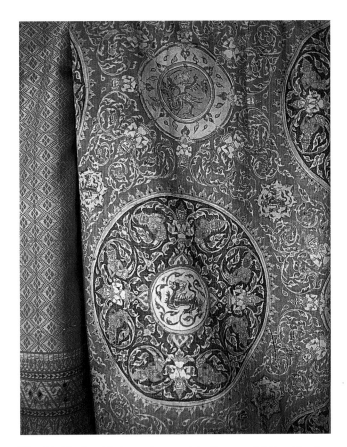

Fig. 14 Textile with decorative roundels. Coromandel Coast for the Thai market. Cotton, painted mordant-dyed and resist-dyed (displayed alongside a locally woven silk brocade). National Museum, Nakhon Sri Thammarat, southern Thailand. Photograph by John Guy

that underpinned this system of patronage. Textiles were to serve as demarcaters of rank, and of special honours granted expressly by the king. The first attempt to systematically describe the intention underlying the complex court hierarchy was, remarkably, written by King Chulalongkorn himself. *A Royal Essay: Traditions of Royal Lineage in Siam*, published in 1878, was a study of Thai royal titles and ranks. The system had been in evidence since the sixteenth century, and was first described by van Vliet early in the following century, as we saw above. As the chief architect of modernisation in Thailand, Rama V recognised the need to elaborate the social hierarchy he had inherited from his father and to situate the reforms within a clearly defined political structure. This essay represented the king's attempt to do this.

In the labyrinthine world of court protocol and rank described by King Chulalongkorn, the accoutrements of rank are referred to but not always specifically named. One exception is the passage that describes those of lesser noble rank *(momraadchawon/momrajawongs)* who wait on the king. They are required to "wear *sompag* (a kind of printed fabric), like the nobles, but each a different kind. They wore a white sash, not a coloured one and they could not wear clothes of varied designs and many colours like those who had truly royal rank. In the royal family those from *momcaw/mom-chao* (rank) and higher could dress in any manner when attending the king without offence" (Jones: 67).

Modernisation

Up until the mid-nineteenth century the essential elements of court dress remained unchanged. Traditional Siamese dress was largely a non-tailored tradition, utilising lengths of cloth. The standard garment, typically measuring 800 cm x 4 metres, was worn in a number of configurations. At its simplest, it was used by both men and women as a waist-cloth *(pha nung)*, or drawn up between the legs in the dhoti-like style known as *pha nung chong kraben*. Women could also wear it as a front pleated skirt *(naa nang)*, as seen in photographs of royal women from the beginning of Rama V reign. A separate cloth, of varying lengths, would be used as a shoulder- or breast-cloth *(phaa sabai krong thong)*.

The waist-cloth drawn up in *chong kraben* style represented more formal dress and was favoured at court until trousers became regulation attire. A young princess of the court in late nineteenth-century photograph wears a trellis-pattern *pha nung chong kraben,* a fitted shirt and two breast cloths *(phaa sabai),* one pleated, the other embroidered or perhaps with applique jewellery (fig. 15). These shoulder cloths were, on occasions, of open-work gold and silver thread, when they were known as *pa krong tong* (fig. 16).

Fig. 15 Princess (Pra-Ong Chao) Thaksincha, the sixth daughter of King Mongkut, born to Chao Jom Chantorn. She is wearing a silk brocade *pha nung chong kraben*-style skirt, a blouse and two *sabai*, one pleated, the other richly appliquéd. c.1870. Private collection, Bangkok

Fig. 16 Breast cloth *(sabai);* open-work textile of gold and silver thread. Bangkok, nineteenth century. Private collection, Bangkok

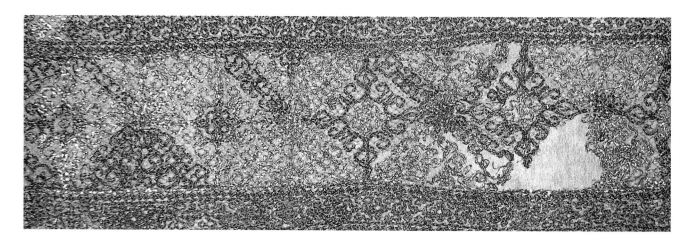

Fig. 17 Mom Rachothai (Kratai Israngkura). Thai nobleman, dressed in a brocade jacket and *pha nung chong kraben;* reign of Rama IV. He served as the official interpreter of the Siamese Ambassador to the Court of St James, London in 1857, and wrote the official account of the mission

Fig. 18 Portrait of the child Pian Bunnag, member of a noble Bangkok family, dressed in formal attire on the occasion of the tonsure ceremony. Reign of Rama V; late nineteenth century. Private collection

The jacket or shirt *(senakut)* had long been introduced for formal wear, believed to have been inspired by attire of the Persian embassies, in the later seventeenth century. Their use was largely confined to formal occasions and winter wear. Nonetheless, in the reign of Rama III (1824-1851) a waist-cloth alone was acceptable at court, presumably worn in the more formal drawn-up manner as *pha nung chong kraben*. A photograph of a senior minister in King Mongkut's reign, Mom Rachothai, shows him in court dress of the 1860s: brocaded jacket, worn with *pha nung chong kraben* (fig. 17). This manner of wearing the *pha nung* persisted until King Chulalongkorn progressively began to institute change. His first move came in 1869, following a state visit to Singapore and Batavia, and was followed by further directives in 1873. These were attempts to introduce a European dress code at court. European-style tailored garments were to be worn – jackets or shirts for men, and

blouses, often combined with lace, for women. At first these were worn with the traditional *pha nung chong kraben* but later King Chulalongkorn's reign were increasingly combined with trousers for men and full skirts for women.

Indian and Chinese silks and gold and silver brocades were still favoured, especially the Indian gold brocade *(zarabaft)*, satin with gold or silver design *(atlas)* and silk with a woven metal thread striped design *(kimbhab)*. These textiles were expensive and were confined to court use. Brocades, imported by the court from Benares, were the preferred fabric for the tailoring of jackets in the reign of Rama V and for the "royal-shirts" *(rajapataen)* devised by King Chulalongkorn for court dress.

The portrait of a young prince at the occasion of his tonsure ceremony, dating from the reign of King Chulalongkorn, shows the traditional constituents of formal dress still intact (fig. 18). Gold and silver brocades were widely favoured for tailored garments, but with designs which carefully preserved the traditional motifs and design schema, as seen in brocades with *thepanom* design. Brocades became increasingly lavish, with quilted appliqué and the applied ornaments, the most elaborate being used for display rather than wear.

Sir John Bowring, the British ambassador, signalled another new development in court textile protocol. He observed in the 1855 that "some of the most costly garments worn by the people of high rank were, as we learnt, manufactured in the homes; and they prided themselves on their being able to produce textiles more valuable than any imported from foreign countries". Delicately embroidered silks were favoured, along with cloths with woven patterns. A red-ground silk with gold thread embroidery of flame and leaf design, known as *pha pak mai thong,* may be an example of such work produced within the home (fig . 19). Other Thai woven textiles were also coming increasingly into fashion, especially the finely worked silk fabrics from the southern provinces. A beautiful *pha yok* displays the best of this work (fig. 20). The woven and supplementary gold thread is careful controlled, creating a delicate trellis pattern centre-field. The design organisation directly follows earlier Indian painted cloths versions, including

Fig. 19 Cloth for use in court circles. Red silk with gold thread embroidered decoration. Thai, 1ate nineteenth century. Private collection, Bangkok

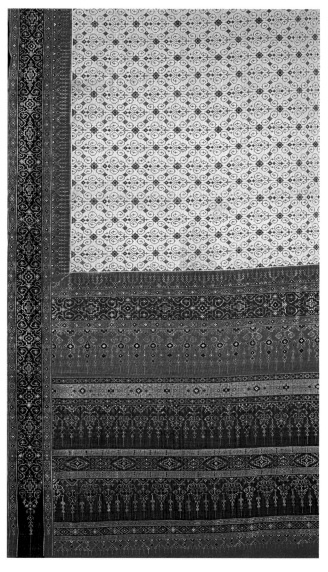

Fig. 20 Ceremonial cloth *(pha yok)* for use as court attire. Silk, with woven warp and supplementary weft gold decoration. Thai, from Chonnabot, early twentieth century. Victoria and Albert Museum, IS 81-1991

the use of a triple end-register, combined with woven border patterns which echoes Khmer silk *mudmee (ikat)* stepped-square designs.

At a number of the court ritual ceremonies observed by Quaritch Wales in the 1920s, both Indian brocades and painted cottons had their appointed roles. These textiles seemed to be assured a place in the royal wardrobe as the embodiments of tradition, as a means of signalling the authority of an unbroken link with the past. In the Ceremony of the Octagonal Throne, a part of the cycle of ceremonies associated with the coronation, the king-designate appears following a ceremonial bath, dressed in a gold embroidered *pha nung* and tunic. The wearing of such robes indicates a king's symbolic re-birth. In the ceremony of the Swinging Festival, in which a senior minister or brahmin enacts the role of Siva on behalf of the king, a brocade *pha nung* is again prescribed. (Wales: 240). At the Ceremony of the First Ploughing *(Rak Na Kwan)*, a Brahmanical ceremony of great import to the welfare of the state - guaranteeing as it does the success of harvest – the Minister of Agriculture substitutes for the king. As 'temporary king', he is required to select an auspicious *pha nung* from those offered to him by the Brahmin priests. The cloths vary in length, and his choice will forecast the length of the rainy season.

Paradoxically, as the pressures on the Thai monarchy to modernise grew, so too did the express desire to preserve aspects of traditional dress in those rituals associated with kingship and the welfare of the state. The Thai monarchy today is still widely seen by the populace as embodying Buddhist virtues of the highest order. It is this reverence and respect which will continue to provide a raison d'être for elements of traditional Thai dress to occupy a place in modern Thai society.

Acknowledgements: First published in *Arts of Asia*, vol. 33, no. 2, 2002; reprinted with kind permission of the author and Arts of Asia. The author wishes to thank Fon Windsor-Clive (Umaworn Hutacharern) for assistance with Thai sources.

REFERENCES

J. Guy, *Woven Cargoes. Indian Textiles in the East,* Thames & Hudson, 1998.

R.B. Jones, *Thai Titles and Rank,* Cornell University, Ithaca, 1971.

H.G.Q. Wales, *Siamese State Ceremonies,* 1931, rep. Curzon Press, 1992.

C.M. Wilson, "Tribute and Gift Exchange in Pre-Modern Thai Political System", *Fifth International Conference on Thai Studies,* London, 1993, u/p.

For full references to the contemporary observations of Duarte Barbosa, John Bowring, Peter Floris, Nicolas Gervaise, Simon La Loubere, Francis Light, Joost Schouten, Father Tachard, Jeremias van Vliet and Zhou Daguan, see bibliography in Guy, *Woven Cargoes. Indian Textiles in the East,* 1998.

LAN NA MALE DRESS IN PEACE AND WAR

Susan Conway

Until the end of the nineteenth century the inland states of Southeast Asia were isolated from coastal Southeast Asia by mountains and primary forest that presented a formidable physical barrier. The rivers were navigable in the rainy season but rapids, rock pools and eddies meant journeys were dangerous. There was the threat of fatal tropical diseases and attack by wild animals that roamed the forests. However, if you made it through these obstacles you discovered a fascinating land and a culture ruled by princes whose power radiated outwards from their valley settlements towards the distant hills. These inland principalities included the kingdom of Lan Na (north Thailand), western Laos, Sipsong Pan Na and Lan Xang. At the beginning of the nineteenth century Lan Na was made up of the major principalities of Chiang Mai, Lamphun, Lampang, Phrae and Nan.

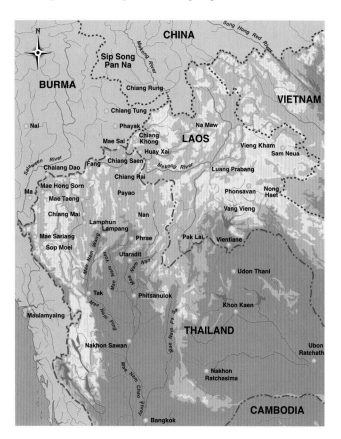

Smaller centres existed in the hinterland, ruled by tributary princes and chiefs. (see map). The Lan Na princes formed political and marital alliances with ruling families in surrounding inland principalities with whom they traded and at times waged war. A complex history involving conquests, movements of people and intermarriage has further contributed to this unique and diverse culture.

The court dress of Lan Na is a fascinating subject for study. The way the royal families were clothed and how they decorated their bodies reflected their view of themselves and the way they wanted to display themselves to others. Through dress they exhibited their Buddhist and spirit religion beliefs, their politics, ethnic identity and their wealth and authority and this in turn defined them as belonging to a particular time in history. As times changed, so did dress and interestingly this affected the princes and senior officials more than their wives and consorts.

The history of Lan Na is full of tales of major wars and local skirmishes. In the sixteenth century the Burmese invaded and occupied the country for over two hundred years, although they often appointed indigenous rulers as governors under their authority. The Burmese were finally expelled in 1774 by the combined forces of the Lan Na Tai, their allies in the surrounding principalities and the Siamese. The Lan Na and Lan Xang princes assembled troops from the major principalities of Chiang Mai, Nan, Phrae, Lamphun and Lampang and from villages whose headmen were expected to provide a quota of military conscripts. They received no formal training and acquired military skills while on the battlefield. They were led by a prince ruler *(chao)* or by his prince deputy *(uparat)*, or by another member of the elite to whom they swore allegiance. The armies crossed the valleys and difficult hill terrain on elephants, on horseback or on foot, with oxen, ponies and human porters carrying supplies (fig.1). Mounted cavalry officers and foot soldiers were armed with swords and spears with dangerous curved and hooked blades. Senior officers carried swords and spears with

Fig.1 Lan Na princes going into battle on elephants, temple mural painting, Wat Buak Khok Luang, Chiang Mai

Fig.2 Soldiers carrying weapons, temple mural painting, Wat Phumin, Nan

tooled silver handles decorated with floral patterns and officers mounted on elephants had swords with elongated shafts and special long-handled spears. The major cities of Lan Na had established districts where skilled silversmiths and metalworkers produced weapons. The princes also had guns and flintlock rifles although they were not always properly maintained and regularly malfunctioned.

We can make informed guesses about the kind of clothing soldiers wore on the battlefield by examining historical sources, including Tai chronicles, temple mural paintings and nineteenth century photographs. Mural paintings portray Lan Na and Shan soldiers without helmets or any kind of body armour (fig. 2). Foot soldiers are often bare-chested although a few, probably officers, wore shirts. Lan Na soldiers wore sarongs *(pha chong kraben)* and had short hair cut in a circle on the crown with the sides shaved. Tai Yai soldiers from the Shan states can be identified by their long hair often coiled in a topknot and secured inside a headband. Prince *(uparat)* Bunthawong, brother of Prince Inthanon Wittayanone of Chiang Mai (ruled 1871-1897) is photographed in clothing that appears totally unsuitable for battle by the military standards of the time (fig. 3). He has no helmet or armour and wears only a plaid *pha chong kraben* and open sandals. His hair is cut in Lan Na style with a short circle on the crown that stands up like bristles on a stiff brush. He holds a sword across his lap and the military attendant at his feet is similarly dressed. Prince Bunthawong was an accomplished soldier who commanded the Lan Na army in campaigns on the northern borders. This type of clothing was worn in battle because the Lan Na princes and their men believed that strong protection was provided by spirit cloths, body decora-

Fig. 3 Prince *(uparat)* Bunthawong of Chiang Mai with his attendant, c. 1875. (National Archives, Bangkok)

113

tion and spirit religion rituals. In fact there was a common belief among the people that charismatic princes like Bunthawong were imbued with supernatural powers that made them invisible to the enemy and immune from injury.

To protect themselves against physical injury many soldiers carried small cloths and wore vests or jackets covered in mystical symbolic diagrams *(yantra)*, drawn in squares, circles and triangles with mythical figures and animals placed strategically among and around them (fig. 4). Some included images of the Buddha and his disciples and angels *(devas)*, others had images of grotesque animals, giants and local spirits. Circles, squares and triangles were filled with letters and symbols that were read or recited as magical incantations *(gatha)*. Numerical symbols in the *yantra* represented stars, suns and planets or their mythical gods and goddesses, selected according to the horoscope of the individual for whom the magic formula was being created.

The earliest known *yantra* is Pa Kua, the Eight Trigrams, created by the Chinese Emperor Fu Hsi around 2852 BC. Lines were drawn in configurations that represented natural energy and the elements and they were inscribed in stone and bronze. The Eight Trigrams were the basis of alchemy and were viewed as a way of channelling positive power in nature and as a means of protecting against negative power. This basic formula evolved and changed to suit the beliefs of individual societies. In inland Southeast Asia, ancestor spirits, ghosts, demons and spirits of the valleys and forests were incorporated in the diagrams. When Buddhism became the prominent religion, images of the Buddha and his disciples were incorporated in the *yantra*.

Spirit doctors composed the *yantra* and skills were passed on from one generation to the next. Induction of a spirit doctor included drinking water in which the ashes of magic scrolls had been dissolved. Some practitioners studied meditation and mysticism with recognised masters and received reference books that contained *yantra* diagrams and texts written in Lan Na, Shan and Burmese dialects. Interestingly Lan Na script was used on old *yantra* cloths found in Sipsong Pan Na, the Shan states and Luang Prabang. If a spirit doctor was very experienced he might draw the *yantra* directly onto a cloth with a stylus, although wood blocks were often used to print frequently repeated images. Reference books and tools were kept on a special altar in the practitioner's house.

Tattooing the skin was also seen as a way of warding off evil spirits, and was common among valley and

Fig. 4 A silk waist decorated with figures of animals, diagrams and incantations. Such waist were believed to protect against numural dangers. (Oriental Collection, The British Library)

hill tribe groups in the inland states. Correctly formulated, tattoos acted like armour and were capable of bestowing special knowledge and guile to defeat the enemy. The earliest record of a people using *yantra* tattoos were the P'u of southern China, referred to in a history of China dating to the 4th century AD. In Lan Na, contrary to many other societies where tattooing was common, there were no special marks or signs to denote rank. This led the diplomat Sir Ernst Satow, who visited Lan Na in the 1880s, to comment that "beggar and king were equal in the hands of the professional tattoo artist". The Lan Na princes employed their own tattoo masters who were considered to be particularly accomplished practitioners of the art. Opium was administered to ease the pain of the process.

Lan Na temple mural paintings portray soldiers with black tattoos on their thighs and around their waists (fig. 5). They wear narrow loincloths *(yak rung)*, drawn tight and twisted between their legs so that the tattoos are clearly displayed. The designs include mythical beasts, animals and birds, contained within a decorative border at the waist and the knee. Some Tai Yai soldiers were tattooed with *yantra* diagrams in red pigment, on the chest and back. Tattoos were considered to have advantages proportional to the pain endured in the process of acquiring them and were therefore a sign of courage. Not all men endured the suffering and some chose to have the designs in isolated areas, others gave up before the tattoos were completed. Foreign observers noted that men were prepared to undergo the pain and discomfort to please women and that in this context, tattoos were perceived as a way of "being made beautiful forever". There is plenty of evidence from oral history that tattoos were seen as an expression of male sexuality and that many women would not marry a man who did not have his thighs tattooed.

Soldiers had other ways of protecting themselves, including inserting objects into skin incisions made in the chest and upper back. Rubies and other precious stones, fine gold wires or small gold and silver discs were the most common. Discs were engraved with symbols of

Fig. 5 A young man with loin cloth twisted high on the hips to reveal his thigh tattoos, temple mural painting, Wat Buak Khok Luang, Chiang Mai

a fish, a monkey, a crab and a peacock. These were the animals whose form the Buddha had assumed in previous lives and their attributes included intelligence and wisdom which soldiers hoped would pass on to them. *Yantra* could also be inserted into metal amulets strung on cord and were worn around the waist, around the upper arm, around the neck and sometimes around each ear. They were put through a kind of test so that they could protect the wearer against bullets and cuts from swords. Amulets were blessed by Buddhist monks and interestingly were not considered truly effective without this blessing. *Yantra* were also punctuated on thin ribbons of silver foil, or written on paper that was rolled up and carried in a small pouch or in a metal container attached to a necklace or bracelet. *Yantra* were often combined with Buddha images and *devas* because a combination of Buddhist and spirit religion iconography was considered a particularly potent force.

There were also strongly held beliefs associated with the protective role of women who performed spirit ceremonies *(suu khwan th-haan)* before men left home to go into battle. A female medium led the chanting to call his spirit and bind it to the man's body. His wrists were tied with a symbolic cord made from hand-spun cotton prepared by older village women. When the soldier returned home a similar binding ceremony was held to ensure that his spirit had not been left behind on the battlefield. Many villagers also put faith in the protective power of a mother's skirt *(phasin)*. A soldier might wear a piece of his mother's *phasin* as an armband or a scarf, or a smaller piece could be inserted in a locket attached to a chain around his neck. This was considered to be particularly potent if it was a *phasin* that had been worn while his mother was in the process of giving birth. Yet although a woman's *phasin* could protect her son, it could also be used as a negative force for other men. This belief is expressed in the *Jinakalamalipakarana* Chronicle that tells the story of Queen Chamdevi of Lamphun who reigned in the seventh century AD, and sent a *phasin* polluted with menstrual blood to an enemy chief. She had disguised the *phasin* as a turban and the chief unknowingly wore it in a battle where he suffered a major defeat. Belief in menstrual pollution is widespread and women's lower garments are hung out to dry on a pole suspended below waist level so there is no chance of a man brushing his head against them.

Of course the Lan Na princes were not always at war and the kind of dress they wore for ceremonial events is also a fascinating area for study. The Chiang Mai Chronicle describes the triumphant procession of

Prince Kawila of Chiang Mai (ruled 1781-1813) into the city following the defeat of the Burmese at the end of the eighteenth century. The prince was publicly acknowledged for his bravery. According to the chronicles the celebrations included poetry readings, musical performances and dancing as well as feasting. The following passage describes the procession:

As for all the officials civil and military, the slaves and freemen, there were elephantry officers and cavalry officers dressed in fine uniforms, like divinities from the Tavadimsa (Tavatimsa) Heaven, the abode of the gods.

The reference to the Tavatimsa Heaven places Prince Kawila in the tradition of Lan Na Buddhist kings portrayed as descendants of the first Prince Lawacangkara who came down to earth from the Tavatimsa Heaven. According to the chronicles, as a legitimate Buddhist Prince Kawila was viewed as a being on the way to enlightenment *(bodhisattva).* Interpretations of the dress worn by *bodhisattva* are portrayed in Buddhist art throughout Southeast Asia, and include representations in sculpture, temple mural paintings and manuscripts. The exterior bas-relief of the fifteenth century temple of Wat Ched Yot, Chiang Mai, and the fifteenth century murals of Wat Lai Hin, Lampang provide examples of early Lan Na style. They portray divinities wearing golden headdresses, bracelets, anklets, and robes with wing shaped scalloped panels on the shoulders, waist and hips. We should therefore expect to see the Lan Na princes similarly attired, as they were in many other courts in Southeast Asia.

There is no evidence that the Lan Na princes actually wore *bodhisattva* style costumes. In an official portrait Prince Kawila is portrayed wearing a simple front-buttoned, round-necked shirt, a *pha chong kraben* and metal belt with an ornate buckle. In a court photograph taken over forty years later, Prince Kawiloros Suriyavong of Chiang Mai (ruled 1856-1870) wore an equally modest outfit (fig. 6). At the beginning of his reign, Prince Indra Witchayanon of Chiang Mai (ruled 1871-1879) also wore a round-necked shirt, *pha chong kraben* and waist sash (fig. 7). The Chiang Mai rulers and senior princes were bareheaded and barefoot, their hair cut in a circle on the crown and shaved at the sides.

Why did the Lan Na princes dress so simply in what were clearly meant as official court portraits? At the time when Kawila was appointed to office the princes lacked funds for expensive display and they did not have an established court infrastructure. However, by the time of Prince Kawiloros (ruled 1856-1870) the princes were

Fig. 6 The sixth ruler of Chiang Mai, Prince Kawiloros Suriyavong (ruled 1856-1870)

relatively affluent and there was a degree of political stability. Perhaps they considered *bodhisattva* style dress as inappropriate because, with the exception of Prince Pana Luang Tin Mahawong of Nan none were related to an earlier Lan Na elite. The princes were descendants of the forester Thip Chang who assumed the title Prince Sulawa Leuchai Songkram when he became ruler of Lampang. Prince Kawila gained the throne because he was an outstanding military leader. It is also likely that Lan Na court dress was more in keeping with the tenets of Yuan Theravada Buddhism that was less hierarchical than other forms of Buddhism practised in Southeast Asia.

If Prince Kawila did not wear ornate *bodhisattva*-style court dress it is probable that the princes of Lamphun, Lampang, Nan and Phrae would not have done so. Chiang Mai was the seat of Lan Na authority from the time of its founding by King Mengrai in 1259 and in the nineteenth century, following the expulsion of the Burmese, resumed its position as first city with its prince as "supreme ruler". This hierarchy was acknowledged within Lan Na, but there were to be later external pressures, particularly from Siam, which judged and rewarded the Lan Na princes according to a different set of criteria.

116

Fig. 7 The seventh ruler of Chiang Mai, Prince Indra Witchayanon (ruled 1871-1897). (National Archives, Bangkok)

Although there is no evidence of *bodhisattva* style costumes worn at the Lan Na courts in the period 1781-1871, we know that the rulers were revered as *bodhisattva* after death. In 1870 the American missionary Daniel McGilvary made a visit to the palace of Chiang Mai to pay his last respects to the deceased Prince Kawiloros, whose face, he reported had been covered in gold leaf. A funeral chariot *(prasat)* built to resemble Mount Meru in the Tavatimsa Heaven, was reserved for the funeral.

The dress of the princes was relatively modest but their regalia was resplendent. There were designated areas in the Lan Na cities where goldsmiths, silversmiths, wood carvers, lacquerware makers, jewellers, weavers and other craft workers lived and worked. A distinctive Lan Na style was evident in their woodcarving, stucco, inlay work and gilding, metalwork, painting and stencilling. Gold and silver water vessels, jugs, betel nut trays and food containers, were proudly displayed in court paintings and photographs. Silver and gold water vessels were of particular significance as they were used to hold sacred water used during the consecration ceremonies confirming a prince-ruler. Special vessels were also used in ritual bathing ceremonies and in allegiance rites. The Chiang Mai chronicle describes a ceremony in

1802 when Prince Kawila was "lustrated with the holy water of consecration" in the presence of the ruling council *(khao sanam luang)*, his family, senior Buddhist monks, court officials and his troops. The pouring of water appears to have been the key ritual because there is no reference to a crowning ceremony.

Some items of regalia accompanied members of the royal family when they went beyond the palace compound. When the fourth Prince of Chiang Mai visited the British explorer Holt Hallett fifteen attendants bearing gold betel boxes, water goblets and other paraphernalia of rank accompanied him. The Prince of Lamphun was carried on a bier with an enormous red umbrella protecting him from the sun. The wedding procession of the Prince of Lampang was equally impressive, led by musicians and dancers followed by attendants carrying flowers, silver-hilted swords and a magnificent red umbrella on a long silver shaft. The whole town turned out to watch the spectacle. When he arrived at Phrae, Sir Ernst Satow was led into the city by an attendant bearing a large silver vase filled with flowers and wax tapers. Servants and porters carrying muskets, silver-shafted spears, drums, gongs and a huge gilt umbrella followed; elephants saddled with gilded howdahs brought up the rear of the procession.

For many years after the war with Burma the Lan Na princes lived in modest dwellings. The Prince of Chiang Rai resided in a bamboo and thatch house before eventually moving to a grander teak building. The Prince of Lampang also lived in a bamboo and thatch dwelling, later also moving to a more substantial building. In 1886 Sir Ernst Satow paid an official call on the Prince of Lamphun who had a new teak palace with a grand audience hall. On a visit to Prince *(uparat)* Bunthawong of Chiang Mai Satow noted that the palace was very impressive with giant teak pillars, bands of carving on the interior and exterior walls and handsome carved wooden screens. The grandest palace of the time belonged to Prince Indra Witchayanon of Chiang Mai, described as a fusion of Chinese and Lan Na style. Holt Hallett wrote that it was a substantial building and the American missionary Emilie McGilvary reported that the house was copied from one the Prince had seen while making a tributary visit to Bangkok. The audience hall had a wooden inlay floor; the ceiling was hung with chandeliers and the walls with gilt framed mirrors. One of the main rooms was papered like an English drawing room. The palace contained European style furniture and elegantly carved latticework partitions that served as screens to the private apartments. Creating an English drawing room style was feasible because of changes in protocol.

In 1868 King Rama V had abolished the custom of prostration and allowed visiting dignitaries and officials to sit on chairs, thus creating a demand for European style seating, tables and other furniture. The costly European furniture in the Bangkok palace was imported from London, probably following the king's visit there. On tributary visits to Bangkok, the Lan Na princes admired the new palace interiors and shipped some pieces of furniture upriver to Chiang Mai where Lan Na craft workers copied them. When Sir Ernst Satow and his colleague W. J. Archer dined with the Prince of Chiang Mai, all the principal guests sat on chairs at a long table and were served from imported china and cutlery. Some Lan Na princes accepted the new European etiquette but others did not. While visiting the Prince of Phrae, Satow and Archer were given chairs while the ruler and his son sat on the floor laid with carpets and cushions. The Prince of Lampang also held audience seated on a carpeted dais reclining on cushions, as did the Prince of Lamphun.

Chewing betel was a social custom practiced among Lan Na royalty and commoners alike. Carl Bock wrote that the people were "perpetually chewing" from infancy to old age, and enjoyed betel at every friendly interaction. As water vessels were a symbol of consecration, so betel box sets represented the sociability of the Lan Na princes. They commissioned designs from local metalworkers who used repoussé (hammering the patterns into relief) and embossing techniques. A betel box set included a number of containers for storing the ingredients of areca palm nut *(areca catechu)*, betel leaf *(piper betle)*, tobacco and white lime. Betel juice stains the mouth and saliva bright red and gold and silver spittoons were provided for expectorating the juice. Decorative cloths were used to wipe the stains from the mouth (fig. 8).

The Lan Na rulers slept on kapok-filled mattresses spread out on a raised wooden dais. Weavers of the royal household produced bed sheets, blankets and pillows, with decorated silver and gold metal thread. Before the fashion for European furniture, the Lan Na princes received their guests from a raised platform, seated on special cloth mats with firm triangular cushions as back rests. They were covered in silk, velvet or cotton and had flat end panels decorated with floss silk embroidery, metal sequins and couched gold and silver metal wire. Floor mats and cushions were also provided for guests.

Fig. 8 A wiping cloth *(pha chet)*, black lacquered cotton panel with red velvet end panels decorated with couched embroidery of silver metal wire inset with mirror glass. Used to wipe betel juice from the mouth. (Khun Akadet Nakkabunlung collection)

New Politics, New Dress Styles

Towards the end of the nineteenth century a shift in power affected traditional political and military alliances in the inland states. The surveyor Nai Banchaphumasathan, sent in the 1890s by Rama V of Siam to inspect the Lan Na-Shan States borders, reported that the Burmese were no longer perceived as threatening stability. Shan rulers had declared independence from Burma in 1881 and a series of feuds and rivalries had broken out between them. The ensuing chaos led to banditry and Lan Na soldiers were involved in quelling the disturbances on the northern borders. Lan Na people in the remote areas were also threatened by bands of Ho (Yunnanese), who came south burning and plundering villages on the way. The Lan Na rulers had also to contend with the colonial ambitions of the British in Burma and the French in Laos.

In this difficult and complex situation Rama V of Siam chose to intervene. He had already appointed a commissioner to Chiang Mai in 1874, accompanied by a group of trained soldiers, dressed in khaki uniforms with white leather helmets and equipped with mountain guns and Snider rifles. In the 1880s a Siamese expeditionary force was stationed on the southern Lan Na borders with a chief of staff trained at the Military Academy, Woolwich in England. Rama V sent more officers for training in Europe including his son Prince Vajiravudh, later Rama VI (1910-1925), who went to the British Military Academy, Sandhurst.

The Lan Na princes were issued with military uniforms some time during the reign of Prince Indra Witchayanon of Chiang Mai (ruled 1871-1897). They were modelled on nineteenth century European uniforms and included jodhpurs and leather riding boots, straight-legged trousers and a range of fitted tunics and helmets set with Siamese insignia, denoting regiment and rank. Prince Chakrakam Kajornsakdi of Lamphun (ruled 1911-1943) was photographed in this style of uniform, a fitted round-necked jacket with gold epaulettes and gold insignia on the collar and sleeves and straight–legged trousers with gold braid down the outside seam. He wears a helmet decorated with ostrich feathers, a silk sash and military medals (fig. 9). In a formal photograph taken in Bangkok, Prince Chai Worachakra wears a white tunic with gold epaulettes, tasselled waist sash, jodhpurs and leather boots. His helmet is decorated with the military insignia of Siam. Military uniforms were ordered directly from Europe or were copied by tailors in Bangkok. It is interesting to note that many leather helmets made for officers bear a label "Made in Britain" in the lining. Radical changes in Lan Na military dress took place towards the end of the century. This is evident if we compare the photograph of Prince Bunthawong of Chiang Mai taken in the 1870s (fig. 3) with that of Prince Chakrakam Kajornsakdi of Lamphun, (fig. 9) taken in the 1900s. Prince Bunthawong wears indigenous dress, a simple *chong kraben* and sandals that carry no symbols of hierarchy. In contrast Prince Chakrakam's Euro-Siamese uniform, insignia and medals establish him within the hierarchy of Siam.

The period 1871-1919 was also a time of change in the style of ceremonial dress. After 1874 as Siam increased her authority in Lan Na, the princes were drawn into a hierarchy of dress codes that had been developed at the Ayutthya court in the 17th century and later revived at the Bangkok courts in the reign of Rama I

Fig. 9 Prince Chakrakam Kajornsakdi, the last prince of Lamphun (ruled 1911-1943). (River Books collection)

(ruled 1782-1809). King Rama V made state visits to Europe and Russia in 1897 and 1907 and one of his letters contains the statement "we do not wish to be Westerners, but wish to know as Westerners know" and is generally quoted as a way of understanding his intentions. He was not interested in slavishly copying Europeans. In the arts, a fusion of European and Siamese style developed, as in the Chakri Maha Prasat throne hall in Bangkok which has a European frame, a Siamese pagoda roof and Siamese and European decorative features. This assimilation is also reflected in the style of court dress that developed at this time.

The transition to Euro-Siamese dress is clearly demonstrated in two formal photographs of Prince Indra Witchayanon of Chiang Mai (ruled 1871-1897). At the beginning of his reign he wore a simple silk shirt, *pha chong kraben* and waist sash and was barefoot, his head shaved at the sides with a circle of hair on the crown. His rank as ruling prince was communicated through the

Fig. 10 Prince Indra Witchayanon, the seventh ruler of Chiang Mai (ruled 1871-1897)

Fig. 11 Prince Suriyapong Paritdej shown wearing his crown and the Chulachomklao sash and decoration (First Class). The photograph was by the German photographer, Robert Lenz. (Payap University Archive, Chiang Mai)

regalia displayed at his side (fig. 7). Later in his reign he wore a white tunic with braided collar and braided cuffs and a silk sash. His *pha chong kraben* was draped and tucked to resemble breeches and he wore white stockings and buckled shoes. He carried a dress sword and wore a white helmet and the medals awarded to him by Rama V (fig. 10). Awards given to the princes of the tributary states included the Order of the Crown of Siam, the Order of the White Elephant, the Chakri Order and the Chulachomklao Order. There were designated classes for each award.

Although Euro-Siamese court dress was worn at official Siamese functions and on tributary visits to Bangkok, the Lan Na princes attempted to maintain their own regalia at court functions that did not involve a Siamese presence. This is demonstrated in a photograph of Prince Suriyapong Paritdej of Nan (ruled 1894-1918) (fig. 11). In Bangkok he posed in front of a painting of the Royal Palace, wearing a dark tunic cut in the style of a Victorian frock coat with matching straight-

legged trousers and black leather shoes. The front panels of his coat, the collar and sleeves are decorated with couched gold wire embroidery and edged with gold braid. The prince wore a three-tiered Siamese crown, a gold chain of office, the Chulachomklao sash and decoration, and medals awarded to him by King Rama V. This Euro-Siamese uniform was worn with a traditional Siamese coat draped over the shoulders.

At home in the Nan palace Prince Suriyapong was photographed sitting on a mattress, supported by a large triangular-shaped embroidered cushion with his Lan Na regalia displayed in front of him (fig.12). He wears a large turban cloth, a plain sash, a *pha chong kraben* and has a sprig of fresh flowers in his right ear. When Suriyapong was on tributary visits to Bangkok he accepted a position in the hierarchy of the Bangkok court. In contrast, when he was resident at the Nan court he presented himself as an independent ruler by wearing indigenous dress and displaying Lan Na regalia. Suriyapong walked a difficult path in his attempt to

Fig. 12 Prince Suriyapong Paritdej of Nan, photographed in 1888 . He is wearing a turban cloth, a sash and *chong kraben* with flowers decorating his right ear. He sits on a mattress leaning on an embroidered cushion, surrounded by his regalia of office. (River Books Collection)

Fig.13 Prince Indra Waroros Suriyavong of Chiang Mai (ruled 1901-1911). (River Books Collection)

separate personal authority from that imposed from Siam and in the long term he did not succeed. French annexation of large tracts of his land on the east bank of the Mekong River contributed to his loss of power. In a photograph taken around 1910 he wears a colonial-style pith helmet with ostrich feathers and his courtiers also wear Siamese dress. At around this time Prince Indra Waroros of Chiang Mai (ruled 1901-1911) made a similar transformation. He was photographed in Chiang Mai in Euro-Siamese uniform also with a colonial style pith helmet (fig. 13).

Court uniforms imposed from Bangkok were modelled on those worn by British officers of His Britannic Majesty's Far East Consular Service, seen in the photograph of Reginald Le May, British Vice Consul to Chiang Mai and Lampang (1913-1915) (fig. 14). Le May wore a white tunic with embroidered and braided collar and sleeve cuffs, straight-legged trousers, a pith helmet bearing the British Imperial coat of arms and insignia, and a dress sword and gloves. The Governors of British colonies wore similar uniforms with insignia designated according to rank, and pith helmets decorated with ostrich plumes. By issuing Prince Indra Waroros of Chiang Mai and Prince Suriyapong of Nan with pith helmets decorated with ostrich feathers, King Rama V was symbolically changing their status as prince-rulers to Governors under his jurisdiction. The decision to model uniforms on those of the British Colonial and Consular Service was a mirror of Siamese government policy. Rama V used the British administrative systems of India and Burma as a prototype for his own reforms. The authority of Bangkok, like that of the British in their colonies, radiated outwards, absorbing former vassals and consolidating administrative control. Queen Victoria lavished titles and honours on the princes of the Raj while her administrators limited their real power. Rama V acted in a similar way in his relationship with the princes of Lan Na.

Fig. 14 Reginald Le May, in the uniform of His Britannic Majesty's Far East Consular Service. (White Lotus)

Fig. 15 A gold coat worn by a member of the royal family or a senior official. Couched gold wire embroidery on a cotton net backing. (Paothong Thongchua collection)

The uniforms were Euro-Siamese but the Lan Na princes continued to receive traditional Siamese exchange gifts, including dress and textiles. They are categorised as Siamese designs, designs made in India to Siamese specifications, Indian designs, Chinese designs and Chinese and Indian designs copied in Siam. The most significant Siamese item of clothing (as opposed to Euro-Siamese), was the gold coat that formed part of court regalia from the time of Rama I (ruled 1782-1809) (fig. 15). Rama V issued gold coats as part of official uniforms worn throughout the tributary states, and to his Ministers of State in Bangkok. Brocaded shirts were also sent as gifts to the rulers of tributary principalities. According to the Chiang Mai chronicle lengths of brocaded silk described as "fabric with gold and silver patterns" were also distributed. Some samples have been identified as *pha yearabab* (*khemkhab* cloth), a type of brocade imported from India. This fabric was used to wrap manuscripts and ceremonial regalia, such as swords and water vessels. Larger pieces were used as floor mats.

On a journey north from Bangkok to Chiang Mai in the late 1880s Sir Ernst Satow noticed that all officials in the towns were now wearing white jackets and *pha chong kraben* with the addition of white stockings and shoes for senior officers. At court the Prince of Chiang Mai "donned a white jacket and a silk sarong, or waistcloth

worn Siamese fashion". However the princes did not always wear white jackets at court and there are many accounts of more colourful dress. When the Prince of Chiang Mai went on a state visit to Chiang Rai he "looked resplendent" in a bright red silk *pha chong kraben*, a blue jacket with gold buttons, and shoes and white stockings. Prince Indra Witchayanon of Chiang Mai (ruled 1871-1897) received tributary offerings from the Lawa wearing a black silk jacket and a silk *pha chong kraben* and was barefoot. His son was dressed in a green satin jacket and a yellow silk *pha chong kraben*. Many princes chose to wear embroidered slippers made in Chiang Mai rather than European style shoes. At his wedding the Prince of Lampang appeared in a blue silk jacket embroidered with gold, a purple *pha chong kraben* and a black velvet cap with a gold band. Many princes continued the custom of wearing flowers and carrying cigars in their pierced earlobes and some kept their hair in traditional Lan Na style.

Senior Siamese princes undertook state visits and inspection tours of Lan Na to boost the profile of the Siamese government. Extensive preparations were made for the state visit of Prince Phichit Preechakorn half brother of Rama V, to Lampang and Chiang Mai in 1876, two years after the appointment of the first Siamese Commissioner. A procession of appropriately adorned elephants, dancers, musicians and regalia bear-

122

ers took part in the ceremony. Although there are no photographs of this event, there are photographs of a state visit to Chiang Mai in 1906 by Crown Prince Vajiravudh, later Rama VI (ruled 1910-1925). The elephant howdah prepared for King Rama VII (ruled 1925-1935), shows the sumptuous decoration associated with such royal events. The way Siamese royalty were now honoured was in contrast to their treatment in 1859 when two Siamese princes on a state visit to Lan Na were virtually ignored by Prince Kawiloros of Chiang Mai and the second prince *(uparat)*.

As part of the changing political climate, ceremonies acknowledging Siamese authority received ever-increasing attention. The bi-annual "Water of Allegiance" ceremony required the participation of all senior Lan Na royalty and government officials as well as Siamese officials serving in Lan Na. Female members of the royal family took the oath to the king at their palace residencies. The photograph of Lan Na and Siamese officials at the ceremony held at Wat Phra Singh, Chiang Mai shows a variety of Euro-Siamese military and government uniforms (fig.16). These uniforms represented civil, provincial authority and cast the princes in the role of state governors rather than independent Buddhist rulers. Some princes attempted to reconcile their traditional authority as "Lords of Life" with the loss of real power, managing to maintain a degree of independence while Siam remained a relatively remote authority. Ancient Lan Na rituals, including the annual ceremony of the Inthakin Pillar and the New Year

dam hua ceremony in which the Lan Na people swore allegiance to their prince, were continued for a time. Other ceremonies that were linked to the traditional *muang* system, like the formal acceptance of Lawa and hill tribe tribute, gradually faded out. As communication with Bangkok improved and as increasing numbers of Siamese officials were stationed in the towns, the Lan Na rulers could no longer avoid their authority.

As Bangkok took power in Lan Na items of regalia that had previously symbolised the authority of the princes were relinquished. Sir Ernst Satow reported the neglect of the Golden Hall (audience hall) of the Prince of Lampang with its red and black pillars decorated with gold leaf, now peeling and fading. The throne of Lampang that he decided "must once have been a gorgeous object" was no longer in use and in a state of disrepair although, significantly, as a symbol of the new order, a photographic portrait of King Rama V of Siam had been placed on the seat. This acts as a perfect symbol for the end of an era.

The Lan Na princes and princesses who look out at us from portraits and photographs account for only a select few. Many lived anonymously leaving few clues, except for perhaps a beautiful item of dress in the possession of a descendant, a faded photograph or passing mention in a traveller's notebook. Although there is so much more to learn, we are fortunate that enough information exists to provide an insight into their fascinating lives.

Fig. 16 The water of allegiance ceremony held inside the *Ubosot* of Wat Phra Singh in front of the portrait of King Rama V. The official group on the left is from the Bangkok court with the princes of Chiang Mai on the right, c.1907. (River Books collection)

CHUAN-TANI OR LIMA CLOTH
Cloth in the Lower Region of Southern Thailand

Somboon Thanasook

Chuan-tani or *Lima* cloth also known as *Tani* brocade, was formerly woven in the lower regions of southern Thailand for personal use. The material, decorated with exquisite designs demonstrates highly sophisticated weaving craftsmanship, which was originally centered in Muang Patani, an area which now covers Pattani, Yala and Narathiwat provinces.

In the past, Muang Patani was a well-known seaport in the eastern part of the Malaya Peninsula. Trade and political relations contributed to the transference and adoption of the culture from the countries with which Pattani came into contact, namely: India, China, Arab countries, European countries, Java and Malaya. It was not clear when the use of cloth and its production commenced in the south, but some experts believe that this began before the Srivijaya Kingdom (8th – 13th centuries A.D) became prosperous.

Through contact and trade with China and India, the natives of Pattani, who might have already been knowledgeable in weaving, were imparted with new weaving traditions. This foreign influence rendered a uniqueness to the newly created textiles. The simple, local fabrics were replaced by intricately woven *mudmee* textiles, with a raised pattern known as *Chuan-tani* or *Lima* cloth, or *Tani* brocade. As the high-quality and beauty of these textiles improved over time, they became widely known during the Ayutthaya period and appreciated by communities in the south, especially in the three southern most provinces on the Thai-Malaysian border.

This type of textile was also referred to in Thai literature as a number of characters adorned themselves in attire made of *Tani* brocade. For instance, an excerpt from *Khun Chang Khun Phaen*, a royal composition by King Rama II, describes an outfit of a character as double layers of *Tani* brocade; the under-layer made of colorful and refined plain silk and the top layer embroidered and perforated into intricate patterns. *Inoh*, a court drama written by King Rama II, describes how one high-ranking character wore a sarong made of *Chuan-tani* silk cloth of a star design. According to the text he let his garment hang loose and fastened it with a gold belt.

Characteristics of *Chuan-tani (Lima)* Cloth

There are two types of *Chuan-tani* cloth:

1. A long strip of cloth with *"long-chuan"* or a strip inserted between the cloth and each end.

Drawing showing *long-chuan* strip

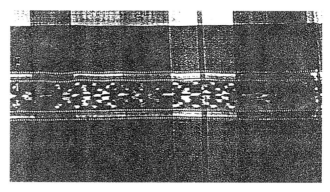

Fig. 1 Detail of textile showing *long-chuan* strip in middle

2. *Chuan-tani* cloth made into a *sarong* with stripe on each cloth end being placed in the seat commonly known as a *"pata"* area.

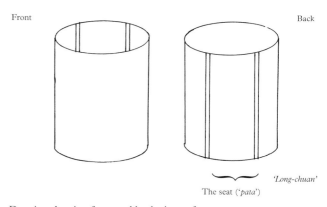

Drawing showing front and back views of sarong

124

The following is the criteria for classification of *Chuan-tani (Lima)* cloth:

1. Composition: *Chuan-tani* cloth, widely-known as a woven textile from Muang Pattani, can be identified by its specific features: the positions of the design, colors, number of designs and design patterns (fig. 2).

1.1 Positions of the designs on the cloth

- "*Long chuan*" or a strip is inserted between the cloth and each end.

- The cloth and both ends are woven into one inseparable piece of cloth.

- Both ends are generally tied and dyed in red color before the weaving process.

Each stripe or "*Long chuan*" consists of three main parts: (fig. 4).

i. "*Pleug*" or a series of outmost broken narrow bands (to border "*panoh*" and "*chai*").

ii. "*Panoh*" or a series of inside broken narrow bands (to border "*chai*").

iii. "*Chai*" or a series of innermost broken narrow bands (bordered by "*panoh*" and "*pleug*").

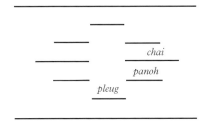

Drawing showing three parts of *long-chuan*

Fig. 2 The "*pata*" must be worn at the seat of the *sarong*

Fig. 3 Detail showing the position of the design

Fig. 4 Textile showing *long-chuan* with strip containing *pleug*, *panoh* and *chai*

Fig. 5 Cloth showing contrasting colors

126

Fig. 6 Cloth showing contrasting colors

Fig. 7 Five colors as seen in this *lima* cloth

Fig. 8 Cloth showing multiple designs in the body and end

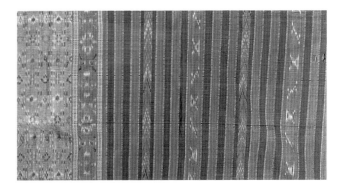

Fig. 9 Cloth showing strips with design

Fig. 10 Pattern showing net or basket weave design

Colors: The main cloth and its ends generally clash in color. The cloth end is usually of different shades of red-bright red, scarlet, fuchsia red and crimson. The main panel is in dark purple, green, dark blue, reddish brown and brown (figs. 5, 6).

Besides clashing colors, it is found that each strip of *Chuan-tani* cloth generally contains five colors. The word "*lima*", which is another name of *Chuan-tani* cloth, is a Malay dialect word meaning "five". In some rare cases this type of textile has more than five colors.

Number of designs: In each piece of cloth, there are five to seven designs, three to five of which are found in the cloth end. A similar type of cloth from other regions has only one to two designs (fig. 8).

Design Patterns
- Strips ("*long chuan*", suggesting the origin of the name "*Chuan-tani*" cloth)
- Meshes/nets/basket weave (fig. 10)
- Checks (fig. 10)
- Stars (golden lanterns) (fig. 12)
- Arabic script (fig. 13)
- Plain end (fig.14)
- Plain cloth (the end being decorated with designs)

Fig. 11 Cloth with checkered pattern

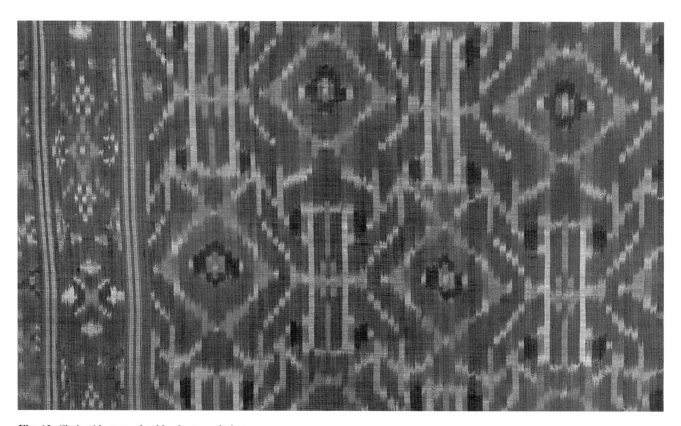

Fig. 12 Cloth with star and golden lanterns design

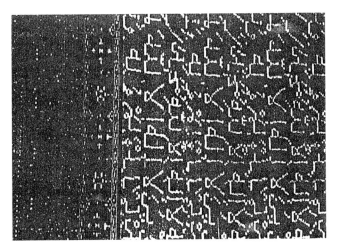

Fig. 13 Cloth with Arabic script

Production Methods

- By a *mudmee* process (only weft yarns being tied and dyed, or both warp and weft yarns being tied and dyed) (fig. 15).

- By raising the designs in the fabric through the *"yok"*, *"chok"* and *"khid"* techniques (continuous or discontinuous supplementary weaving techniques).

Fig. 14 Cloth with plain end without design

Fig. 15 Cloth woven with *mudmee (ikat)* process

Fig. 16 Detail of *phasin* showing supplementary weave

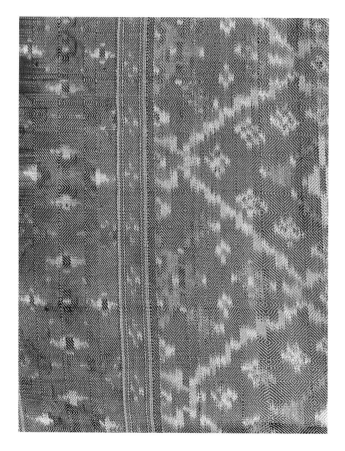

Design Methods

Weaving Method: Using two-ply weaving, three-ply weaving or four-ply weaving. Additional design is added by raising the designs in the fabric through the *"yok"*, this can be either through *"chok"* (discontinuous supplementary technique) or *"khid"* (continuous supplementary technique) (figs. 18, 19).

Dyeing Method

- *Tani* threads obtained from *tani* banana trunk are used to embroider the design onto the cloth before the cloth is dyed (fig.20).

Fig. 17 Cloth can be woven using various ply threads

130

Fig. 18 Weaving with supplementary design

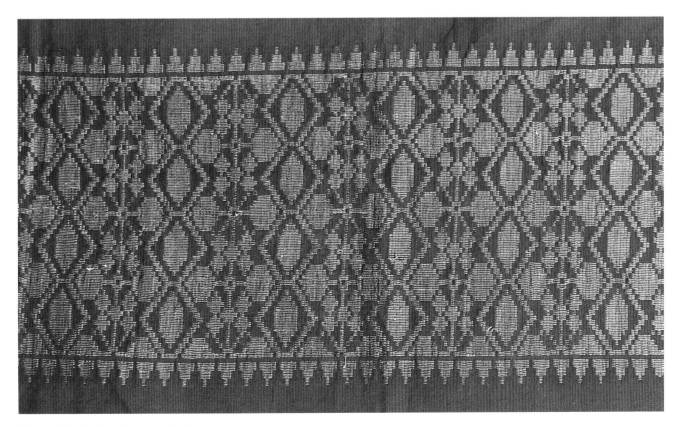

Fig. 19 Detail of supplementary design

Fig. 20 Design made by using *tani* threads to embroider pattern design before dyeing

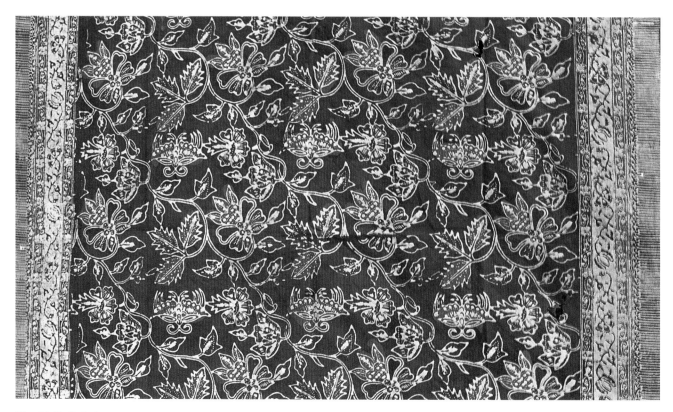

Fig. 21 Batik design

- The method of making batik (fig. 21)

Classification by fibers used for cloth weaving
- Silk
- Cotton
- Gold or silver threads

Dyeing process
- Natural dyes from indigo, lac, straw, cumin wood, jackfruit wood and balsam leaves
- synthetic dyes imported from India and China.

Weaving apparatus: a loom

Uses
- To cover the head (fig. 23)
- To wear around the neck (fig. 24)
- To wear as a top: tucked in under the arm (for women) (fig. 25)
- To wear on top of trousers (for men)(fig. 26)
- To use as shroud.

Chuan-tani or *Lima* cloth is associated with the upper classes as it was difficult to obtain. Thus this textile was used only on special occasions, for instance, weddings or festivals to celebrate the birth of Mohammed.

At present, the tradition of weaving *Chuan-tani* cloth has died out in the lower regions of the south of Thailand and its production has stopped in the southern communities. The making of this unique cloth, of such high aesthetic beauty, has gradually disappeared over the past eighty to one hundred years due to the influence of free trade and the use of machinery in the textile production process. Yet, it is not too late to revive the study of this marvelous hand-woven material and preserve the memory of this unique textile for future generations. A number of elderly persons, who are now of eighty to ninety years of age, can still give information on the glorious past of *Chuan-tani* cloth.

Fig. 22 Variety of textiles worn in a procession

Fig. 23 Cloth used as head cover **Fig. 24** Cloth used as shoulder cover

Fig. 25 Cloth used as bodice wrap **Fig. 26** Cloth wrapper over man's trousers

THE REPRESENTATION OF TEXTILES IN CHAM SCULPTURES

Emmanuel Guillon

My topic belongs partly to archaeology and partly to the history of cloth and the use of textiles. Thus it may be somewhat austere, or a little abstract, in comparison with some of the papers in this volume.

In brief, I shall present what we can glean on the Indianized roots of contemporary, or recent, Cham textiles. Between those roots and these present-day textiles there is a long gap. The purpose of my paper is to fill this gap of more than five hundred years, and, at the same time, to show how vast is the field of research still to be done. For instance, dozens of inscriptions have not yet been read nor translated. And, regarding Champa, one does not find the same continuity as in the Khmer tradition.

In fact, on the sculptures we see attire and not textiles. There are no single fabrics in Cham sculptures, but rather various kinds of clothing and costumes. And because almost all that remains of the ancient Cham civilization is of a religious nature, I would like to subtitle this paper "The Clothes of the Gods and their Attendants in Old Cham Sculptures". In a sense, traditional textiles are always concerned with the supernatural, or with sacred values.

As almost no research has been done on this topic, I begin with an overview of the clothing portrayed in the sculptures before delving deeper into the topic proper. The structure of my talk appears in the summary in figure 1.

After a short introduction discussing old Chinese sources and stressing the importance of the textiles in the representation of movement in these sculptures, I shall, in part one, look at the clothes of ascetics and of servants and attendants. Then in part two, I will show that the clothes were closely related to their function and correspond to four types. Afterwards, in part three, I shall show how changes in fashion can be used to help date sculptures. In part four, I speculate as to the colour and motifs of these old textiles, what they indicate concerning their manufacture, and their various thicknesses. Part five will briefly discuss the clothing of the Cham

The Representation of Textiles in Cham Sculptures

or

THE CLOTHES OF THE GODS

An ancient tradition of textiles in the art of movement

1. The simplest garments: ascetics, servants, children

2. Dancing, standing, sitting, lying

3. The fashion and its dating

4. Motifs and thickness of the fabric

5. The clothing of war

6. Sculptures of the supernatural and the role of textiles

Fig. 1 Textiles represented in old Cham sculpture

warriors and of their Khmer neighbors. Finally, I will finish with a few more general reflections on the textiles in these classical sculptures.

The role of fabric in the development of art styles

The old Kingdoms of Champa were very famous for their wonderful fabrics, their woven silk and cotton, and for their embroideries. This information comes from the fifth century, and from as far as Japan. Therefore apart from the sculpture that we can see, we know of textiles in old Champa thanks to the accounts of Chinese travellers or historians.

For instance, we can read in the Leang Chou that as early as the 5th century, the Cham people cultivated mulberry trees for silk and cotton bushes for cotton. The women spun and wove the threads. They are known to have added golden threads in the weft. They knew how to weave fabrics with different motifs on each side. They perfumed their clothing with musk. Ordinary people usually wore a large piece of cotton from the waist to the feet, which was wrapped around their body from right to left.

Later, in the year 1076 AD the Song Che described the Cham King Harivarman IV as follows: "The king is 36 years old. He eats much. He wears a robe or a long tunic of damask with flower motifs on black or green backdrops. This tunic was fastened up with seven golden ties, not with buttons. The undergarments were of very thin white cotton, trimmed with embroidered braids or golden fringes".

Later still at the end of the 13th century the Chinese traveller Zhou Daguan noted that Cambodia wove only cotton and canvas and imported textiles from Siam and from Champa. But now let us leave the subject of old texts, and turn to looking at the sculptures (almost all of which are in sandstone, with some rare bronze exceptions.)

The sculptures of Champa mainly represent religious subjects, and the clothing plays a very important part in the meaning and in the composition of the scene. Figure 2 represents one of the masterpieces of this art, and one of the oldest. It is a detail of one of the risers of a Shivaite pedestal dating to the middle of the seventh century. It was found in a temple at My Son in central Vietnam, 20 kilometers southwest of present-day Da Nang. This temple was called My Son E1 by the first European archaeologists and belongs to the style of the same name E1.

The scarves indicate the vertical lines, and when the faces of the dancers look upwards, the meaning is that they are looking towards the gods. The cloth is a *sampot* of which the upper part is tucked back up in the belt, while the other tail forms an oblique pleat. This drape is typically Cham, (derived originally from India) and the stages in its evolution can help to date the sculpture.

The three drawings, taken from Cham sculptures, shown in figure 3 (page 136) show clearly how the cloth is adjusted (note the belt). These designs, based on the the work of the late Professor Boisselier, also illustrate the horizontal folds of the *sampot*. This detail is important, because it also existed at the same time, in the representation of *sampot* in pre-Angkorian Khmer art. However in Khmer examples this style soon disappeared, to remain only in the art of Champa. Most important are the long, narrow strips, which may help us to learn which kind of textile was used.

Fig. 2 Stone carving Da Nang Museum, photo credit V. Combré

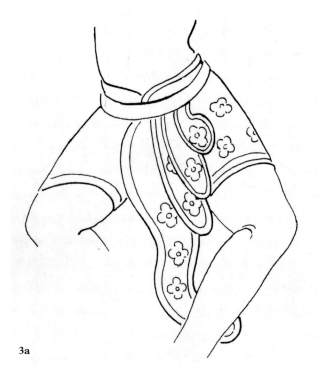

3a

3b

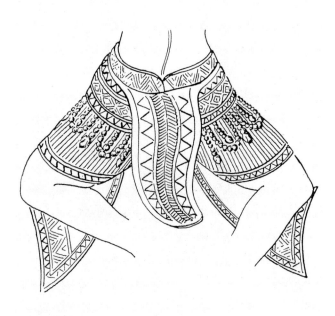

3c

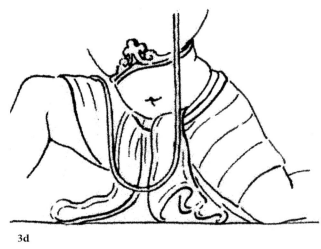

3d

Fig. 3a, 3b, 3c, 3d. Three ways of draping different kinds of cloth

Simple Clothing: Ascetics and Servants

In drawings based on the seventh century pedestal we have already seen (fig. 4), we can find some representations of ascetics shown in their caves, on the mythical mountain, praying, playing the *vina* or flute, reading manuscripts and so on. Other examples of ascetics show similar garb. Their clothing is as simple as possible: it is made of a short strip which hangs down and is held in position by a thin string used as a belt. We do not even

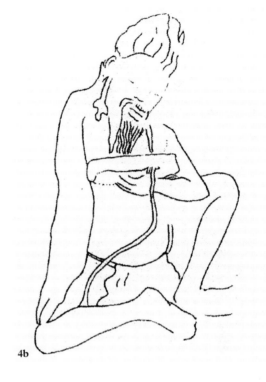

4a

4b

4c

Fig. 4a, 4b, 4c. Ascetics in different poses

Fig. 5 Detail from the Tra Kieu stone pedestal, Da Nang Museum

know if this very rudimentary clothing with the appearance of a loincloth is a textile or made of leather.

We also find this elementary costume on the curious rider squatting down on the horse and dancing or making a sort of acrobatic movement (fig. 4c), a representation unique in Cham sculpture. The original piece from which these drawings were made is now in the museum in Da Nang and dates back to the beginning of the 10th century.

Such elementary items of clothing (fig. 5) were used by servants and by attendants of the gods or demigods. We can see here side A of the pedestal of Tra Kieu, dating back to the middle of the 10th century. Two male attendants, possibly children, join their hands to pay respect to the other people in the scene of the breaking of the bow. They are both wearing what appear to be small briefs. However, their belt is a double woven cord or braid, more decorative than functional.

Fig. 6 Stone carving My Son museum. (Photograph: I. Pignon)

Sitting, dancing, lying down and standing

Figure 6 shows a tympanum from temple C1 at My Son, which is now stored in a small museum at the site. It is dated to the end of the 7th century. The piece shows Shiva dancing with Skanda and Parvati. There are also two musicians and a skeleton-like figure.

Shiva is dancing on a pedestal behind his mount, Nandi. He wears a kind of short *sarong* with a long tail with several pleats hanging from a belt made of fabric. We can also see this kind of belt on the non-identified attendants on the right.

In a detail from the tympanum (fig. 7) we see Parvati sitting with the child Skanda under a tree. Her apparel is one of the oldest representations of feminine dress in Cham art. Clearly visible are the vertical bands of her skirt and the hanging ribbon or scarf, the evolution of which has helped to determine the successive periods of Indianized art.

Usually the three types of clothing (fig. 8) represented in these sculptures are functional and very realistic. Each corresponds to a position of the body. So we have three kinds of clothes for the three main positions: dancing, standing and sitting.

Dancers (fig. 9) wear a kind of undergarment, which is very tight. The three drawings shown here are not in chronological order, but rather show the develop-ment from simpler to more sophisticated designs. One should stress the design of the middle figure: it belongs to the *aspara* of the pedestal of Tra Kieu dated to the middle of the 10th century. The richly decorated cloth, is skin-tight and fits closely to the legs. This type of clothing is unknown in Southeast Asian art outside of Champa. It was borrowed from the south of India, where it appeared frequently in the sculptures representing dancers and even female deities of exactly the same date, the 10th century. This style is famous and is known under its Sanskrit name as *Candataka*.

I use the term *sarong* (fig. 10) because of its common use, even if I find the word imprecise and possibly misleading. These *sarong* were used when representing female persons like Trivakra or Mahishamardini or other goddesses. Avalokitesvara also wears a *sarong*, usually decorated.

Other standing figures wear a *sampot* (figs. 11) turned up between the legs. They represent Dvarapala, or door guardians, in ceremonial dress, with ornate belts similar to those made by a goldsmith.

We can identify the period of a sculpture (figs. 12) by the clothing of the seated persons in three different stages of developement: Parvati of the 7th century; a *deva* of the 9th century; and Shiva of the 15th century.

138

Fig. 7 Detail of stone carving My Son museum.
(Photograph: I. Pignon)

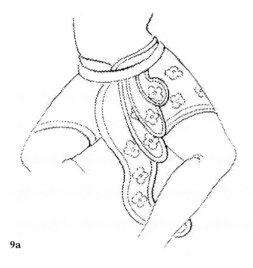

9a

9b

Three Kinds of Cloth

A. Dancing: Pair of tights

B. Standing 1: Sarong

   Standing 2: *Sampot* turned up between the legs

C. Sitting and lying

Fig. 8 Three kinds of cloth

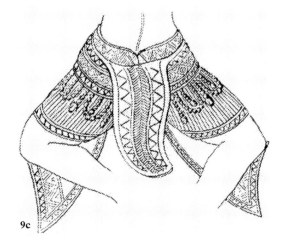

9c

Fig. 9a, 9b, 9c. Drawings showing dancing figures

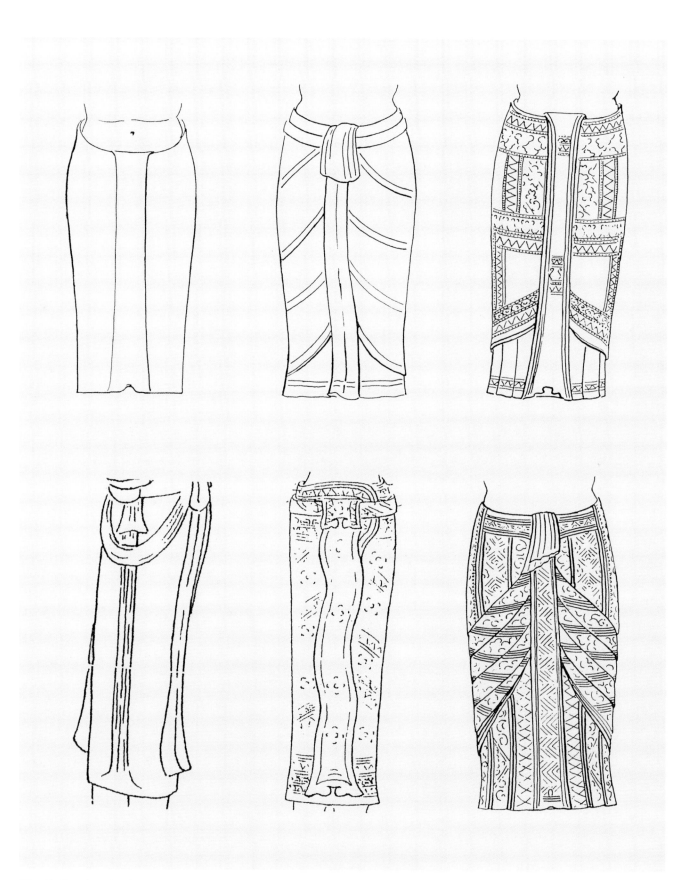

Fig. 10 Drawings showing various types of *sarong* found in Cham sculptures

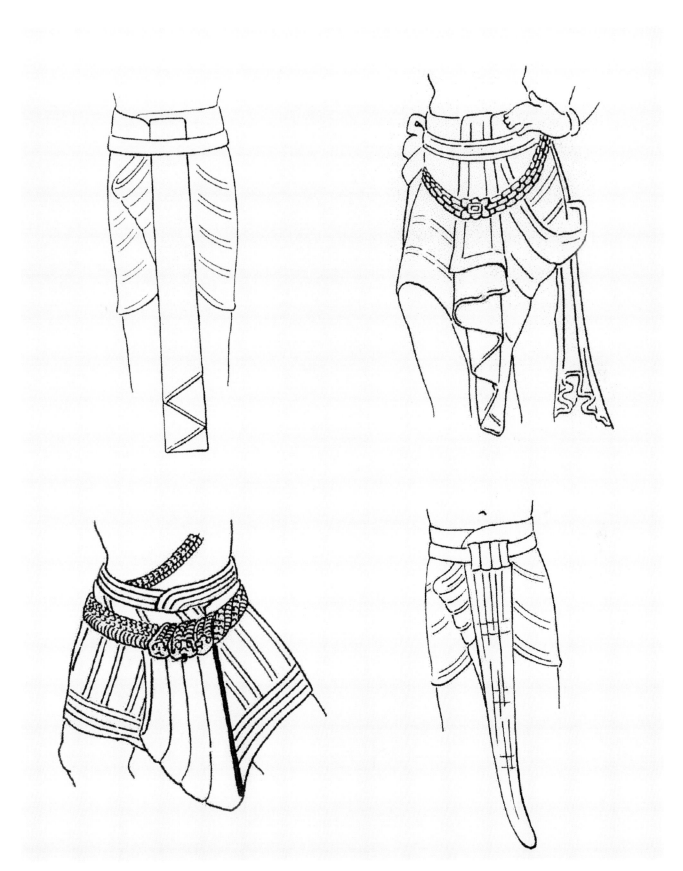

Fig. 11 Drawing showing various styles of *sampot*

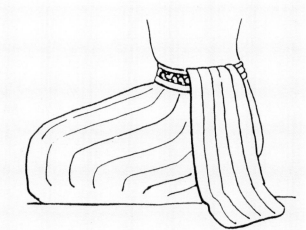

Fig. 12a Parvati, 7th century

Fig. 12b A 9th century *deva*

Fig. 12c Shiva, 15th century

Fig. 12d Reclining Vishnu, 8th century

Fig. 13 16-armed dancing Shiva, Da Nang Museum

Fig. 14 Stone statue of Dvarapala in garden of Da Nang Museum, (Photograph: V. Combré)

Fig. 15 Stone relief of Dvarapala from Marble Mountain

The reclining Vishnu, celebrating the birth of Brahma, represents an intermediate step of the 8th century.

I shall complete my survey by showing three instances which indicate the complexity of this classification. Figure 13 illustrates a tympanum from Da Nang Museum showing a 16-armed dancing Shiva. The image dates to the beginning of the 10th century. The *sampot* is unusual, in that it is not decorated, so we see here more clearly the triple belt and the thick textile used.

This *dvarapala* shown in figure 14 dates to the end of the 9th century, only a few decades earlier than the previous image. The clothing is quite simple, with a band hanging between the legs. Nevertheless, this is also a kind of ceremonial dress.

From the same period is a strange *dvarapala* (fig. 15) from the so-called "Marble Mountains" near Da Nang. This appears to be a woman, and her large multi-folded band is also unique. This figure has never been studied properly.

Clothing styles can also be studied on Buddhist subjects. The seated Bodhisattva (fig. 16) from the Dong Duong site in central Vietnam shows a geometrical and floral design on the horizontal bands of his tights.

Fashion and Styles

Most experts in the art of Champa have concentrated more in the styles of clothing seen in the sculptures than in the textiles themselves. Professor Boisselier the prime exponent of Cham art, has theorized that as at the Indianized courts, Cham clothing would develop over time. Comparison with the Indian and Indo-Javanese evolution of clothing tends to support this theory. If we examine the development of the different styles, we can discern seven periods.

As you can see in figure 17, the classification of the different styles begins in the middle of the 7th century and finishes at the end of the 16th century, thus covering almost one thousand years. All of the style bear names of archeological sites. The third style is essentially Buddhist, and the golden age dates to the 10th century. The patterns of the Chan Lô style, at the

Fig. 16 Stone Bodhisattva, Da Nang Museum

The Seven Styles of Champa

1. Mid-VII Cent.	My Son E 1 style
2. VIII Century	Hoa Lai style
3. Second half of IX Cent.	Dông Duong style
4. X Cent.	My Son A 1 style
4.a	Khuong My style
4.b	Tra Kieu style
5. End X Cent./1st half of XI Cent.	Chan Lô
6. End XI Cent./beginning XIV Cent.	Thap Mam style
7. End XIV Cent./early XVI Cent.	Late styles
7.a	Yang Mum style
7.b	Po Rome style

Fig. 17 The seven styles of Champa

Fig. 18 *Avalokitesvara*, Saigon Historical Museum

beginning of the 11th century, were later borrowed by the Khmer. The latter styles show that Indian inspiration and beliefs had gradually been forgotten. The Chams had moved from the world of palaces and rich temples to village life.

A small bronze (fig. 18) showing Avalokitesvara with four arms indicates the Indo-Javanese influence of a Mahayanist representation. This figure dates to the middle of the 9th century. He wears a draped *dhoti* of Indian origin, with a large, twisted double belt-scarf.

On the pedestal of the *vihara* of Dong Duong, at the northern stairs there is a *Dvarapala* (fig. 19) in a Buddhist context, with an unusual *sampot* folded up

144

Fig. 19 Stone Dvarapala in situ Marble Mountain

Fig. 20 Stone dancing figure Saigon Historical Museum, photo credit I. Pignon

between the legs. This image shows how Buddhism has borrowed from the Brahmanic fashions.

A different type of figure is this dancer (fig.20), of which we can find similar examples in the Historical Museum of Saigon, in the Paris Guimet Museum, and in Toulouse in France. The dancer, standing on one foot, brandishes a long scarf, with one end held above her head, the other at knee height. I believe we can compare this with the modern "dance of the scarf", found here and there (in Burma for instance).

Fig. 21 Stone fragment of musician in the garden of Da Nang Museum

Fig. 22 Stone pedestal from Tra Kieu

Fig. 23 Dancing figure Da Nang Museum.
(Photograph: V. Combré)

A recently unearthed fragment (fig. 21), shows a musician playing a *vina*. His *sampot* is quite unusual for the period, with its narrow belt. It can be dated to the end of the 10th century.

Returning to the pedestal of Tra Kieu (fig. 22), we can see at the right of the upper part a standing Trivikra, wearing a single decorated *sarong* to show her rank. Here, as elsewhere, we can see that cloth and textiles are used as an indication of social level.

The dancing figure belonging to the Chan Lô style, (fig. 23) is very sensuous. During this period the movement of the hips is contrapuntal to the position of the dancer's legs. The central band of the cloth emphasizes the unusual stance.

A comparison of three dancing Shiva figures is instructive. The dancing Shiva (fig. 24) with four arms now in the Da Nang Museum, belongs to the Thap Mam style, and dates to the end of the 11th century. The embroideries and jewels have become more important than the cloth itself, a characteristic that marks the beginning of a more decadent style.

146

Fig. 24 Dancing Shiva, Da Nang Museum

Fig. 25 Dancing Shiva, Hanoi Museum. (Photograph: I. Pignon)

Fig. 26 Shiva Da Nang Museum, (Photograph: V. Combré)

Another dancing Shiva in the Hanoi museum (fig. 25) shares similar characteristics.

The culmination of this more decadent style may be seen in figure 26, a Shiva belonging to the Yang Mum style. The legs are no longer shown. We cannot study the cloth, because it completely disappears behind the three large embroidered bands.

Motifs and Thicknesses of Fabrics

The main types of material found in Cham sculpture are bands of fabric which are draped vertically, laterally and horizontally. Unfortunately, the colour can only be conjectured at because we have not found any painted sculptures. However, the earliest evidence of red, Indian Carnelian beads were reported in excavations of the Huyn culture, which immediately preceded the Champa. We have already seen that there were green, red and

Fig. 27 Prajnaparamita from Dai Hui.

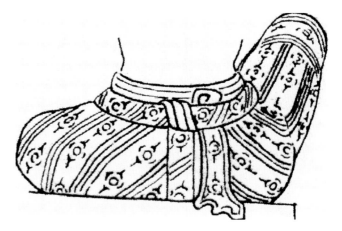

Fig. 28 Drawing showing symbolic flower design

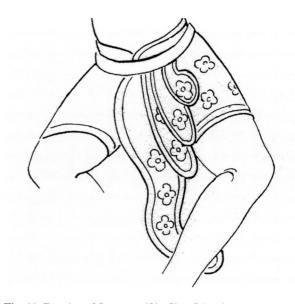

Fig. 29 Drawing of flower motif in Chan Lô style

yellow textiles, local indigo blue, and tumeric used as the sacred colour and dye for Vishnu. But this is a terra incognito. In addition, for various reasons most notably political ones, there have not been serious archeological excavations for almost 70 years. As a result, we can only assume that the old Indianized courts of Champa depended upon maritime activities and thus received trade textiles from abroad.

According to Robin Maxwell, figures wearing textiles with stripes running vertically indicate weft decoration, and the passage from warp decoration to weft décor. As for the patterns or motifs, three are clearly distinguishable: geometric, four-petal flowers and star shapes of various kinds.

This *sarong* of the Prajnaparamita from Dai Hui (fig. 27) dating to the end of the 9th century is decorated with carved geometric motifs, diamond tips, circles

with a dot in the middle, symbolic flowers and so on. It is the most common design found in the sculpture of Champa.

Another symbolic flower design (fig. 28) can be found in this drawing of a *deva* from a Buddhist temple dating to the end of the 9th century seen earlier. The floral design is clearly against the plain background.

A more obviously floral motif (fig. 29) appears in the Chan Lô style, and these simple flowers with four petals, were probably a sign of social rank. They were often found later in the sculptures of Angkor up to the Bayon period.

Unusually, flower motifs are also found on this Brahma (fig. 30) in Thap Mam style. Additionally we can find this motif (fig. 31) on a carving also in the Da Nang Museum suggesting that these flowers were sometimes sewn on the textiles.

Fig. 30 Brahma, Da Nang Museum. (*Photograph: V. Combré*)

Fig. 31 Stone carving showing flower motif, Da Nang Museum

Fig. 32 Stone carving showing textile covered saddle

The poor quality of figure 32 makes it difficult to discern but nevertheless the textile covered saddle on an animal which looks like Nandi is just visible. Nowadays, symbolic clothes or sumptuous embroideries are still used to adorn certain mythological animals, such as the extravagant *gajasimha*, half-lion, half-elephant.

The thickness of the textiles shown in the sculptures vary with the thinnest resulting in skin-tight clothing as seen in the famous dancer (fig. 33) from the 10th century Tra Kieu pedestal, called the "pedestal of dancers". The dancer is not naked, but is portrayed wearing a very thin, almost invisible cloth, whose diaphanous appearance is reminiscent of fine muslin.

The large bronze statue of Tara (fig. 34) was found in 1978 in Dong Doung. In contrast to the dancer, her *sarong* is very thick, even stiff, more suitable for formal regalia. No motif is discenible on the fabric.

The dress of war

In the art of Champa there are few representations of aggressive human beings, instead we see this in standing lions, especially of the 10th century. Curiously enough, with the exception of one or two sculptures, war is not represented, nor the warriors, even in mythical scenes. To know a little more about the attire of warriors, we must refer to the neighboring Khmer art.

At the Bayon in the heart of Angkor Thom (fig. 35) reliefs portray the battles between the Khmer and the Cham. In the outer gallery, north aisle, east side, we can see a figure with a kind of jacket, which we might call a "jacket of war", which had the power of magical protection.

Fig. 33 Dancer, Da Nang Museum. (Photograph: V. Combré)

Classical sculpture and textiles

As we have seen, the sculptures of Champa are mainly concerned with the world of the gods, as these two Gandharvas from the pedestal of Tra Kieu remind us (fig. 36). These demigods are celestial, represented flying and delighted at the miracle of the hunchback of Trivikra. This is shown mainly by the scarf, which at the same time indicates that the Gandarvas are in the air, and is used to fill the space of the sculpture. Here, the representation of the textiles plays a crucial role in creating the art. In this example the art of textile, the art of dance and art of carving are united in a magnificent piece.

I would like to finish with one masterpiece of Cham art, which shows wonderful embroidery. Now at the Da Nang Museum, this goddess (fig. 37 and fig. 38) dates to the end of the 10th century. Her double skirt carved in light relief marvellously epitomises ancient Cham textiles evoked in stone.

Fig. 34 Bronze Tara, Da Nang Museum

150

Fig. 35 Stone carving, the Bayon, Angkor Wat. (Photograph: Dolias)

Fig. 36 Celestial gandharvas from the stone pedestal of Tra Kieu

Fig. 37 Goddess, Da Nang Museum. (Photograph: V. Combré)

Fig. 38 Another view of the goddess from the Da Nang Museum

CHAM WEAVING IN VIETNAM

Gerald Moussay

Today the Cham people have been reduced to a small ethnic minority found almost exclusively in the area around Phanrang/Phanri in southern Vietnam. However, they remain attached to the memories of the Hindu culture and religion of their ancestors, and continue to observe numerous traditions that recall their glorious past.

The Cham are particularly devoted to the worship of all the divinities in their pantheon. Of special importance are the deified kings and legendary heroes of Cham history and literature.

Each year, at the Cham New Year, religious ceremonies are held in honor of the gods at the three chief cultural sites in the region: Po Nagar, Po Klaung Girai and Po Rome. In addition to ceremonies performed in the temples, the Cham also ensure harmonious relations with their gods through rituals marking major events in human life (birth, death, cremation) and through seasonal celebrations (repairing dams and canals, irrigating rice fields, planting crops). A significant religious clergy is responsible for these ritual observations.

In the 16th or 17th century, the Muslim religion spread through much of Champa, and approximately one-third of the Cham community was converted to Islam. Since that time, the descendants of these Muslim converts (called *banis*) have lost contact with the Islamic world. As a result, they have forgotten certain fundamental rules of Islam, such as circumcision, fasting at Ramadan and the pilgrimage to Mecca. However, they have retained the memory of other Muslim rituals and continue to worship in mosques (*sang magik*), where there is a permanent clergy specializing in the *bani* sect.

The clergy of both religions co-exist peacefully, sometimes within the same village. Each avoids holding ceremonies at times that are seen as inconvenient to followers of the other sect. There are also special persons who can perform various functions in both the traditional Cham religion and the *bani* faith.

Clergy of the traditional Cham religion

The clergy of the traditional Cham religion, which centers around ancestor worship and the worship of ancient Cham kings, consists of: the high priest, *Po Adhia;* his assistant, *Ong Bac,* and the officiating priest, *Ong Baseh,* all three of whom are identified by their long hair. They are sometimes assisted in the performance of their duties by the following: *Ong Chamnei,* the temple keeper; *Ong Ka-ing,* the fire-walker, whose annual firewalk *(rija nagar)* commemorates the victories of ancient Champa heroes; *Ong Kadhar Gru,* who recites the great deeds of legendary Cham kings and heroes, and *Ong Kadhar Pahuan Anik,* who assists the *Kadhar Gru.*

The Cham priests also preside over the rituals associated with the cremation of the dead. In this, they are assisted by a number of other religious dignitaries, notably *Ong Daoh,* who performs the traditional funeral chants; *Ong Hang,* who adorns the coffin; *Ong Gru Kaleng,* the exorcist (in the event of a violent death*);* *Po Damân,* who represents the matrilineal clan at the ceremony, and *Hala Car,* who carries the body of the deceased on the day of the cremation.

Clergy of the *Bani* religion

Depending on its importance, a *bani* village may have between 10 and 25 religious dignitaries, with each of the matrilineal clans represented by one or two members. Recognized by their cleanly shaven heads, these dignitaries may perform one of the following five functions: *Po Gru,* head of the *bani* community; *Ong Mâm,* the *imam,* who presides over prayers at the village mosque, commonly held twice a month; *Ong Katip (khatib)* and *Ong Mâdin (muezzin),* who assist the *imam,* and *Ong Acar Jamaah,* novices receiving religious instruction.

Clergy members common to both religions

In addition to the clergy, whose roles are clearly defined within the religion to which they belong, there are other religious dignitaries who perform activities common to both the traditional Cham and the *bani* religions. These include the *Ong Mâduen, a rebab* player and one of the principal celebrants of the traditional *"rija"* ceremonies. In a language derived from ancient Malay, the *Ong Mâduen* recites the adventures of a Malay hero who came to wed a Cham princess. His recitation is accompanied by a ritual dance performed by an older woman called the *Muk Rija*. Other dignitaries common to both religions are: *Ong Ganuer Ripaong*, who is responsible for irrigation canals; *Ong Banâk*, who presides over purification rituals meant to ensure the soundness of dams; *Ong Danaok*, who represents the matrilineal line at seasonal ceremonies; *Ong Pal*, who watches over food offerings made to the gods; *Muk Pajaw*, a female seer and magician, sworn to celibacy, who assists other clergy members; and *Muk Buh*, a woman appointed to prepare the offerings of food, betel nut and flowers used during traditional rites.

Attire of the religious dignitaries

All religious dignitaries wear specific clothing, which indicates their status and function, and distinguishes them from other members of the community. Individual dignitaries can be identified by the width and design of the border adorning their turban or sarong. The form, color, pattern and size of their clothing is dictated by Cham custom and tradition. This is equally true for both everyday clothing and ceremonial attire.

Clothing of the traditional Cham clergy

The everyday costume worn by the two principal priests of the traditional Cham religion, *Po Adhya* and *Ong Bac*, consists of 11 items: a white turban, a turban trimmed with a red border or a fringe made of red threads, a sash, short trousers, a *sarong* with a red or gold hem, a woven cloth belt with a diamond-shaped design, a white tunic, a red scarf, a headscarf, a sash referred to as "an eel bone" and a betel nut pouch (see fig. 1).

The *Basaih*, who assist the chief priests, wear the same costume, except that their *sarong* has no decorative border. Instead, it is trimmed with a lateral strip of lace.

Fig. 1 Po Adhya

The temple caretaker, *Ong Camnei*, wears an outfit consisting of eight items: a turban with a red and gold border or a fringe made of red threads *(khan mâtham taibi)*, a headscarf *(kadung gibak)*, a red scarf *(siaip phong)*, short trousers *(tarapha panak)*, a *sarong* trimmed with lace *(khan marang)*, a plain woven cloth belt *(talei ka-ing mrai)*, a short, white tunic *(aw sah lakei)* and a betel nut pouch. The *Ong Ka-ing*, or firewalker, wears eight articles of clothing, namely: a turban with a red and gold border or a fringe made of red threads *(khan mâtham taibi)*, a red scarf *(siaip phong)*, short trousers *(tarapha panak)*, a lace-trimmed sarong *(khan marang)*, a plain woven cloth belt *(talei ka-ing mrai)*, a short, white tunic *(aw sah patih)*, a short, red tunic *(aw sah phong)*, and a betel nut pouch.

The costume worn by the *Ong Kadhar*, who recites the royal genealogies, consists of eight items: a turban with a red and gold border or a fringe made of red threads *(khan mâtham taibi)*, a headscarf *(kadung gibak)*, a long red scarf (*siaip phong*), short trousers (*tarapha panak*), a *sarong* with a red and gold hem (*khan mbar jih*), a woven belt with a diamond-shaped design (*talei ka-ing bingu tamul*), a short, white tunic (*aw sah*), and a betel nut pouch. Two other costumes are used strictly to dress statues of Cham divinities on the country's national holiday. The first of these, called *as po yang lakei*, is composed of a ceremonial *sarong*, a red tunic with gold flowers, a multicolored belt and a tiara, and is used to dress statues of male gods. The other (*aw po yang kamei*) is used for female gods and consists of a dark-colored *sarong* with a lateral border, a floral tunic, and a braided red crown.

Clothing of the *bani* religious dignitaries

The principal *bani* dignitaries: *Po Gru, Ong Mâm, Ong Mâdin, and Ong Katip* wear a uniform comprised of seven articles of clothing: a white turban (*khan mbram*), a turban with a red and gold decorative border or with a fringe made of red threads (*khan mâtham twak*), a head-scarf (*kadung gibak*), short trousers (*tarapha panak*), a *sarong* with a red and gold hem (*khan mbar jih*), and a woven belt with a diamond-shaped design (*talei ka-ing bingu tamul*). *Bani* novices (*Acar Jamaah*) wear a similar costume, but their *sarong* has no border, and their woven belt lacks the diamond-shaped motif. (see fig. 2)

Clothing of the officiants of both religions

The costume worn by *Ong Maduen*, who presides over the traditional "*rija*" ceremonies, consists of seven items: a silk head cover (*siaip kabuak*), a turban with a red and

Fig. 2 *Acar bani* in a cemetery

gold border or with a fringe made of red threads (*khan mâtham taibi*), a *sarong* with a lace border (*khan marang*), a plain, woven belt (*talei ka-ing mrai*), a white tunic (*aw maduen*), a betel nut pouch (*tanyrak hala*) and a fan (*tadik*).

During the performance of the ceremonial "*rija*", the sacred dancer, *Muk Rija*, wears a succession of four different costumes to represent the different characters she portrays.

The first of these costumes (*aw muk rija*) consists of a plain, white veil (*kahn luh putih*), red thread earrings (*bruei tangi*), a dark-colored *sarong* trimmed with a red decorative border (*khan mbar jih*), a white tunic (*aw tuak patih*), and a betel nut pouch.

The costume of the princess (*aw patri*) consists of a red veil trimmed with a red and gold border (*khan matham tuak bhong*), a dark-colored *sarong* with a red hem (*khan mbar jih*), a red tunic with a red border (*khan mbar jih*), and a red tunic trimmed with a gold border and gold flowers (*aw tuak bhong bingu*).

In the costume of the prince (*aw patra*), the *Muk Rija* wears a white veil trimmed with a narrow border (*khan matham bingu pathap*), a white *sarong* with a red and gold hem (*khan matham jih*), a belt with a diamond-shaped design (*talei ka-ing bingu tamul*) and a white tunic (*aw lah*).

The costume of the ancestors (*aw ataw*) includes a red veil with a red border around the edges (*khan matham tuak bhong*), a red band to tie back the hair (*ginreng*), red earrings (*bruei tangi*), a red *sarong* (*khan bhong*) and a red tunic (*aw tuak bhong*).

The other women who play secondary roles in the performance of religious or magical rites *Muk Pajaw* and *Muk Buh* also wear distinctive costumes, consisting principally of a veil, red earrings, a white *sarong*, a white tunic and a betel nut pouch.

Those persons responsible for agricultural rituals wear almost identical clothing, namely a white turban with red and gold trim, a white *sarong* trimmed with lace, a short white tunic, a white belt and a betel nut pouch.

Clothing for ordinary people

At public ceremonies and celebrations, ordinary people, regardless of their religion, also wear distinctive clothing: (see fig. 3).

a) Traditionally, the women wear a two-colored outfit, called an *aw kuak kuang*, over a one-piece *sarong* trimmed with a decorative hem (*khan mbar jih*) and

Fig. 3 Cham women in everyday clothing

Fig. 4 Weaver using a back-strap loom

Fig. 5 Weaver using a back-strap loom

secured by a woven sash (*talei ka-ing*) tied around the waist. They also wear a simple, borderless turban (*khan luh bar*), red thread earrings (*bruei tangi*), and a necklace (*talei tamrak*).

b) The men wear a silk or cotton turban with a fringe (*siaik kabuak*), a white, lace-trimmed sarong (*khan mârang*), a cloth belt (*talei ka-ing mrai*), a short tunic (*aw lah mbar*), and a pouch for betel nut (*kadung hala*).

Looms for weaving

The clothing worn by the Cham is made from home-spun cloth that the villagers weave themselves. Two types of looms are used to weave this cloth. One, the *back-strap loom*, is used to produce the large pieces of fabric needed to make *sarongs,* turbans and scarves. The second type, the *horizontal loom*, is used to make the narrow pieces of cloth for belts, sashes, decorative hems and ribbon.

The back-strap loom *(danang manyim ban khan)*
The body of the weaver serves as the frame for this loom. Two cords connect the heddle to a bamboo pole, which functions as the tensioning rod. The breast beam, which rests on the weaver's knees as she sits, is connected by a strap to a piece of wood that hugs the small of the weaver's back.

The shuttle is passed through the shed, first, from left to right and then from right to left. The weaver uses a wooden beater to press the newly-inserted weft into the weave, and then to separate the alternating threads of the warp. As the shuttle is worked back and forth, the textile gradually comes into being. Shed sticks are used to create decorative patterns (figs. 4 and 5).

The back-strap loom is used to make the following:

turbans (khan, khan matham)

khan caro	one-piece turban with a fringe
khan mâtham	turban with a red and gold decorative border and a red fringe
khan mâtham taybi	type of turban with red and gold border and a red fringe (fig. 6)
khan pwah	white turban worn by *Basaih* priests
khan njram	turban worn by women and by *Acar*
khan balo kabuak	one-piece turban made of silk

men's *sarongs* (khan)

khan mârang	*sarong* with a lateral lace border
khan mbar jih	*sarong* worn by religious dignitaries

women's skirts (aban, ban)

aban gauh	plain *sarong*
aban tuk	patterned *sarong*
aban tuk hop	seed motif
aban tuk hop saw	variation of seed motif
aban tuk hop wil	variation of seed motif
aban tuk tamul	diamond-shaped design
aban tuk parik	checkerboard pattern
aban tuk kacak	gecko motif

and various other patterns, such as: *tuk tapit, tuk the, tuk bamak, tuk tam-un, tuk wang tam-un, tuk mbem,* etc.

Fig. 7 Weaver using the horizontal loom

Fig. 6 *Khan mâtham*

Fig. 8 Weaver using the horizontal loom

156

The horizontal (long) loom
(danâng mânyim jih dalah)

In this loom, the warp is tensed between the two beams of the frame. The heddle is attached to one of these beams, while the breast beam is joined to the other by means of a support. The top of the frame, which connects the two vertical beams, is made from a thick piece of bamboo, and supports the pulley to which the main heddle shafts (*cakauw hala*) and the shed sticks (*cakauw bingu*) are joined. (figs. 7 and 8)

The main heddle shafts are raised and lowered by two-foot treadles. The shed sticks are controlled by counter-weights, according to the pattern being made. The weaver sits on a stool, facing the warp. From this position, she inserts the shuttle, first, from front to back and then from back to front, before using a wooden beater, which she keeps close at hand, to press the weft into the weave.

The number of shed sticks depends on the complexity of the design, which tends to be formed by the warp (*bingu tak*) rather than the weft (*bingu cuk*). Two or three weavers may be required to complete a particularly intricate design. The horizontal loom is unique to the Cham. It is used by no other ethnic group native to Indochina. The loom is joined to the human body, and its constituent parts bear the names of body parts:

rup danâng, the body of the loom: the entire frame
akauk danâng, the head of the loom: support for the breast beam
takuai danâng, the neck of the loom: tenon for the breast beam support
takai danâng, the foot of the loom: the base of the beam

This loom is used to make the following:

a) wide bands of cloth (*dalah*) with patterns on either a light (*yor*) or dark (*klam*) background

The best known patterns are:

dalah 7 cakauw	7 heddle design
dalah 9 cakauw	9 heddle design
dalah 12 cakauw	12 heddle design
dalah 13 cakauw	13 heddle design
dalah kacak	gecko motif
dalah bauh m,bai	bean motif
dalah kacak-bauh m,bai	gecko and bean motif
dalah tamul takai asau	diamond and dog-leg motif
dalah tamul kacak sa	diamond and gecko motif
dalah tamul kacak dua	diamond and double gecko motif

Fig. 9 Diamond and bean motif

b) sashes *(talei ka-ing)*

talei ka-ing manikam	sash with various patterns
talei ka-ing pok	overlapping diamond pattern
talei ka-ing kacak	gecko motif
talei ka-ing tamul	diamond-shaped pattern
talei tamul-takai asau	diamond and dog-leg motif
talei tamul luak	variation on diamond-shaped pattern
talei bamâk	zigzag design
talei seng	banyan leaf design
talei haraik	vine motif
talei baoh m,bai	bean motif
talei tulang lanung	eel bone design

c) decorative borders for turbans *(khan mâtham)*

These borders have gold patterns on a red background and are decorated with a fringe made of red threads. One can notice a blue thread called "the navel" running in the direction of the warp. The designs differ according to the function and nature of the person for whom they are intended.

taibi	for the turbans worn by *Po Dhia* and *Ong Camnei*
taibi pabon	worn by *Ong Bac,* on the day of his appointment
binguw tathap	worn by the *Kadhar* and his assistant
tuak	worn by the *Po Gru* (Cham *bani*)
tuak lieng	
patrun	
lieng	
haling mâtham liêng	

Fig. 10 The *tuak lieng* design

158

d) braid on skirts *(biyon)*

These decorative borders, worn exclusively by women, are sewn on to the sides of skirts. A narrow hem, of the same color as the main border, is sewn on to the bottom of the skirt. The best known of these decorative borders are:

biyon rup	Shiva dancing on a peacock, alternating with a dragon design (fig. 11)
biyon mrak	peacock-like design
biyon hiep	dragon-like design
biyon hang	dragon-like design
biyon saharaik	vine pattern (fig. 12)
biyon 3 haraik	three vine pattern
biyon padaong	zigzag pattern of triangles and lines
biyon 13 cakauw	13-heddle shaft design

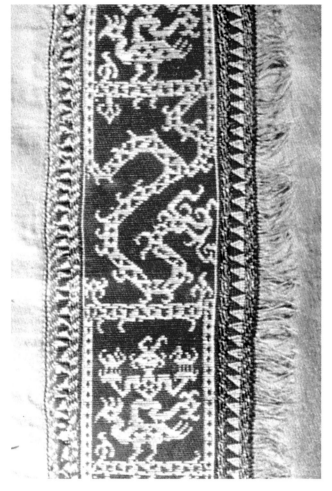

Fig. 11 Design of Shiva dancing on a peacock

Fig. 12 Vine Pattern

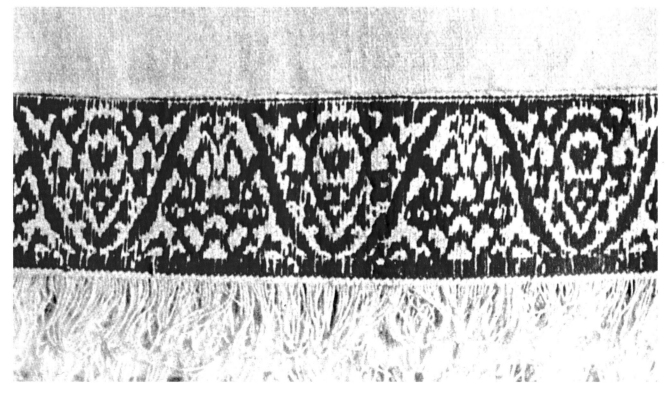

159

e) narrow hems *(jih)*

These are sewn on to the bottom of women's skirts and the sides of men's sarongs.

jih bamâk/wang/tamul	zigzag/circular/diamond-shaped design
jih tamul/kakei asau/kacak	diamonds, dog leg, gecko
jih wang	small, rounded diamond-shaped design
jih baoh mabai	bean pattern
jih 9 cakauw	9-heddle shaft design
bar jih	border sewn on to the bottom of men's *sarongs*

Fig. 13 Dragon design

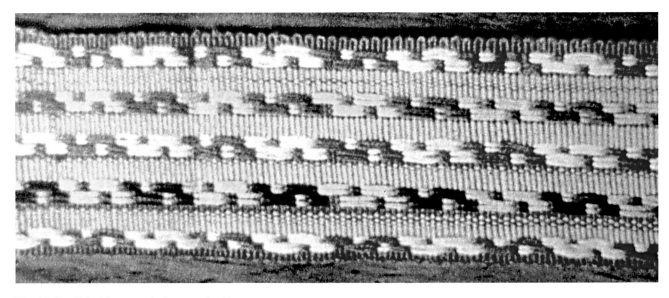

Fig. 14 *Bar jih* braid sewn at the bottom of a skirt

160

Reflections on the future of Cham textiles

In the past people were largely unfamiliar with Cham textiles, probably because the Cham people themselves felt no need to make their textiles known outside their own community. After all, their textiles were made almost exclusively for the priests and other religious dignitaries. It was not until 1968 that the Cham Cultural Center of Phanrang, with the opening of an important textile exhibition in Saigon, brought attention to the community and their traditional weaving. The exhibit proved to be a great success with foreign visitors and quickly convinced the Cham that their textiles could be exported and become a major source of income. Initially, a number of the Cham elders disapproved of putting their textiles to non-religious uses, but these objections were easily overcome by the weavers themselves, who command considerable influence in the matrilineal Cham culture. The weavers began to produce new patterns and designs adapted to the tastes and demands of the marketplace. This new trade in Cham textiles flourished and continued to expand up until the Communist takeover of Vietnam in 1975.

When the new rulers came to power, they pursued a policy of national unity, which actively suppressed the country's ethnic minorities and discouraged the practice of all customs and traditions seen as not complying with Communist Party ideals. Yet despite the restrictions, the Cham managed to preserve what remained of their glorious past: for example, their language, which they were allowed to teach in primary school; the status of their religious dignitaries and their traditional festivals, which survived in spite of strict government control.

Gradually, however, the political leadership realized the importance of tradition for the Cham people, and rather than hinder the expression of traditional beliefs and practices, the authorities began to portray themselves as the saviors of the ancient Cham culture. They even went so far as to participate in organizing religious festivals (perhaps in order to exercise more effective control over them!).

Eventually, such expressions of cultural identity were given legal status, and this opened the door for the Cham people to revive their traditional craft of weaving.

The Cham have also taken advantage of Vietnam's opening up in the 1990's, to produce textiles for the tourist trade. They began creating a range of new items, such as tablecloths, napkins, backpacks, and handbags, all adapted to the demands of customers. Around 1995, a group of weavers formed a small cooperative in the village of My-Nghiêp, near Phanrang. The cooperative gathers together woven goods from individual producers, which it displays and sells. Today, there are even two or three shops in Saigon selling Cham textiles.

Let us hope that this traditional craft survives all the country's recent upheavals since Cham textiles are undoubtedly among the most beautiful and the most original found in Southeast Asia.

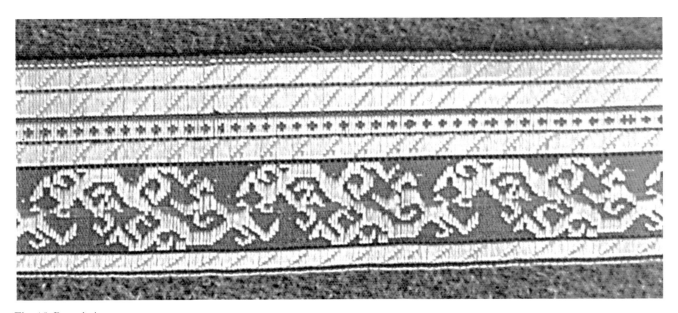

Fig. 15 Bean design

TRADITIONAL COSTUMES OF THE HMONG OF VIETNAM

Christine Hemmet

The group of people in China known as the Miao actually consists of several communities and minorities; among them, the Hmong who were the most important community to emigrate to Vietnam, Laos and Thailand at the end of the 19th century. There are today approximately 9 millions Miao: 7,383,600 in China (in 1990), 787,604 in Vietnam (in 1999), 315,465 in Laos (in 1995), and around 111,677 in Thailand (in 1995).

The diversity of the sub-groups of Miao is clearly illustrated by the abundance of their distinctive traditional costumes. Their dress plays an important part in their family and social relations. From the beginning of the 20th century until now, these traditional costumes have changed tremendously. Analyzing this evolution will demonstrate how these hilltribe people, who have been considered "traditional", are far from being fixed in the past. In fact, they have experienced and been influenced by fashion.

For the most part, the Hmong people live at the highest altitude of mountainous regions, scattered over areas which are at times difficult to access. Their ancestral way of life depends fundamentally on a slash and burn existence. When the land becomes infertile, they will leave and migrate to other areas. This completely nomadic way of life, where people carry their belongings with them, places an important role on costumes and jewelry in the social and cultural life of such communities. Thus as a result of the uniqueness of their dress and the way they wear their hair, these minorities have been differentiated as White Hmong *(Hmong Dawb)*, Black Hmong *(Hmong Du)*, Flowered Hmong *(Hmong Lenh)*, names which the Hmong of Vietnam use today among themselves.

For a long time the Miao have had a reputation in China as masters of textile handicraft. They excel in this field compared with most of their neighbours and at

Fig. 1 Returning from the field. Hmong in Vietnam still wear their traditional dress and jewelry. 1993, Moc Chau, Son La province

Fig. 2 Detail of the jacket's sleeve with embroidery and appliqué work. 1993, Moc Chau, Son La province

Fig. 3 For festivals or ceremonies, women add a high indigo dyed turban. Nowadays earrings are still made in their original style, although now some are made of aluminium instead of silver. 1993, Moc Chau, Son La province

Fig. 4 Day market in Sa Pa, Lao Cai province. These Hmong are called Hmong Du (Black Hmong) because of their dark indigo garments. Mostly made of hemp, the shiny appearance is done by pressing the cloth between two stones with wax. 1993, Sa Pa, Lao Cai province

times even with the Chinese. The variety of their styles and the extreme diversity of their techniques are impressive. Already in the 17th century when Qing Dynasty began to be interested in the wealth of the Guizhou Province, the Chinese were amazed at the splendour of what they called at that time "Miao brocade". All during their long history, women have dedicated their artistic skills and their activity to the development of an astonishing variety of techniques, the most ancient of which is the wax-resist dyeing, called "batik". The Hmong are also masters of needlework, using a variety of stitching techniques and designs. Most of their dresses have embroidered adornments or appliqués.

The making of clothing is the exclusive work of women. This activity takes up all of their free time; they spend their free moments between farming, housework and children's education for this. Their hands are permanently coloured in blue indigo; they braid hemp or spin cotton thread while walking. At home, they weave and embroider with no rest because they are in charge of making all the family clothing. Costumes for women and also those of men, are abundantly decorated with representations of the cross, rolled snails, stylized flowers or geometric designs symbolizing objects, animals or plants which play an important part in Hmong daily life. Those made for wedding ceremonies, funerals and festivals, particularly the New Year Festival, are the most valuable ones, requiring high skills, great care and artistic feelings.

For a young woman, the dress she wears can be seen as a method of seduction and a sign of wealth. To wear a beautiful dress during a festival is not only a ceremonial practice of Hmong social life. It is also considered a way to show courteousness, and respect when visiting relatives and friends. A Hmong woman is always concerned with being elegant. Along the trails of North Vietnam, Hmong woman going to the fields with their husbands, generally wear a nice dress and keep an older one in their basket for working in the fields. Others create certain types of dresses which are entirely reversible. One side, which has no decoration, is worn for work which is dirty, while the other side is decorated for public show.

From the age of six or seven little girls begin to sew with their mothers. By the time they reach adulthood, they have already completed a trousseau that includes all the dresses needed for the first years of their adult life. Young women of marriageable age wear their most beautiful clothes during festivals or when going to the market. Their talent is confirmed by the workmanship they develop during all their years of making dresses and adornments. The beauty and the number of dresses made before marriage allows a young woman to demonstrate her ability. Her enthusiasm, determination, and sense of taste are the qualities which testify to her character. Her work also serves to indicate the rank and wealth of her family. For all these reasons she will be appreciated by a young suitor and his family.

Hmong place great importance on their traditional costumes. Today many communities both in China and Vietnam still wear them in their daily life. Such continuity in this tradition permits us to understand not only the evolution but also the fashion trends.

In the mountains of North Vietnam, from one Hmong village to another, hairdos vary and the colors of clothing change. At one place the coiffure is adorned with an aluminium comb, at another with a single indigo turban, or elsewhere, red wool threads. Each village is a center of homogenous culture where disharmony is rare. Always present, fashion trends are a collective effort, never from an isolated member. A dress design will first be adopted by a small group of younger people from the same generation before the whole village will reproduce it. An individual never tries to stand out. It is the entire village that makes this effort as a whole.

The Hmong have always known how to intertwine the threads of their traditions and beliefs with the ever changing weft of the world in which they live. Thus their techniques as their tastes are in constant evolution. Younger generations spend much less time than older ones in the making of clothing. They prefer brighter colors and synthetic textiles from China which are available in the local markets. Although taste and fashion may vary among the young Hmong communities, symbolic functions of their costumes still remain and perpetuate their beauty. Still today, baby-carriers and child-caps are specially adorned because their patterns bring protection and blessings. Costumes created for wedding, New Year and funeral ceremonies remain artistic achievements.

These works of art are in great demand around the world; and their costumes and textiles have become works found in both private and public collections. More and more, exhibitions show the workmanship, the impressive visual effect and the artistic sensibility of the Hmong. Nonetheless, these works of art should not disappear from their villages (as has happened to some African sculptures), becoming objects only found in museums or collections in western countries.

Fig. 5 Women and young girls always work on costumes. After the market, they join hemp fibers. 1993, Sa Pa, Lao Cai province

Fig. 6 Wax-resist dyeing with indigo (batik) is practised on hemp and cotton by most of the Hmong groups. *Hmong Du* baby carrier is made of cotton decorated using the wax-resist technique with embroideries and appliqué. 1993, Sa Pa, Lao Cai province

Fig. 7 Embroideries evolved significantly over the past 80 years. On the right, a 1900 silk pattern and, on the left, a recent one. *Hmong Du*, Lao Cai province

Fig. 8 Detail of the wax-resist design on a new pleated skirt. Mu Cang Chai, Yen Bai province

Fig. 10 Young Hmong ladies wear a short bolero under which they show modern tee-shirts made in China. 1997, Muong Hum, Son La province

Fig. 9 Marriage outfit decorated with elaborate embroidery patterns and French Indochina silver coins (still made today for decoration). The bride must keep it until death when she will wear it again. 1994, Mu Cang Chai, Yen Bai province

Fig. 11 Their spectacular hairdressing is enlarged with the actual hair they inherited from their mothers. Hair adorned with black and red wool from the market. 1997, Muong Hum, Son La province

Fig. 12 The wealth of a young White Hmong woman is her turban made with as many Chinese headscarves she can afford. 1996, Meo Vac, Ha Giang province

Fig. 13 Upper back panel of this everyday jacket is wax-resist, the yellow is further painted by hand. 1994, Mu Cang Chai, Yen Bai province

Fig. 14 Tradition and modernity blended in a new White Hmong young lady's costume. Traditional are the large turban, the jacket, apron, thick belt, heavy white skirt (the white skirt, made of undyed hemp, has given its name to this Hmong group) and especially the thickness of the leg cloths with yards and yards of textiles wrapped around the legs, as old photographs show. Modern aspects are the synthetic shining velvet bought at the market, used to make the turban, jacket and apron. This velvet, imported from China, is very fashionable in those provinces of Northern Vietnam. 1996, Meo Vac, Ha Giang province

Fig. 15 The younger, the wealthier you are, the richer your hairdo. 1997, Muong Hum, Son La province

Fig. 16 Embroidery patterns on a White Hmong collar. 2000, Phong To, Lai Chau province

Fig. 17 In Lai Chau province, *Hmong Dawb* (White Hmong) ladies show their skills through belts and especially collar decorations. 2000, Phong To

Fig. 18 *Hmong Lenh* (Flowered Hmong) in Lao Cai province. The name of this Hmong group stems from the plentiful colours and decorations on their garment. In fashion today are red and flowered textiles imported from China. They are used as belts and decoration on the edges of the jacket instead of embroidery or appliqué. 1997

Fig. 19 A richness of colours. Patterns almost entirely cover the jacket and the skirt of young *Hmong Lenh*. 1997, Bac Ha, Lao Cai province

Fig. 20 In the twenties, the same *Hmong Lenh* costume was decorated with reverse appliqué on the jacket; embroidery and appliqué on apron; batik, appliqué and cross-stitched embroidery on the hemp and cotton pleated skirt. Lao Cai province

Fig. 21 In the beginning of this century, the navy collar was entirely adorned with very refined appliqué patterns. Nowadays embroidered patterns are a lot more common. Embroidery is easier to do and can be made everywhere

Fig. 22 Detail of the reverse appliqué technique on the *Hmong Lenh* jacket showing snails and tiger teeth patterns. Lao Cai province

Fig. 23 In the fifties, the appliqué pattern is enriched with handmade embroidery. The more complicated design today has become a flower. *Hmong Lenh*, Bac Ha, Lao Cai province

Fig. 25 In 2000, *Hmong Lenh* young girls prefer flowered velvet jackets decorated with plastic beads strings coming from China. Lao Cai province

Fig. 24 In the nineties, this *Hmong Lenh* jacket is entirely sown with a machine using very flashy colours. The design is still a flower. Bac Ha, Lao Cai province

Short bibliography

Costumes traditionnels de la Chine du Sud-Ouest,
Catalogue of Musée des Textiles de Lyon, L'Objet d'Art, 2002.

Eric Boudot - "Minority Costumes and Textiles of Southwestern China", *Orientations,* Hong-Kong, March-April 1993.

Gina Corrigan – *Miao Textiles from China.* The British Museum Press, London, 2001.

Zhang Fumin, Lin Yaohua, Theresa M. Reilly - *Richly Woven Traditions. Costumes of the Miao of Southwest China and Beyond.* Catalogue d'exposition, China House Gallery, New York, Oct 1987 - Jan 1988.

Jacques Lemoine - *Un village hmong vert du Haut Laos.* CNRS, Paris, 1972.

- "Les ethnies non Han de la Chine", *Ethnologie régionale II,* Encyclopédie de la Pléiade, Paris, 1977.

Paul and Elaine Lewis - *Peoples of the Golden Triangle.* River Books, Bangkok, (Olizane, Genève, 1986).

Claudine Lombard-Salmon - *Un exemple d'acculturation chinoise : la province du Guizhou au XVIIIème siècle.* EFEO, Paris, 1972.

Jane Mallinson, Nancy Donelly, Ly Hang - *H'mong Batik. A Textile Technique From Laos.* Silkworm Books, Chiang Mai, 1996.

Vo Mai Phuong et Claire Burkert - *A Yao Community in Sapa, Vietnam.* The Vietnam Museum of Ethnology, Hanoi, 2001. (Hmong in Sapa to be published soon).

EXHIBITION
THE TILLEKE & GIBBINS COLLECTION

In 1989 the Bangkok-based law firm Tilleke & Gibbins acquired a private collection of textiles. Since then, the firm has actively acquired textiles in order to assemble a museum-quality collection. Today, the collection consists of more than one thousand pieces, which are displayed on rotation in the firm's offices. The textiles include both typical and rare examples of weavings of the Tai, an ethnolinguistic group living in regions of Thailand, Laos, northern Vietnam, southern China and Myanmar. The collection also includes many pieces made by Khmer weavers, Burmese ethnic groups, Vietnamese ethnic minorities and hill tribe peoples. Included here are a few of the pieces belonging to the collection.

Head Cloth *(Pha Piao)*
Laos, Sam Neua
Tai Daeng, late 19th century
Supplementary weft,
warp 215 cm x weft 40 cm

Head Cloth *(Pha Piao)*
Laos, Sam Tai
Tai Daeng, late 19th century
Supplementary weft,
warp 197 cm x weft 44 cm

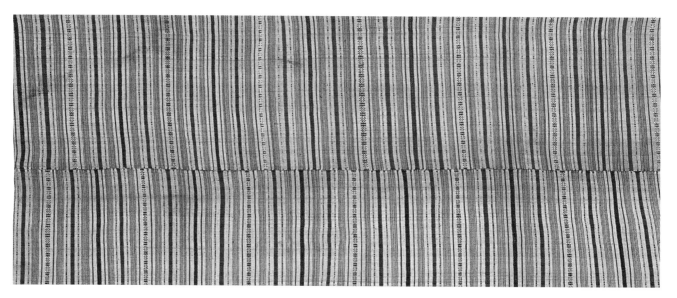

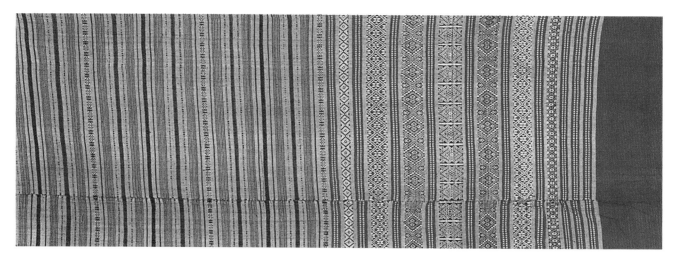

Funeral Cloth *(Pha Pok Long)* Laos, Luang Prabang (?)
Tai Lue (?), late 19th century
Continuous supplementary weft, warp 413 cm x width 95 cm

Door Curtain *(Pha Gang)*, Laos, Sam Neua
Tai Daeng, late 19th century
Supplementary weft , warp 183 cm x weft 44 cm

Tube Skirt *(Pha Sin)*, Laos, Sam Neua
Tai Kao, early 20th century
Supplementary weft, warp, weft *ikat*, warp 138 cm x weft 70 cm

Blanket *(Pha Hom)*, Laos, Sam Neua
Tai Daeng, mid 20th century
Supplementary weft, length 197 cm x width 89 cm

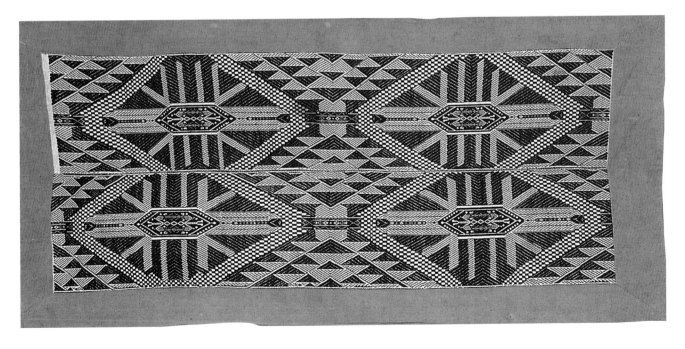

Baby Wrapper *(Pha Tuum)*
Laos, Oudomxai
Tai Phuan, mid 20th century
Supplementary weft
Warp 151 cm x weft 52 cm

Skirt *(Pha Sin)*
Laos, Tai Daeng
Early 20th century
Supplementary weft, weft *ikat*
Warp 145 cm x weft 72 cm

Head Cloth *(Pha Piao)*
Laos, Sam Tai
Tai Daeng, late 19th century
Supplementary weft
Warp 225 cm. x weft 50 cm

176

Tube Skirt *(Pha Sin)*
Laos, Lao Krang
Mid 20th century
Weft *ikat*
Warp 74 cm (sewn tube) x weft 73 cm

Head Cloth Panel *(Pha Piao)*
Laos, Sam Neua
Tai Daeng, early 20th century
Supplementary weft
Warp 101 cm (with fringe) x weft 53 cm

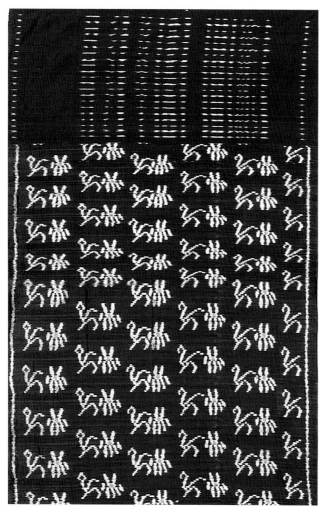

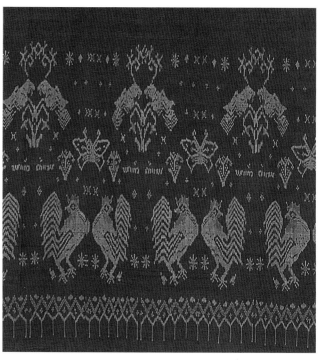

Tube Skirt *(Pha Sin)*
Thailand, Surin
Khmer Esarn, mid 20th century
Weft *ikat*
Warp 93 cm (sewn tube) x weft 92 cm

Skirt *(Longi)*
Burma, Shan State
Shan mid 20th century
Weft *ikat*
Warp 156 cm x weft 101 cm

Skirt
Cambodia, Pratabong?
Khmer, early 20th century
Weft *ikat*
Warp 177 cm x weft 83 cm

Hip Wrapper *(Sampot Hol)*,
Cambodia
Khmer, early 20th century
Weft *ikat*
Warp 310 cm x weft 93 cm

Temple Hanging *(Pidan)*
Cambodia
Khmer, late 19th century
Weft *ikat*
Warp 199 cm x weft 88 cm

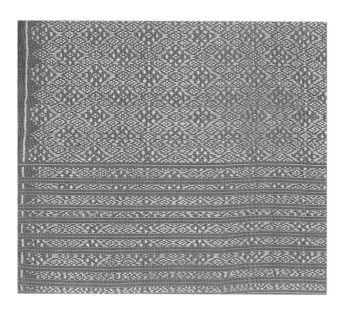

Skirt *(Longi)*
Burma, Shan State
Shan, mid 20th century
Weft *ikat*
Warp 76 cm (sewn tube) x weft 98 cm

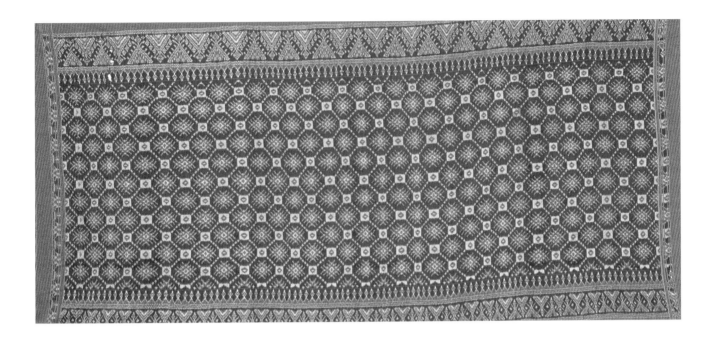

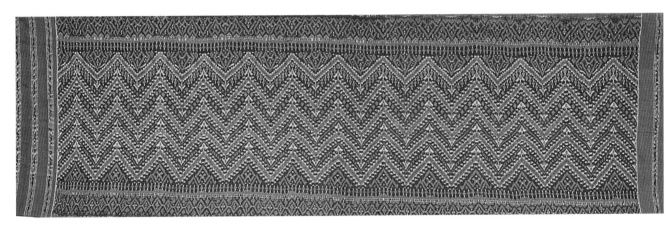

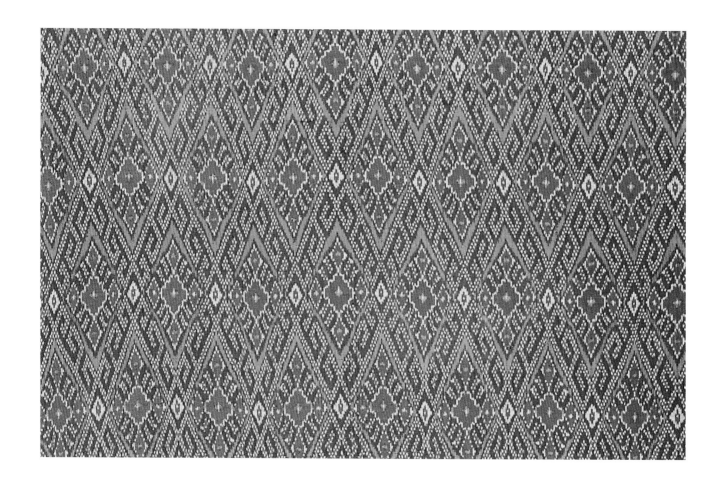

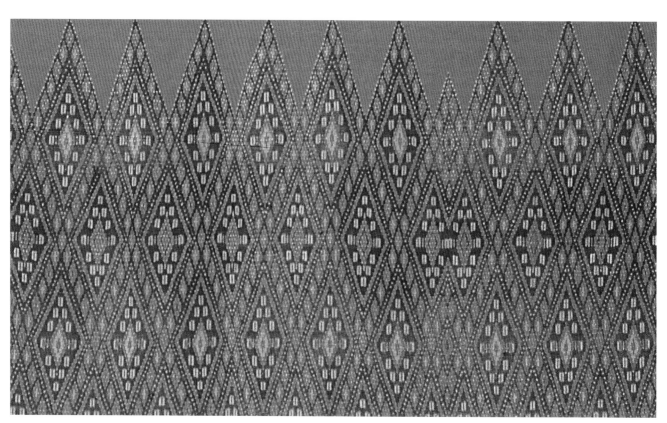

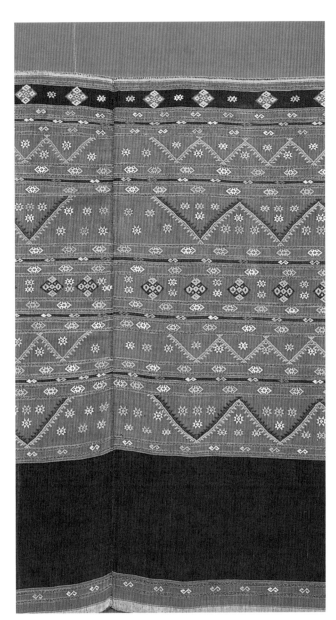

Tube Skirt *(Pha Sin)*
Thailand, Rajburi
Tai Yuan, late 19th century
Supplementary weft, weft *ikat*
103 cm (waist to hem) x warp 65 cm (seam to seam)

Tube Skirt *(Pha Sin)*
Thailand, Rajburi
Tai Yuan, mid 20th century
Supplementary weft
95 cm (waist to hem) x weft 70 cm (seam to seam)

Tube Skirt
Cambodia, Pratabong
Khmer, mid 20th century
Weft *ikat*
Warp 94 cm (sewn tube) x weft 86 cm

Tube Skirt *(Pha Sin Teen Daeng)*
Thailand, Burirum
Khmer Esarn, mid 20th century
Weft *ikat*
Warp 85 cm (sewn tube) x weft 78 cm